The Church and
the Market

Studies in Ethics and Economics
Series Editor: Samuel Gregg, Acton Institute

Economics as a discipline cannot be detached from a historical background that was, it is increasingly recognized, religious in nature. Adam Ferguson and Adam Smith drew on the work of sixteenth- and seventeenth-century Spanish theologians, who strove to understand the process of exchange and trade in order to better address the moral dilemmas they saw arising from the spread of commerce in the New World. After a long period in which economics became detached from theology and ethics, many economists and theologians now see the benefit of studying economic realities in their full cultural, often religious, context. This new series, Studies in Ethics and Economics, provides an international forum for exploring the difficult theological and economic questions that arise in the pursuit of this objective.

Titles in the Series

The Church and the Market

A Catholic Defense of the Free Economy

By Thomas E. Woods, Jr.

LEXINGTON BOOKS

Lanham • Boulder • New York • Toronto • Oxford

LEXINGTON BOOKS

Published in the United States of America
by Lexington Books
An imprint of The Rowman & Littlefield Publishing Group, Inc.
4501 Forbes Boulevard, Suite 200, Lanham, Maryland 20706

PO Box 317
Oxford
OX2 9RU, UK

British Library Cataloguing in Publication Information Available

Library of Congress Cataloging-in-Publication Data

Woods, Thomas E.
  The church and the market : a Catholic defense of the free economy / by Thomas E.
Woods, Jr.
    p. cm.
  Includes bibliographical references and index.
  ISBN 0-7391-1035-7 (hardcover : alk. paper) — ISBN 0-7391-1036-5 (pbk. : alk.
paper)
  1. Economics—Religious aspects—Catholic Church. 2. Free enterprise—Religious
aspects—Catholic Church. 3. Catholic Church—Doctrines. I. Title.
BX1795.E27W66 2004
261.8'5—dc22

2004019346

Printed in the United States of America

⊗™ The paper used in this publication meets the minimum requirements of American
National Standard for Information Sciences—Permanence of Paper for Printed Library
Materials, ANSI/NISO Z39.48-1992.

To my father,

Thomas E. Woods, Sr. (1951–1996)

Requiescat in pace

Contents

Acknowledgments

I am very happy to have the opportunity to acknowledge my indebtedness to the scholars and friends who have taught me so much over the years. I am profoundly grateful to David Gordon, Jeffrey Tucker, Guido Hülsmann, and Leonard Liggio for reading portions or the entirety of the manuscript and offering their valuable insights. I have also benefited from conversations with Jeffrey Herbener and Shawn Ritenour of Grove City College, and Christopher Westley of Jacksonville State University. Responsibility for any errors of fact or interpretation is, of course, solely my own.

I am also grateful to Thomas McArdle for urging me to write this book. I had received e-mail correspondence from time to time from people who had read my economic articles and hoped I might write a book on the subject, but it was only when Tom implored me that I gave the matter serious consideration. Were it not for him, this book would not have been written.

I feel compelled to make mention of the inspiration I have derived from the personal and professional example of Murray N. Rothbard (1926–1995), one of the great economists of the twentieth century and a scholar whose learning and productivity, in several different disciplines, was staggering. I consider myself very lucky to have had the chance to meet Murray a number of times in the early 1990s, and to have had the opportunity for lengthy conversations with him in person and on the telephone. (While still a kid, I felt like a big shot when he insisted I call him Murray.) Murray refused to compromise on principle even though to do so would have meant winning the prestigious academic posts for which lesser men sell their souls. He threw himself into his work with gusto and joy, and could produce more scholarly output in a few years than most professors do in a lifetime. Murray's example of what one man can do has inspired me in my own work.

Thanks are also due to those periodicals that have permitted me to use material I originally wrote for their pages. *Ideas on Liberty*, the monthly periodical of the Foundation for Economic Education, has kindly granted me the use of relevant portions of "A Myth Shattered: Mises, Hayek, and the Industrial Revolution" (November 2001), "The Economics of Infantilism" (June 2002), "Race, Inequality, and the Market" (October 2002), "Why Wages Used to Be So Low" (June 2003), and "The Fallacies of Distributism" (November 2003). A portion of chapter 1 originally appeared on SeattleCatholic.com as "Economics and Profit: A Final Word." A substantial portion of chapter 2 appeared as "Catholic Social Teaching and Economic Law" in the June–September 2003 issue of the *Journal des Economistes et des Etudes Humaines* (France). Another portion of chapter 2 originally appeared in *The Free Market* as "The Non-Crime of 'Price-Gouging.'" A portion of chapter 3 appeared as "Money and Morality: The Christian Moral Tradition and the Best Monetary Regime" in *Religion & Liberty*, the bimonthly publication of the Acton Institute, and a portion of chapter 6 appeared on Mises.org as "Bring Back the Guild System?" Throughout the text I have drawn on my article "Cobden on Freedom, Peace, and Trade," which appeared in *Human Rights Review* in October–December 2003.

I also wish to thank Doreen Munna, Dolores Perilo, and Marilyn Ventiere of my college's interlibrary loan department. Likewise, I extend my thanks to the staff of Lexington Books, with whom it has been a pleasure to work.

Above all, I wish to thank my wife, who was her usual encouraging self during this project, even though we were expecting our first child during most of that time. I am happy to say I married the woman I'd always wanted to marry but wasn't sure really existed.

This book is dedicated to my father, the late Thomas E. Woods, Sr., whose hard work and sacrifice (along with those of my mother, of course!) made it possible for me to be where I am today. I will never forget being seven years old and being terribly upset about some trivial thing. After Dad had sat me down and put everything into perspective, he told me that I was going to go to Harvard University someday, and that, well, he would pay for it somehow. In December 1989 his prediction came true when the Early Action letter arrived.

It was Dad, a blue-collar worker who worked as a forklift operator in a food warehouse for fifteen years, who first got me interested in politics and economics. I was the most politically aware ten-year-old around. We talked about these things regularly until his untimely death in 1996, and we typically agreed on just about everything. (I may have been a bit more pro-market, but not by much.)

Thanks, Dad. May perpetual light shine upon you.

Introduction

After years of lackluster economic performance in Japan, Western Europe, and the United States, and with more and more people, clergy included, increasingly prepared to discuss fundamental economic questions, cultivating ties of mutual understanding between religion and economics is as urgent as ever. Moral principles and economic science are meant to play complementary roles. A sound moral foundation can help us to evaluate existing economic institutions in light of genuine principles of justice. Without economic knowledge, on the other hand, the moralist's advice can prove profoundly misguided, even destructive.

Yet among the leadership of the various Christian churches as well as within popular preaching and writing, we continue to see the same prejudice in favor of the state and against the market that perhaps first emerged with the coming of the Social Gospel movement in the late nineteenth century. A 2001 study of 251 Christian seminaries in the United States only confirmed what most people already suspected: "[T]hose [seminaries] that place the heaviest emphasis on 'social justice and economic issues'" were found to be "most hostile to the free market."[1]

It is within the Catholic Church that discussions of economics and religion have perhaps been most robust over the past century. Important papal encyclicals have spoken forcefully and effectively against Marxism and socialism and in favor of private property. They have likewise emphasized the important Catholic principle of subsidiarity, whereby no function should be assigned to a higher or more remote institution (the bureaucracy of a distant central government, for example) that can be effectively carried out by a smaller and more immediate social unit (families, churches, and the like). These principles were not always fashionable during the twentieth century.

and Catholics rightly took comfort and satisfaction in knowing that the supreme pontiffs were consistently defending them.

Here, too, however, the same hostility toward the market, while far from universal, has been pervasive, notwithstanding Pope John Paul II's favorable references to the market economy in his important encyclical *Centesimus Annus* (1991). Pope Pius XI's *Quadragesimo Anno* (1931), promulgated during the Great Depression, was notoriously hostile to market economics, and skepticism about the market can be found in numerous other papal statements.

This relatively widespread suspicion of the market may help to account for why Catholic supporters of the market economy have at times been willing to make so many concessions to their opponents. They have adopted a middle-of-the-road position on such issues as labor unions, wage rates, monopoly theory, and a variety of other matters, perhaps in order to appear to be arguing from a position of wise moderation. The net effect of these concessions, however, has been to yield the moral high ground to the interventionists, who are essentially told that their arguments for intervention into the market, rather than being qualitatively mistaken, are simply quantitatively too extreme—i.e., they are mere errors of degree, not of kind. The argument in this book may well be unique in Catholic literature in that it makes no such concessions, offering instead a principled and unapologetic defense of the free market.

In defending the market, I have not taken the relatively easier road of critiquing the socialists "of the left" who look forward to a collectivist utopia. I have instead chosen as my principal foils those Catholics "on the right" who regard the market society with suspicion. These are not socialists or collectivists but people faithful to the Church who reject free enterprise and favor a wide array of interventions into the marketplace. They often favor these interventions because they believe Church teaching requires them. As a fellow Catholic of orthodox belief, I am in profound sympathy with such people, and it is with their concerns in mind that I have formulated my argument.

In the course of building up what I believe is an overwhelming case for the market, I shall be challenging not so much the doctrinal position of these Catholics as their practical application of economics, which is often notably deficient. In taking this approach, I hope to build a stronger case for the market, clarify common misunderstandings, and ultimately to push laymen and clergy alike to become more informed on economic matters.

The Catholic Church has taken a particularly vigorous and active role in debates over economic affairs ever since Pope Leo XIII issued the encyclical *Rerum Novarum* in 1891. In what a future pope would refer to as his "immortal document,"[2] Pope Leo began by condemning socialism as incompatible with the rights of private property. Yet while he refrained from a similarly sweeping criticism of capitalism, the Pope argued that such a system was nevertheless susceptible to abuses that required correction. Undesirable working conditions and inadequate wage rates were perhaps the two most important to which *Rerum Novarum* directed the attention of the faithful.

Since then, additional encyclicals have pointed to still other areas in which the market is said to require correction. Pope Pius XI suggested, among other things, that "certain kinds of property . . . ought to be reserved to the State."[3] Pope Paul VI argued in *Populorum Progressio* that Western taxpayers were morally obligated to support less developed nations, and suggested a number of economic policies that these nations should follow in order to achieve prosperity. Pope John Paul II, in turn, has gone well beyond his predecessors in suggesting that workers have a *right* to inexpensive or free health care as well as a right to rest, a paid vacation, and a pension.[4]

Few would question the good and humane intentions that motivated such economic counsel. For decades, however, a great many Catholics with backgrounds in economics have been concerned that the means recommended by the popes may not have the results intended for them, and were even likely to make the condition of workers and the poor still worse. Meanwhile, though, the impression has been given that to voice these misgivings is to involve oneself in some kind of disobedience to Church teaching. It is this unresolved difficulty that this book aims to address in the course of its defense of the market.

The type of question to which Catholics who support a free-market economy have never received a straightforward reply is as follows: If I can show that coercive labor unionism must have the overall effect of impoverishing society more than in proportion to any "gains" won by unionized labor, and that unionized labor itself would be better off in a society with a free labor market, how can I be obliged *in conscience* to believe coercive labor unionism to be a boon to workers and an indispensable institution to whose defense I must be committed?[5] This is one of many questions whose answer the social teaching leaves ambiguous. The Catholic social principle that avows the right of free association is an aspect of Catholic social teaching on which practically everyone can agree; analysis of the *economic consequences* and desirability of labor organization, however, is very far from the Church's competence.

LAWFUL DIVERSITY OF OPINION

It is eminently sensible for the Church to describe the ideal situation for a workingman to be one in which his wage is sufficiently high to provide adequately for his family. But any statement that purports to indicate *the most effective way* to bring about this desirable outcome — by means of labor unions, for example — is several levels removed from the areas of faith and morals. It is in this realm that people of good will may legitimately disagree, since nothing in the Pope's charism of infallibility gives him any unique insight into specific matters of economic policy. This is why Pope Leo XIII once said, "If I were to pronounce on any single matter of a prevailing economic problem, I should be interfering with the freedom of men to work out their own affairs. Certain cases must be solved in the domain of facts, case by case as they occur. . . . [M]en must realize in deeds those things, the principles of which have been placed beyond dispute. . . . [T]hese things one must leave to the solution of time and experience."[6]

This is an important point. As he was about to embark upon his own political and economic analysis of recent history (in particular, the recent collapse of Communism), Pope John Paul II issued a similar caution: "It goes without saying that part of the responsibility of Pastors is to give careful consideration to current events in order to discern the new requirements of evangelization. However, *such an analysis is not meant to pass definitive judgments since this does not fall per se within the Magisterium's specific domain.*"[7] "The Church," he went on, "has no models to present; models that are real and truly effective can only arise within the framework of different historical situations, through the efforts of all those who responsibly confront concrete problems in all their social, economic, political and cultural aspects, as these interact with one another. For such a task the Church offers her social teaching as an *indispensable and ideal orientation. . . .*"[8] In his most important economic encyclical, Pope Pius XI spoke of "matters of technique for which she [the Church] is neither suitably equipped nor endowed by office."[9]

Consider another example. Pope Paul VI recommended an approach to foreign aid for the developing world that has proven ineffective and in some cases even calamitous in practice. It was logically possible at the time to predict that the outcome of such a policy would not be a happy one, and indeed a number of development economists, such as Peter Bauer, were issuing such warnings. Now while the Pope doubtless has the right to instruct the faithful on matters of morality, and to remind them of their obligations toward the less fortunate, surely nothing in the doctrine of papal infallibility guarantees that the Pope's suggestions for economic policy must always bear good fruit. If that were true, no one would need to study economics at all.

A final example may help to clarify the diversity of opinion that of its very nature Catholic social teaching certainly permits. Most people, including numerous recent popes, take for granted that the government must enact legislation on behalf of worker safety or for decent working conditions in general. The point appears obvious, and to argue otherwise may even seem perverse.

But consider: in this world, nothing is without cost. Since there is no limit to the standards for working conditions that we might hope for (who would not want an office in Hawaii and a beautiful new company car every year?), at some point additional improvements become counterproductive even from the point of view of the workers themselves, who are priced out of the market by the high labor costs these requirements impose on employers. Certainly the popes would oppose state-mandated safety requirements so stringent as to cause serious disruption in employment.

Chapter 2 demonstrates that there is only one nonarbitrary way of making such determinations, and of making them in such a way that increases in working conditions do not come at the expense of other goods that society at large as well as workers themselves value more highly. That way is the market mechanism, as I then proceed to demonstrate. Now if it can be shown that any arrangement other than that achieved on the unhampered market must make workers worse off, there can hardly be a reasonable objection to my suggesting the market as the best way of implementing the popes' concern for working conditions, even if this particular solution may not have occurred to them (as indeed it does not occur to most people).

Pope Pius XI made a potentially significant concession in his encyclical *Quadragesimo Anno* (1931), which marked the fortieth anniversary of the issuance of *Rerum Novarum*. He acknowledged that limits must exist to what the moral theologian may legitimately say within the economic sphere, since "economics and moral science employs each its own principles in its own sphere."[10] To be sure, the Pope then went on to deny that "the economic and moral orders are so distinct from and alien to each other that the former depends in no way on the latter."[11] But once it has been conceded that economics is a bona fide science possessing an internal coherence of its own, problems immediately arise for those who would claim that Catholic social teaching definitively settles all major economic matters in an absolute and binding way. As A. M. C. Waterman points out, this concession by Pius XI "throws doubt on the authoritative character of that very substantial part of Catholic (or at least papal) social teaching which consists not of theological and ethical pronouncements, but of empirical judgments about the economy."[12]

This is the fundamental issue, as yet unresolved, in Catholic social teaching from the perspective of the supporter of the market. The moral argument advanced in favor of such teachings as the "living wage" is inextricably bound to certain economic preconceptions. But if those economic preconceptions are incorrect, what happens to the moral analysis whose conclusions are based on them? For instance, churchmen have wanted to increase the material well being of workers, and have not ruled out the imposition of a government-mandated "living wage" in order to do so. But what if such legislation increases unemployment? Should this not be a factor in our moral evaluation of living-wage legislation? Furthermore, what if we can show that real wages are reliably increased across the board not by intrusive legislation but by an economic order that leaves capital accumulation unhampered, thereby increasing the productivity of labor? Facts like these must inform our judgment of such important matters.

This is the difficulty with some of what goes by the name of Catholic social teaching. And it is this, rather than any lack of loyalty to the teaching office of the Church, that accounts for why so many genuinely faithful Catholics have had difficulty lending their wholehearted support to these positions.

William Luckey shares this concern: "The fact that Catholic economic teaching, put forth as unchanging and required of belief, did not square with what Austrian [that is, free-market] economists know to be true, has created an agonizing crisis of conscience for such economists."[13] All these economists have tried to say is that if churchmen wish to weigh in on important economic questions, they cannot do so in a way that legitimately binds the conscience unless they pay very serious attention to what the secular discipline of economics has to say.

It is perfectly unobjectionable for churchmen to say that churches should be built with the sturdiest materials in order that they might remain standing for as long as possible. But they go beyond their competence *as churchmen* and their ability to bind the faithful on pain of mortal sin as soon as they say, "The best building materials are A, B, and C, and the wisest techniques to use are X, Y, and Z." A churchman qua churchman has been vouchsafed no particular insight into such a question.

The Church has always maintained that faith and reason are not in conflict, but rather constitute two harmonious paths to truth. That is the approach toward the secular world that makes most sense for a Catholic, and for which there exists considerable precedent throughout history. In the second century, St. Justin Martyr spoke of the "seeds of the Word" to be found in the ancient Greeks, and Clement of Alexandria insisted that the great works of the Greeks be studied at his renowned catechetical school. St. John of Damascus (John Damascene) adopted the same attitude. He favored the study and use of what was good in Greek philosophy because "whatever there is of good has been given to men from above by God, since 'every best gift and every perfect gift is from above, coming down from the Father of lights.'"[14] Thus while it is certainly true that such thinkers as Mises and Hayek were themselves agnostic, their insights into human action are not for that reason alone to be ignored or despised. Just as St. Thomas Aquinas built on the philosophical reasoning of the pagan Aristotle, present-day Catholics may appropriate a broad range of sources in their attempt to understand the working of the economy.

In my book on Catholic intellectual life during the Progressive Era, I showed that the same type of interaction with secular knowledge was at work in the early twentieth century as well. It is simply not possible to question the doctrinal orthodoxy of the men I profiled in that book. At the same time, they were not afraid to engage in selective appropriation of the best of secular thought wherever it contained an insight that might be of benefit to the Church, all the while keeping the Faith itself free from profanation.[15]

Yet while the Church has not hesitated in the past to make use of whatever secular knowledge has to teach, what is especially interesting about the present case is that the secular truths that economic theory has to teach were in some cases anticipated or even discovered by some of the Church's own theologians. The story is still being written of how the sixteenth-century Spanish scholastics anticipated the best of modern economics, and even managed to avoid some of the errors into which Adam Smith would fall in the eighteenth century. Opponents of the market, knowing very well that such thinkers can scarcely be dismissed as "liberal," have not known quite how to treat such figures, who represent something of an embarrassment to their insistence that theirs is the only legitimate Catholic view. Although perhaps the most accessible treatment of the scholastics' views appeared in Alejandro Chafuen's outstanding *Christians for Freedom: Late Scholastic Economics* (1986)—republished in 2003 as *Faith and Liberty: The Economic Thought of the Late Scholastics*—a very substantial literature exists on the subject, including important work by Joseph Schumpeter, Marjorie Grice-Hutchinson, and Raymond de Roover.[16]

AUSTRIAN ECONOMICS

The particular school of economic thought to which this book shall have recourse is known as the Austrian School of economics. The distinctive features of the school will unfold over the course of the book, beginning in a special way with chapter 1, so a brief overview will suffice for now. For Austrians, economics is the science of individual choice. The act of choice involves a great many fundamental economic concepts, including valuation, utility, cost, and profit (to be understood not in an exclusively monetary sense). It is upon the implications of choice, and indeed of human action itself, that Austrian economics is built. The standard Austrian treatises present their subject through verbal reasoning and without recourse to the vast mathematical apparatus that has overtaken the rest of the profession. The Austrians offer unique contributions to many aspects of economics, including money, business cycles, so-called public goods and "externalities," and monopoly theory.

The founder of the school was Carl Menger (1840–1921), a professor of economics at the University of Vienna, whose *Principles of Economics* (1871) had considerable influence. He contributed mightily to what became known as the "marginal revolution" in economics, and made important contributions to the methodology of economics (discussed here in chapter 1) and the theory of the origin of money. Another important member of the school, Eugen von Böhm-Bawerk (1851–1914), is perhaps best remembered for his critique of Marxism as well as for his work on interest rate determination.

Böhm-Bawerk's great student, in turn, was Ludwig von Mises (1881–1973), whose contributions to the discipline were legion, ranging from epistemology to monetary theory, from business cycle theory to the socialist calculation problem. After arriving in New York in 1940, Mises picked up the practice he had developed in Austria of holding a private seminar for interested students. A number of the most important and accomplished developers of the Austrian school would come out of that seminar, including Murray N. Rothbard (1926–1995), George Reisman, and Israel Kirzner. The school has enjoyed something of a renaissance since 1974, when Austrian economist F. A. Hayek (1899–1992), a colleague of Mises, won the Nobel Prize in economics for his work on business cycle theory.

That Catholicism and much of Austrian economics are eminently compatible I shall attempt to demonstrate throughout the book. For now, consider the following testimony regarding the scholastic origins of Austrian economics, drawn from the introduction to a common history of the school:

> The story of the Austrian School begins in the fifteenth century, when the followers of St. Thomas Aquinas, writing and teaching at the University of Salamanca in Spain, sought to explain the full range of human action and social organization. These Late Scholastics observed the existence of economic law, inexorable forces of cause and effect that operate very much as other natural laws. Over the course of several generations, they discovered and explained the laws of supply and demand, the cause of inflation, the operation of foreign exchange rates, and the subjective nature of economic value — all reasons Joseph Schumpeter celebrated them as the first real economists.

Nevertheless, traditional Catholics can be found who condemn free-market economics as nothing more than a form of liberalism, and look with amused condescension upon their brethren in the Faith who, they believe, are too naïve or ignorant to perceive that they have been duped by modernity. It is partly to address this misconception that I have written this book.

Let me state at the outset what this book is not: it is not a line-by-line refutation of the likes of Hilaire Belloc, Amintore Fanfani, and Fr. Vincent

McNabb. At times I shall quote from such figures by way of contrast (though occasionally in agreement) with my own position. Neither is it a textual analysis of papal encyclicals. What I have aimed to do instead is to provide a positive statement of the pro-market position, rather than to be purely defensive, answering critic after critic. The approach I have adopted is, I think, more effective and to the point, not to mention more pleasant and interesting to read.

I have nothing but the most profound respect for the pre-Vatican II popes whose economic commentary I regret having to criticize in the present study. They were good, holy, and courageous men who governed the Church with great skill and courage and from whose writings I have profited immensely. Yet great as they were, merely by virtue of occupying the Chair of Peter they did not inherit any particular *economic* insight over and above what any intelligent layman might possess. It should be obvious that although in this book I hold up some of their economic statements to careful scrutiny, I am in no way criticizing them as popes.

Some of Pope John Paul II's *Centesimus Annus* (1991), particularly its understanding of the role of prices, entrepreneurship, and market exchange in general, reveals a far greater understanding of market mechanisms than is evident in earlier encyclicals, although it would be dishonest not to concede that this document, too, is disappointing in certain ways. Still, it is an encouraging sign. Gregory Gronbacher points to "a central problem with many schools of Catholic social thought, namely, the inability to integrate both the logic of the market and the logic of morality." If the Church is to be taken seriously in these matters, he cautions, then "it must understand basic economic theory. There are foundational market realities that cannot be ignored for any reason, including moral concerns, because, in so doing, further harm may result to both market mechanisms and morality." This critical point can no longer be overlooked. As Etienne Gilson put it, "Piety is no substitute for technique."[17]

NOTES

1. "Religious Hostility to the Free Market," National Center for Policy Analysis, August 16, 2001, <http://www.ncpa.org/pd/social/pd081601e.html> (July 8, 2004); see also John Green and Kevin E. Schmiesing, *The State of Economic Education in United States Seminaries* (Grand Rapids, Mich.: Center for Economic Personalism, 2001).

2. Pius XI, *Quadragesimo Anno* 39; John Paul II, *Centesimus Annus* 1. Citations from papal encyclicals in these notes refer to the numbering system used at the Vatican website, http://www.vatican.va.

3. Pius XI, *Quadragesimo Anno* 114.

4. John Paul II, *Laborem Exercens* 19.

5. It might be argued that the form that labor organization should take is not expressly delineated in the social encyclicals, and that strictly voluntary unions, employing no coercion of any kind or any threats of violence, may fulfill papal expectations. But bishops' conferences as well as standard treatises on Catholic social teaching appear to take coercive unionism for granted and have never been contradicted or rebuked by the Vatican, and it is through these media that the faithful come into closest contact with the social teaching.

6. Quoted in Katherine Burton, *Leo the Thirteenth: The First Modern Pope* (New York: David McKay Co., 1962), 171.

7. John Paul II, *Centesimus Annus* 3; emphasis added.

8. John Paul II, *Centesimus Annus* 43; emphasis in original.

9. Pius XI, *Quadragesimo Anno* 41.

10. Pius XI, *Quadragesimo Anno* 42.

11. Pius XI, *Quadragesimo Anno* 42.

12. A. M. C. Waterman, "Property Rights in John Locke and in Christian Social Teaching," *Review of Social Economy* 9 (October 1982): 112–13.

13. Ever since the Industrial Revolution, Luckey writes, Christians "have clung like sloths to thinkers [such as Thomas Carlyle and John Ruskin] who caricature modern economic systems as dehumanizing slave systems, accelerating the impoverishment of the poor, so that the factory owner can live more splendidly." Such critics, he says, tended "to ignore empirical evidence [and] were ignorant of cause and effect relationships in economics." William R. Luckey, "The Intellectual Origins of Modern Catholic Social Teaching on Economics: An Extension of a Theme of Jesús Huerta de Soto" (paper presented at the Austrian Scholars Conference, Ludwig von Mises Institute, Auburn, Alabama, March 23–25, 2000).

14. Edward Grant, *God and Reason in the Middle Ages* (Cambridge, UK: Cambridge University Press, 2001), 35.

15. Thomas E. Woods, Jr., *The Church Confronts Modernity: Catholic Intellectuals and the Progressive Era* (New York: Columbia University Press, 2004).

16. Raymond de Roover, "The Concept of the Just Price: Theory and Economic Policy," *Journal of Economic History* 18 (1958): 418–34; idem, *Business, Banking, and Economic Thought in Late Medieval and Early Modern Europe: Selected Studies of Raymond de Roover*, ed. Julius Kirshner (Chicago: University of Chicago Press, 1974), esp. 306–45; Alejandro A. Chafuen, *Christians for Freedom: Late Scholastic Economics* (San Francisco: Ignatius Press, 1986); Marjorie Grice-Hutchinson, *The School of Salamanca: Readings in Spanish Monetary Theory, 1544–1605* (Oxford: Clarendon Press, 1952); idem, *Early Economic Thought in Spain, 1177–1740* (London: George Allen & Unwin, 1978); Joseph Schumpeter, *History of Economic Analysis* (New York: Oxford University Press, 1954). Rothbard's most in-depth treatment of the late Scholastics appears in Murray N. Rothbard, *An Austrian Perspective on the History of Economic Thought*, vol. 1,

Economic Thought before Adam Smith (Hants, England: Edward Elgar, 1995),
99–133.

17. Gregory M. A. Gronbacher, "Economic Personalism: A New Paradigm for a
Humane Economy," in *Centesimus Annus: Assessment and Perspectives for the Future of Catholic Social Doctrine*, ed. John-Peter Pham (Vatican City: Libreria Editrice
Vaticana, 1998), 67–68.

Chapter One

In Defense of Economics

One of the characteristic features of Catholic thought over the centuries has been its emphasis on reason. Man's mind, according to this tradition, is capable of apprehending a world of order that exists outside itself. Man is able to abstract "universals" from the myriad objects and sense data that appear to him and thus bring order to the chaos of mere data above which mere brutes can never ascend.

Throughout the Bible and the Church Fathers, the regularity of natural phenomena is described as a reflection of God's goodness, beauty, and order. For if the Lord "has imposed an order on the magnificent works of his wisdom," that is only because "He is from everlasting to everlasting" (Sir. 42:21). "The world," writes Stanley Jaki, summing up the testimony of the Old Testament, "being the handiwork of a supremely reasonable Person, is endowed with lawfulness and purpose." This lawfulness is evident all around us. "The regular return of seasons, the unfailing course of stars, the music of the spheres, the movement of the forces of nature according to fixed ordinances, are all the results of the One who alone can be trusted unconditionally." The same holds for Jeremiah's citation of the faithful recurrence of harvests as a demonstration of God's goodness, or the parallel he draws "between Yahweh's unfailing love and the eternal ordinances by which Yahweh set the course of stars and the tides of the sea."[1]

Likewise, God and the Bible are teleological; things have purposes. It is not for man to define the purposes of marriage and sexuality, for instance, according to his arbitrary will; God punishes men who substitute their whims for the order and purpose He has built into His creation. Catholics generally did not consider God's will to be absolutely unfathomable or his moral laws ultimately arbitrary. Actions were not good simply because God had said so;

God had said so because they were good. Thus from the physical world to the world of moral precept, God was nothing if not rational and orderly.

During the eighteenth century, thinkers impressed by the elegant regularity of phenomena and the beautiful order that Isaac Newton had described in the physical world looked in the social world for similar lawlike relationships. And indeed, as Ludwig von Mises explains, the founders of political economy perceived "regularity in the operation of the market." People came to realize "with astonishment that human actions were open to investigation from other points of view than that of moral judgment. They were compelled to recognize a regularity which they compared to that with which they were already familiar in the field of the natural sciences."[2] The analogies to the natural sciences were readily drawn. As Josiah Tucker explained, "The Circulation of Commerce may be conceived to proceed from the Impulse of two distinct Principles of Action in Society, analogous to the Centrifugal and centripetal Powers in the Planetary System." Adam Smith appealed to this very model, describing prices as "continually gravitating, if one may say so, toward the natural price."[3]

Although the rise of what might be called economic thought had long preceded the Enlightenment, the attempt to systematize observations of economic activity into a coherent discipline reflected the intellectual life of the eighteenth and nineteenth centuries at its best. They found natural harmonies at work in the market order, and concluded that ill-considered efforts to improve the economic well-being of certain groups by means of government intervention were bound to have deleterious consequences, often exactly contrary to the stated wishes of their proponents. As Mises points out, many of these thinkers found the hand of divine providence in the beautiful order and harmony created by the free market and the division of labor—a supplement to the order in the physical realm that St. Paul and Catholic theology as a whole had always pointed to as evidence of God's existence and goodness. Eighteenth-century thinkers viewed the regularity of natural phenomena as "an emanation of the decrees of Providence," and when these same thinkers discovered a like regularity in human action and the economic sphere, they "were prepared to interpret it likewise as evidence of the paternal care of the Creator of the universe." "Observe the functioning of the market system," some classical liberals put it, "and you will discover in it the finger of God."[4]

The nineteenth-century classical liberal economist and writer Frédéric Bastiat described the consequences of this insight in his posthumously published *Economic Harmonies*:

> For if there are general laws that act independently of written laws, and whose action needs merely to be regularized by the latter, we must study these *general*

laws; they can be the object of scientific investigation, and therefore there is such a thing as the science of political economy. If, on the contrary, society is a human invention, if men are only inert matter to which a great genius, as Rousseau says, must impart feeling and will, movement and life, then there is no such science as political economy: there is only an indefinite number of possible and contingent arrangements, and the fate of nations depends on *the founding father* to whom chance has entrusted their destiny.[5]

The methodology of Austrian economics aims to discover these laws and to put them on a sound theoretical footing. In claiming that such laws exist at all the Austrians found themselves, beginning in the late nineteenth century, in an intense philosophical clash with the German Historical School. The Historical School, which included Adolf Wagner, Karl Knies, Gustav Schmoller, and Werner Sombart, rejected the idea of universally valid economic law that admitted no exception across nations and epochs, and thereby effectively denied the possibility of economics as such. They rejected even such standard relationships as supply and demand.[6] Thus the famous *Methodenstreit*, or debate over method, which has in one form or another continued to the present day, began in the late nineteenth century when Carl Menger argued, contrary to the claims of the Historical School, that economic law was something universal and accessible to reason.[7]

In searching for and establishing these laws, Mises rejected the idea that economics should be modeled after physics and the hard sciences. For one thing, the very existence of human choice and free will precluded basing social analysis on such a model, since human beings are fundamentally unlike inanimate objects. One cannot study social interaction the same way he would the flight of a projectile, since the behavior of the latter, devoid of reason and will, occurs in a manner that can be exactly predicted by the natural scientist. The same is not true for the behavior of human beings. There are no constants in human action as there are in physics.[8]

Not surprisingly, then, Mises argued that the predictive power of economics was comparative rather than absolute—that is, while economic theory can tell us that a ten percent increase in the supply of money will tend to raise prices higher than they otherwise would have been, it cannot tell us the precise extent of this increase in prices. It cannot say that prices will rise by ten percent, or five, or three, whenever the money supply is increased by ten percent. Human beings do not lend themselves to mathematical exactitude in this sense.[9] Hence the mathematization of the profession that has proceeded rapidly over the course of the twentieth century, and which has rendered the professional journals all but unreadable, was not a trend that Mises could favor. As if to drive home the point, he included not a single equation, chart, or graph in all 900 pages of his outstanding economic treatise, *Human Action*.

PRAXEOLOGY

Economics, Mises said, was the best-developed branch of a wider science of human action known as praxeology. Praxeology begins with an axiom that is surely incontestable: *human beings act.* From this basic starting point, Mises, Murray N. Rothbard, and other Austrians have proceeded to deduce an entire edifice of economic truth. Hence the status of this original claim, on which rest the truth of the conclusions derived from it, should be examined.

Much has been written about how Mises and Rothbard justified the action axiom. Mises did so on Kantian grounds, arguing that this truth about human action was an example of the Kantian synthetic a priori: a statement which, made prior to experience, is both substantive and true. Rothbard, on the other hand, took a different approach. "My own epistemological position rests on Aristotle and St. Thomas," he explained, and thus was broadly empirical, resting on reasoned generalization from the constant testimony of sense experience.[10] Both agree that the attempt to deny the existence of human action would be self-refuting, since the denial itself would constitute an action.

Having established the truth of the action axiom, Mises proceeds, with the help of a few subsidiary postulates derived from experience (such as the disutility of labor—i.e., that people prefer leisure to work), to deduce the entire edifice of economic thought. It is through analysis of human action that praxeology functions. Here we shall draw out bits and pieces of the implications of human action in order to show the praxeological method at work.

Human action, says Mises, "is an attempt to substitute a more satisfactory situation for a less satisfactory one."[11] Here we can call upon St. Thomas to lend support to Mises' analysis.[12] St. Thomas observes in his *Summa Contra Gentiles* that "in acting every agent intends an end" and that "every agent acts for a good." Indifference between alternatives, Aquinas says, does not give rise to action: "Now, he who looks upon a manifold number of things with indifference no more succeeds in doing one of them than another. Hence, from an agent contingently indifferent to alternatives no effect follows, unless he be determined to one effect by something. So, it would be impossible for him to act."[13]

Since man acts for a good, says St. Thomas, his action involves moving from a less satisfactory situation to a more satisfactory one. "The less satisfactory situation," explains Gabriel Zanotti, author of a study of the Thomistic foundations of praxeology, "is the situation of privation with respect to that for which the agent acts, and the more satisfactory situation is the acquisition of the good—which thus implies a passage from potency to act."[14]

Human action, moreover, involves choice: man's time, his resources, and indeed his body are scarce, and thus by acting he must choose among alternative employments of these things. The very act of choice, moreover, implies the concept of *cost*, since in choosing to do one thing man must forego some alternative. That in acting man must forego alternatives implies that he possesses an ordinal ranking of ends, which is revealed in action. The available choices that he forgoes are ranked lower on his value scale than the one he actually pursues. Naturally, man pursues his most highly valued end.[15] If that pursuit should for some reason become impossible, he pursues his second most highly valued end, and so on.

We can see just from this brief analysis why the Austrians have always insisted so strongly on the concepts of subjective value and the subjective nature of costs. While we can know that a man prefers *a* to *b* because we observe his preference expressed through his action—when he in fact chooses *a* over *b*—we cannot know how much more intensely he prefers *a* to *b*. It is impossible for human beings to quantify precisely the intensity of their desires; at best they can speak in terms of much more, a little more, and so on (and even here, these evaluations cannot be compared across human beings). Men's value scales consist not of cardinal rankings but of ordinal ones—e.g., first, second, and third most valued ends.

Perhaps surprisingly, we have already derived the law of diminishing marginal utility; all we need do now is make that derivation explicit. The law itself can be stated simply: the (marginal) utility of each additional unit of the homogeneous supply of a good decreases as the supply of units increases.[16] (Stated more colloquially but less precisely, the more water I have, the less urgently I desire additional water.) This conclusion follows directly from what we have said thus far, since in line with his ordinal ranking, man will put the first unit of a good toward the satisfaction of his most urgent need. The second unit, therefore, must be desired less insofar as it satisfies a need felt not as urgently as that to which the first unit was directed. Additional units, being used for still less urgent purposes, will be valued correspondingly less. (Note that at no point in this demonstration does Mises or any other praxeologist have recourse to explanations from psychological or physiological satiety to substantiate the law.[17] The entire demonstration is a strictly logical elaboration of the implications of human choice.)

For example, suppose my value scale for the use of water is such that I use my first unit of water for drinking, the second unit for bathing, the third for watering my plants, the fourth for washing my car, and so on. If I begin with four units of water and for some reason have to give up one unit, I do not go without drinking. I simply refrain from applying any of my remaining units of water to the least urgent end that I could have satisfied had I had the fourth (or marginal) unit—that is to say, I go without washing my car.

All of this information, in turn, implies the direction of the supply and demand curves used in all standard economics. The law of marginal utility states that a person's demand for a particular good decreases with each additional unit (since each additional unit will be applied to a less-valued end); it follows, therefore, that it is only at lower and lower prices that he will be willing to acquire more units of the good. And indeed the more money he spends on the good, the greater the marginal utility of the lesser cash reserves remaining to him, a factor which also contributes to his decreasing desire for additional units of the good. An individual's demand curve for a particular good must, therefore, be downward sloping to the right—that is, as the quantity of goods he acquires increases, the price he is willing to pay declines. The curve depicting total demand for this good, as the summation of the demand curves of all individuals, must itself be downward sloping to the right. The vertical or upward sloping supply curve is derived from similarly subjective considerations. A seller of some good is faced with the option of consuming the good himself, selling it at present, and selling it in the future. The more units he sells, the greater the utility of the remaining units in uses other than current sale, and therefore the higher the price he will demand in order to part with additional units.[18] (Since it is very often the case that sellers have practically no use for the goods they sell, and therefore these goods, as Carl Menger would say, have next to no use value and possess only exchange value, the supply curve may well be vertical.) Given this analysis it necessarily follows that a legally imposed increase in wage rates independent of an increased demand for labor (which in turn is related to the productivity of labor) must lead to unemployment, as an increased number of workers present themselves for fewer available jobs. The downward-sloping demand curve, derived above, tells us that at a higher wage fewer workers will be demanded. (Stated more precisely, the artificially increased wage rate will lead to more unemployment *than there would have been in the absence of the intervention*, since countervailing forces, such as increases in productivity, could to some degree offset, counteract entirely, or even overcome the effects of the wage increase.)

Since these principles (and a great many others, which curious readers may discover in Mises' and Rothbard's great treatises) are established on the basis of logical deduction from an irrefutable axiom, they are, to use Mises' words, apodictically true. They are not falsifiable by experience. Economic law is not disproved if no change in unemployment is observed after an increase in the minimum wage to $25 per hour. All we can say is that unemployment is higher than it would have been in the absence of the minimum wage.

Mises argues that praxeology and history constitute the two main branches of the sciences of human action, and that these two branches are conceptually distinct from each other. History "cannot teach us any general rule, principle, or law."[19] Indeed it is only with the kind of sound theory with which praxeology provides us that we can make sense of history. Without some coherent theory, Hans-Hermann Hoppe observes, it is impossible to make sense of empirical data. Was a society prosperous because of economic regulation or in spite of it? Did a socialist society suffer a decline in living standards because the state owned the means of production, or in spite of that fact? Nothing in the historical data themselves can provide irrefutable answers to these questions, and therefore, without some theory with which to understand historical events, we must resign ourselves in such cases to endless arguments over how the data should be interpreted.[20] As Mises summed up the matter, the statements and propositions of praxeology "are not derived from experience. They are, like those of logic and mathematics, a priori. They are not subject to verification and falsification on the ground of experience and facts. They are both logically and temporally antecedent to any comprehension of historical facts. They are a necessary requirement of any intellectual grasp of historical events."[21] Mises' system, therefore, amounts to a wholesale assault on logical positivism, according to which only those statements that can be tested by experience can provide us with genuine knowledge.

CATHOLICS AND AUSTRIAN ECONOMICS

Needless to say, there is a great deal in all this that Catholics should find congenial. The Austrian approach to economics rejects the scientism that has crept into so many disciplines and indeed into virtually all of economics itself; instead, the Austrians insist upon a methodology that respects the uniqueness of man as a creature with free will. Additionally, the Austrians posit a universe of order that reason, properly exercised, is able to apprehend. And they reject the argument that the only kind of meaningful knowledge is that derived by means of the induction and empirical investigation of the scientific method.

Regrettably, it is often the case that those who are most vocal in their opposition to Austrian economics and most insistent on its incompatibility with Catholicism who turn out to know the least about it. Not long ago, for example, John Sharpe, the head of a publishing house dedicated to books on Catholic social teaching, described "[t]his infatuation with Austrian economics" as "a strange phenomenon among Catholics." It is practically certain that at the time he made that remark he had read essentially nothing by Mises or Rothbard. Yet he felt qualified to conclude:

Many of the critics of Distributism repeatedly cite the words of Murray Rothbard, Ludwig von Mises, and others of the Austrian school in defense of their
position. . . . The Austrian economists were liberals, plain and simple, following
on the heels of the French Physiocrats and the liberal English Political Economists. They opposed socialism *not* because it violates the natural law as taught
by true philosophy and confirmed by Revelation, but because it is less efficiently productive of material wealth than the free market.[22]

No one who had ever read anything by Mises, or especially by Rothbard,
could have made such a remark. We find here no acquaintance with the basic
ideas of the Austrian School of economics, let alone the distinction between
the Austrian and Chicago schools (the latter of which does indeed place great
emphasis on economic "efficiency"). St. Thomas Aquinas went out of his way
to understand his opponents' arguments in order better to refute them. He
demonstrated this kind of charity even when dealing with the arguments of
outright heretics. Surely we have a right to expect that *our fellow Catholics*,
before launching such attacks, likewise acquaint themselves with the matter
at hand.

Mises did, of course, point out the inefficiencies of socialism, though why
this should render him suspect is far from clear: even Aristotle implied the inefficiency of socialism when he spoke about the extra care with which we
treat property that is our own. Economists' preoccupation with "economic efficiency" is routinely cited as evidence of their moral perversity—do they not
know that there is more to life than mere efficiency? But surely efficiency is
a value. It is simply the avoidance of waste. Any conception of man's stewardship of the things of the earth must inevitably involve a concern for the
avoidance of waste. As historian Ralph Raico has noted, it is a good thing that
the capitalists of the eighteenth century were every bit as committed to cost-
cutting and efficiency as their modern-day critics claim they were, since in a
society as poor as theirs any waste came at the expense of the well-being of
the great mass of the population.

Moreover, Mises' economic argument against socialism went far beyond
the mere question of efficiency as that term is popularly understood. His intellectual demolition of socialism constituted a work of such genius that one
can scarcely imagine grounds on which an intelligent Catholic could simply
dismiss it as a product of "liberalism" unworthy of his attention.

THE SOCIALIST CALCULATION PROBLEM

Mises' argument might be explained as follows. The existence of money
prices for the means of production—raw materials, machinery, physical plant,

and the like—allows entrepreneurs to calculate profit and loss. A business earns a profit if it earns more from the sale of its product than it expends on the inputs that go into its production. Profit informs the firm that it has employed resources in conformity with consumer desires, taking raw materials valued less and transforming them into finished products that consumers value more—and which they value more than the use of those raw materials in alternative production processes.[23] These facts assist entrepreneurs in their task of appraising future conditions and of pursuing production plans that conform to what they anticipate the level of future prices to be.

In the absence of money, moreover, we are dealing with inputs and outputs that are inherently incommensurable—there is no nonarbitrary way to compare wood and rubber, for instance. Money prices allow incommensurable goods to be expressed in terms of a common unit: a unit of currency (which, ideally, represents a certain weight in gold), thereby rendering economic calculation possible. Furthermore, practically every good possesses myriad uses, and could be used in many different lines of production and in combination with many potential complementary factors of production. Money prices tend to direct these factors of production toward their most urgently needed uses.

Imagine, for example, the case of a stereo manufacturer. A considerable variety of materials, from plastic to platinum, could be used as the casing of a stereo. Since platinum is relatively scarce, it carries a high price—which tells entrepreneurs that if they are planning to use platinum, they had better need it for something urgent, lest they divert it from some other industry for which platinum is among the only materials that could make its production process profitable.[24] The high price of platinum, a price that the stereo manufacturer almost certainly cannot afford to pay, is a reflection of the fact that the platinum is more urgently needed in some other sector of the economy, and its profitability there allows users of platinum to bid up the price to a point at which it is no longer feasible for a stereo operator to compete for this scarce resource.

The stereo manufacturer, of course, probably does not know exactly why the price of platinum is so high, or what other uses in the economy platinum serves that are so urgent that they have bid platinum away from him altogether. All he knows is that platinum is expensive—and he therefore adjusts his production plan accordingly. He will now use some other material, like plastic, whose greater abundance and/or less intense need elsewhere makes its use more feasible and reasonable for him. Myriad production decisions of this kind are made every day with the help of the price system, and without the producers involved having to know anything about the economy-wide conditions that make prices what they are.

Now prices emerge as a result of the ongoing interaction of buyers and sellers, each exchanging his private property. But if the state owns all the means of production, no such exchanging takes place, and the process that gives rise to prices in a capitalist system, therefore, simply does not exist. So without private ownership of the means of production, there can be no prices for capital goods, and without such prices the socialist planning board must literally grope in the dark in its allocation of capital.[25] The central planners are faced with "the impossibility of . . . performing the arithmetic of profit and loss computations in pure socialism which, in turn, makes it impossible for them to engage in entrepreneurial appraisals necessary to give meaning to profit and loss, and, thus, rationally allocate factors of production."[26] As Murray Rothbard observed, "It is precisely this central and vital role of the *appraising entrepreneur*, driven by the quest for profits and the avoidance of losses, that cannot be fulfilled by the socialist planning board, for lack of a market in the means of production. Without such a market, there are no genuine money prices and therefore no means for the entrepreneur to calculate and appraise in cardinal monetary terms."[27]

In the absence of prices, the socialist planning board has no rational way of choosing between the practically limitless ways in which the various factors of production at their disposal can be employed. Faced with a choice between two simple production processes, one employing ten units of steel and nine units of rubber, and the other employing nine units of steel and ten units of rubber, socialist planners have no way of knowing which is more efficient—that is, which involves the most economical use of resources in terms of the alternative uses in whose service those resources might have been employed. Is it less wasteful in terms of the economy as a whole for this industry to use the process requiring the extra unit of steel or the one requiring the extra unit of rubber? Without being able to express the value of these resources in terms of a common unit (dollars, for instance), there is no way in which they can be rationally compared in the process of entrepreneurial appraisal. Without a price system, there is no way to know that a particular resource is especially urgently needed here or there, or that a resource's use in industry A is a net loss for the economy since it is more efficiently and rationally used in industry B. Industry B has no way of bidding resources away from sectors in which they are less urgently needed, as platinum users were able in our earlier example to bid that resource away from manufacturers of stereo equipment.

If this problem exists even in the case of relatively simple production processes, imagine an entire economy run along these lines. Instead of trying to decide between two processes, one of which uses more steel and the other of which uses more rubber, imagine planning an entire economy and trying to decide between a practically infinite possible combination of factors of production, with hundreds or thousands of variables in every single industry. In that case, it is inescapable that the entire economy will be run with a total lack of regard for rational resource allocation, since no mechanism exists by which such allocation could be achieved. Every single industry will be run inefficiently and wastefully.

Mises' great insight thus went well beyond standard arguments against socialism. Plenty of people had figured out that an incentive problem would exist under socialism, a system organized according to Marx's slogan "from each according to his ability, to each according to his need." Under such a system, an especially skillful worker reaps no particular benefit from his increased production; he is simply saddled with a higher production quota in the future. On the other hand, there is plenty of incentive to drop out of the economy and emphasize one's "needs." Mises showed that even if this problem could be solved, even if human nature could somehow be changed, socialism would still be a catastrophe.

Another scholar has nicely summarized the problem:

> Given, therefore, the infinitude of the relationships of complementarity and substitutability simultaneously subsisting among the various types of productive resources, a single human mind—even if it were miraculously endowed with complete and accurate knowledge of the quantities and qualities of the available factors of production, of the latest techniques for combining and transforming these factors into consumer goods, and of the set of all individuals' rankings of consumer goods—would be utterly incapable of determining the optimal pattern of resource allocation or even if a particular plan were *ludicrously and destructively uneconomic.*[28]

Thus even if all raw information could be known, economic calculation would still be impossible for lack of a method by which entrepreneurs, looking to the future, could compare the value and cost of different courses of action.

Clearly, we are not dealing here with the standard argument that capitalism is more efficient than socialism. Mises' position is far more significant and profound. Consider how Mises describes the choice with which society is faced when adopting either socialism or capitalism:

> Socialism cannot be realized because it is beyond human power to establish it as a social system. The choice is between capitalism and chaos. A man who chooses between drinking a glass of milk and a glass of a solution of potassium cyanide does not choose between two beverages; he chooses between life and death. A society that chooses between capitalism and socialism does not choose

between two social systems; it chooses between social cooperation and the disintegration of society. Socialism is not an alternative to capitalism; it is an alternative to any system under which men can live as *human* beings. To stress
this point is the task of economics as it is the task of biology and chemistry to
teach that potassium cyanide is not a nutriment but a deadly poison.[29]

Surely there is room enough in the Catholic worldview for Mises' bril-
liance to take its place among the reasons that a Catholic should oppose
socialism. In the past, a number of Catholic philosophers have argued against
certain philosophical systems they considered erroneous by arguing that their
logical consequence was skepticism, which could be shown to be self-
refuting and absurd.[30] In like manner, since socialism must lead to the breakdown of society, and since the well-being of society is obviously necessary
for man's flourishing, then one might similarly argue that any economic system whose tendency is toward socialism must also be rejected, or at least held
in profound suspicion.

Yet Mises' critique of socialism went well beyond its economic shortcomings; he also demonstrated how it threatened the social and moral foundations
of society. In *Socialism* (1922), Mises warns that "proposals to transform the
relations between the sexes have long gone hand in hand with plans for the
socialization of the means of production. . . . Marriage is to disappear along
with private property."[31] Socialists, he argued, exploited the struggles of some
men in keeping the sexual instinct under control by holding out the prospect
of a society in which such struggle would no longer be necessary. Such a
strategy "was the more to be expected since many of them [the socialists]
were themselves neurotics suffering from an unhappy development of the
sexual instinct."[32]

After a spirited defense of marriage, Mises engages in a critique of feminism. "By 'abolishing' marriage one would not make woman any freer
and happier; one would merely take from her the essential content of her
life, and one could offer nothing to replace it."[33] Feminism, when "it attacks the institution of social life under the impression that it will thus be
able to remove the natural barriers," reveals itself as "a spiritual child of
socialism. For it is a characteristic of socialism to discover in social institutions the origin of unalterable facts of nature, and to endeavor, by re-
forming these institutions, to reform nature."[34] Yet another reason for opposing socialism, therefore, was that it carried social revolution in its train.
It hardly needs pointing out that this is rather a different claim from the one
ascribed to Mises by the critic above, according to which the great Austrian economist opposed socialism simply because it was economically
less efficient.

AUSTRIA VS. CHICAGO

As for Murray Rothbard, nothing could be further from the truth than to suggest that he opposed socialism because of its inefficiency. In fact, Rothbard wrote a well-known paper called "The Myth of Efficiency," in which he questioned the analytical usefulness of the very concept of efficiency as understood by the neoclassical mainstream.[35] Much of his career was dedicated to exposing the injustice of socialism and making the moral case for private property, and in fact he explicitly rejected the utilitarian case for the free market.[36] So committed was he to the question of justice, in fact, that he found himself in frequent opposition to the so-called Chicago School of economics, a school of thought associated with the University of Chicago, whose free-market credentials Rothbard threw into serious question.

The classic case in Chicago law and economics, famously described by Ronald Coase, is the example of the train that emits sparks that set fire to a farmer's crops. (The example occurs prior to the introduction of diesel engines.) Either the farmer or the train will have to bear the cost of this damage. On the basis of strict liability, of course, the farmer has the right to the property in question and therefore the right to enjoy its fruits unmolested. The train should compensate him for his loss or install some kind of spark retarding device. But Chicago decides this case on the basis of pure economic efficiency: the judge should decide the case in such a way that overall wealth is maximized.[37]

Austrians have objected to the Chicago approach on both positive and normative grounds. First, they have pointed out the difficulties inherent in attempts to measure efficiency without engaging in interpersonal comparisons of utility. In the case of purely voluntary exchanges, we can be certain that *ex ante* the utility of each party increases since otherwise they would not have made the exchange. The only way a coerced outcome could be judged "efficient" would be if it were philosophically (not to mention morally) legitimate to claim that the losses imposed on one party were more than offset by the gains to the other and/or to society as a whole. Since utility is inherently subjective and incommensurable, no such claims are permissible.[38]

Some Austrians have also been skeptical of Coase's claim that judges should take into account the economic consequences of their decisions "insofar as this is possible without creating too much uncertainty about the legal position itself."[39] The fact is, a policy of deciding cases on the basis of maximizing social wealth instead of on the much more straightforward (and just) basis of strict liability for damages to private property has to undermine the security and predictability that a private-property regime is supposed to provide, and makes individual planning far more precarious and uncertain.[40] It will inevitably create "uncertainty about the legal position itself."

More importantly, however, economists working within the Austrian tradition have offered a profound *moral* critique of Coase's entire approach, arguing that the rights of property should not be compromised in order to satisfy any wealth maximization calculus, and that as a rule strict liability should be observed.[41] (They offer these critiques in their capacities as moral philosophers rather than qua economists, a point to which we shall return in our discussion of economics as a value-free science.) Walter Block has described it as "*evil* and *vicious* to violate our most cherished and precious property rights in an ill-conceived attempt to maximize the monetary value of production."[42]

And make no mistake: Chicago economists do speak this way. In his original article delineating this approach, Coase formulated the problem as follows:

> The question is commonly thought of as one in which A inflicts harm on B and what has to be decided is: how shall we restrain A? But this is wrong. We are dealing with a problem of a reciprocal nature. To avoid the harm to B would inflict harm on A. The real question that has to be decided is: should A be allowed to harm B or should B be allowed to harm A? The problem is to avoid the more serious harm.[43]

To appreciate what Coase is saying here, imagine the train in our above example as A and the farmer as B. The traditional way of looking at the situation, says Coase, is that the train should be held strictly liable for damages to the farmer's crops. But the "real question," he insists, is whether the train should be allowed to harm the farmer (by setting fire to his crops) or whether the farmer should be allowed to harm the train (by demanding that the train either install a spark retarding device or compensate him for the damaged crops). The "more serious harm" is to be avoided by encouraging judges to decide a case like this on the basis of the economic consequences for society as a whole. In defense of Coase, Chicago economist Harold Demsetz argues that "[e]fficiency seems to be not merely one of the many criteria underlying our notions of ethically correct definitions of private property rights, but an extremely important one. It is difficult even to describe unambiguously any other criterion for determining what is ethical."[44] *Here* is efficiency analysis with a vengeance.

The idea of strict liability, championed by the Austrians, does not require that in every case the party suffering harm should be legally entitled to compensation. Surely it would be absurd for someone to build a house adjacent to an airport runway and demand that the airport respect his right to live free from excessive noise. In a case like this, Rothbard proposes the use of the "easement" concept, by which the airport, having preceded other comers to the area, is entitled to a noise easement corresponding to the level of noise that its normal operations have typically produced over the course of its existence. Noise emitted up to this level would not be actionable by later arrivals to the area. In a Lockean sense, the airport would have homesteaded a right to emit a certain level of noise, what we might call an easement right to noise emission. Now should the airport exceed its entitlement under the easement and begin emitting still louder noises, then either the airport may be ordered to cease and desist, or the newer arrivals could be entitled to compensation. It is hardly necessary to point out that none of this analysis has anything to do with "efficiency."[45] It has to do with maintaining a legal order based on principle and justice.

The point of this discussion is that it is not the Austrians who point to "economic efficiency" as the supreme value. Rothbard's Austrian treatment of law and economics has nothing whatever to do with efficiency and everything to do with *justice*. At no time in his entire career did he so much as hint that an alternative way of conceiving of the situation could be acceptable. Rothbard's opposition to socialism rested on similarly moral grounds. Unfortunately, a commentator who presumes to tell Catholics which economists they may and may not admire informs his readers that Rothbard cared only about efficiency. That is not even close enough to Rothbard's position to qualify as a caricature.

Rothbard's consistent commitment to justice should also put to rest once and for all the misunderstanding of the Austrian view of economics as a value-free science: that they considered the science itself to be value free at no time implied that *as men*, rather than as economists, they themselves ought to consider economic *policy* as a matter of indifference. As Rothbard himself put it:

> I conclude that we cannot decide on public policy, tort law, rights, or liabilities on the basis of efficiencies or minimizing of costs. But if not costs or efficiency, then what? The answer is that only *ethical principles* can serve as criteria for our decisions. Efficiency can never serve as the basis for ethics; on the contrary, ethics must be the guide and touchstone for any consideration of efficiency. Ethics is the primary. In the field of law and public policy . . . the primary ethical consideration is the concept that "dare not speak its name"—the concept of justice.[46]

We shall return once again to the topic of economics as a value-free science.

ECONOMIC LAW

The same figure who unfortunately dismisses Mises and Rothbard then goes on to condemn the Austrian position on economic law. The "original Austrian crusade," Sharpe writes, "was to assert the validity of economic 'law' against the German Historical School of economics, which maintained that such laws were a fiction. But the 'laws' which the Austrians maintained have *nothing* whatsoever to do with the Natural Law of philosophical realism and the Catholic Faith."[47]

It is difficult to decipher what Sharpe could mean when he claims that the Austrians' laws of economics "have nothing whatsoever to do with the natural law of philosophical realism and the Catholic Faith." He could mean it in the trivial sense that the law of diminishing marginal utility, for example, has nothing directly to do with the Catholic faith. Certainly true, but neither do many things of temporal value. Moreover, the laws of economics are derived from an axiom that is easily justified on the basis of St. Thomas. In any case, surely there is nothing wrong with studying a variety of subject matter, whether or not it bears directly on the Faith.

Perhaps, on the other hand, he means that the Austrians' laws of economics, and the philosophical method by which they are derived, are in fact somehow antagonistic toward or incompatible with the Catholic faith. What would be especially ironic about such an attack is that the most common criticism of Mises has come precisely from "modern" thinkers who consider him *too scholastic*. As David Gordon explains, "It is largely owing to the logical positivist influence on American philosophy that most American economists reject praxeology. *They regard Mises' method as old fashioned and scholastic, allegedly not in keeping with the dictates of scientific philosophy*."[48] Likewise, Sam Bostaph considers the *Methodenstreit* to have been primarily a battle between Humean nominalism and nineteenth-century neo-Scholasticism and Aristotelianism.[49] Philosophically, then, the laws of economics as derived through praxeology have in fact a great deal to do with philosophical realism and the Catholic faith.[50]

It is very significant that Richard Weaver, one of the great thinkers of the conservative intellectual renascence following World War II, considered praxeology a quintessentially conservative approach to economic thinking. The conservative, says Weaver, accepts reality as it is. He resists calls to remake human nature or the structure of reality around him. He acknowledges the existence of natural constraints that limit what is possible in this world. Praxeology, he writes, is but an extension of these insights. It teaches us "how things work because of their essential natures." It is, therefore,

> not only presumption, it is folly to try to interfere with the workings of a praxeology. One makes use of it, yes, in the same way that a follower of Bacon makes use of nature by obeying her. The great difference is that one is recognizing the objective; one is recognizing the laws that regulate man's affairs. Since the conservative and the libertarian believe that these cannot be wished

away through the establishment of a Utopia, they are both conservators of the real world.[51]

For that reason, real economists have often been disliked by heads of state. Mises once wrote that an economist "can never be a favorite of autocrats and demagogues. With them he is always the mischief maker, and the more they are inwardly convinced that his objections are well founded, the more they hate him."

> Princes and democratic majorities are drunk with power. They must reluctantly admit that they are subject to the laws of nature. But they reject the very notion of economic law. Are they not the supreme legislators? Don't they have the power to crush every opponent? No war lord is prone to acknowledge any limits other than those imposed on him by a superior armed force. Servile scribblers are always ready to foster such complacency by expounding the appropriate doctrines. They call their garbled presumptions "historical economics." In fact, economic history is a long record of government policies that failed because they were designed with a bold disregard for the laws of economics.[52]

We have already seen examples of economic laws, from supply and demand curves to the law of diminishing marginal utility. Many others might be cited, some of which are immediately evident even to those with no economic background (for instance, that the amount of production will be greater when two people specialize and take advantage of the division of labor than if they remain isolated in autarkic production). An increase in the demand for a good will tend to increase the price of that good to a level higher than it would otherwise have reached. A greater supply of a good will tend to decrease its price to a level lower than it would otherwise have reached. An increase in the quantity of money will tend to increase prices to a level higher than they would have been in the absence of the additional money.[53] None of these seems incompatible with, let alone actually hostile to, the Catholic faith. And if our critic simply meant to say that these laws have nothing directly to do with the Faith, it is not at all clear why a Catholic or anyone else would not still want to learn from them or make informed economic decisions on the basis of the knowledge they provide.

It is all very well to say that economic law is "fundamentally subordinate to moral law," and that man should not be "crushed by abstract and rationalist economic law, the way he is crushed by the law of gravity, should he find himself under a falling rock!"[54] But if economic law exists, then it no more makes sense to say that economic law should be subordinate to moral law than it does to say that physical laws should be subordinate to moral law. If they exist, they exist. Economic law cannot possibly be contradicted by the moral law. The moral law tells us what we ought to do. Economic law, on the other hand, is purely descriptive and necessarily amoral, having nothing to do with morality one way or the other.

Any reasonable application of moral law in concrete circumstances must take into account all the facts of those circumstances. Economic law is one of those facts, whether its opponents like it or not. If economic law tells us that the consequences of rent control will be shortages of rental housing (compared to the stock of rental housing that would have existed in the absence of rent control), it is completely senseless to argue that this economic law should be subordinate to moral law. It is a fact of reality. Policy makers who think they are subordinating economic law to moral law when they impose rent control in defiance of the economists' advice will be in for a very great disappointment.

What is probably happening here is that our critic, unfamiliar with the authors he is criticizing, simply assumes he knows what the Austrians mean by economic law when in fact he does not. It obviously makes no sense to say that the law of diminishing marginal utility should be subordinated to moral law, or that the economic law that a division-of-labor economy will produce more material wealth than one that lacks the specialization of tasks should be subordinated to the moral law. The only way his comments can make any sense is if he believes that the idea of "economic law" involves normative (that is, value-laden) statements, rather than merely positive (factual) statements. But absolutely nothing in the body of economic law derived through praxeology involves normative claims. For example, if a man wants to live in relative isolation from his fellows, spurning the material advantages of the international division of labor in order to pursue what he considers a more fulfilling and humane form of existence living self-sufficiently in the countryside, neither Mises personally nor Austrian economics as a whole has anything to say about his decision. All that economics can do is to outline for him the economic consequences of that decision. It can tell him that he will possess less material wealth outside the division of labor than he would within it. But if the man is aware of this factor and is willing to sacrifice material wealth in order to pursue his vision of the good life, there is nothing more that economics per se can say to him.

ECONOMICS: A VALUE-FREE SCIENCE?

This point leads us to another disputed question regarding economics: its value-free nature. A number of sources can be cited in favor of the idea that economics ought to be subordinate to ethics, or that the idea of economics as a completely autonomous science is a materialistic and liberal innovation that a Catholic cannot accept.[55] Again, however, this objection misconceives the very nature of economics as a science.

Economics is a discipline that reckons with the fact of scarcity in the world, and which demonstrates to man, *given his ends*, how they can or cannot be achieved. Thus if our end is to improve the lot of the least fortunate, economics can tell us whether a $25/hour minimum wage will or will not achieve that end. Economics, therefore, does not presume to dictate to us what our ends should be. Neither does it attempt to claim, by being "value free," that all values are equal, or that morality does not matter, or that all that matters is money. It is simply delineating the limits of its subject matter: it is a science whose purpose is to employ human reason to discover how man's ends can be reached. What those ends should be is a matter for theology and moral philosophy to decide. Father James Sadowsky, S.J., professor emeritus of philosophy at Fordham University, expressed it well when he said that ethics is *prescriptive* while economics is *descriptive*. "Economics," he says, "indicates the probable effects of certain policies, while ethics determines what one should do."[56] These are two very distinct things.

Every academic discipline, while making its own contribution to knowledge, is necessarily limited in the amount of the truth with which it can enlighten us. Catholics have rightly complained that for too long, natural scientists have neglected this principle, arguing from the fact that they themselves study observable phenomena that observable phenomena are all that exist. Moreover, while scientists can tell us what is scientifically possible or how a certain scientific goal might be reached, they can properly tell us nothing, qua scientists, about the *morality* of any of these things (e.g., *should* we investigate human cloning?).

As any genuine science should, therefore, economics properly acknowledges its limits. Again Rothbard:

> [E]conomists have been long engaged in what George Stigler, in another context, has called "intellectual imperialism." Economists will have to get used to the idea that not all of life can be encompassed by our own discipline. A painful lesson no doubt, but compensated by the knowledge that it may be good for our souls to realize our own limits—and, just perhaps, to learn about ethics and about justice.[57]

As men, of course, economists can and should take moral positions in favor of this or that proposal. Mises certainly did. Rothbard, his great student, wrote of him: "Economic science may be value-free, but men can never be, and Ludwig von Mises never shirked the responsibilities of being human."[58]

Inevitably, the values of the economist will influence the topics to which he devotes his attention. Thus it is unlikely that a properly informed Christian would spend his time trying to come up with the most effective way of debasing the monetary unit. To the contrary, he would be interested in how to establish an economy in which no government-induced inflation was possible.[59] But as Rothbard explains, "the unquestioned fact that values and ethics are important in guiding the attention of scientists to specific problems is irrelevant to the fact that the laws and disciplines of the science itself are value-free."[60]

Critics of this approach typically claim that to divorce ethics from economics is somehow anti-Christian, and that such allegedly artificial "compartmentalization" is a typical modern error.[61] This criticism misfires. It is rhetorically impressive to call for the insertion of a moral dimension into economics, but how exactly this "moral dimension" would figure into economic *method* is rarely explained. Is it the analysis of supply and demand curves that needs moral correction? Is it economists' understanding of the complementarity of capital structure? Is it their analysis of the economic effects of inflation that needs a moral dimension? In this latter case, the effects of inflation themselves certainly do hold important moral implications for policy making, as I show in chapter 3, but how could the *technical* analysis of these effects require a moral dimension?

Let us have some specifics: what, exactly, would be substituted for the value-free science of economics? Shall economists say, "Since a 90 percent tax rate would be immoral, we shall not even study what its consequences would be"? When opponents of value-free economic analysis are thus pinned down, their position disintegrates into incoherence.

Shawn Ritenour, defending *Wertfreiheit* (value freedom) against its critics, correctly observes: "It is not clear that the choice of the proper method depends on value judgment. It more likely depends on economists' opinions regarding the nature of reality. The belief that humans act is not a value judgment, but an opinion regarding the nature of man. The fact that ceteris paribus, if the demand for a good rises, its price will follow suit does not depend on the values of the economist. It is a deduction from the axiom that humans act purposefully."[62] An economist's *analysis*, as Professor Ritenour rightly argues, is either *correct* or *incorrect*, and not typically moral or immoral.

The economist, therefore, can describe for us the logically necessary consequences of raising a tariff, but he cannot tell us whether we should be more concerned about protecting jobs in domestic industries than with the lower standard of living and higher prices that consumers will face as a result. Describing the consequences of dropping a safe from a twenty-story building is a qualitatively different task from telling us whether or not we should drop a safe on someone's head, just as describing the effects of high marginal income tax rates is qualitatively different from advocating or condemning them.

Similarly, nuclear physics can tell us *how to construct* a nuclear missile, but it can tell us nothing about the circumstances, if any, in which it would be morally licit to use one. Such a question is, to say the least, at least as important from a moral point of view as any economic decision any of us will ever make, yet the critics of value-free economics refrain from criticizing nuclear scientists for not being moralists as well. If everyone in every discipline were expected to be an amateur moral philosopher in addition to a practitioner of his own field, we would wind up with a lot of perfectly useless moral advice from people who lacked the training to make such judgments.

If economics is a science, then *as a science* it must be permitted its autonomy. This is why Benjamin Rogge once asked:

> What can we find in the Bible on the ethical rightness of the statement that two plus two equals four? What do the Papal Encyclicals tell us of the justice of Boyle's Law, that the volume of an ideal gas varies inversely with its pressure, other things being equal? Does Christian doctrine tell us that it is fair for a hydrogen atom to contain three isotopes while a fluorine atom contains but two? Or, to approach my own topic, is it Christian or un-Christian for a demand curve to be negatively inclined from left to right?
>
> Let me now put the general case: What does Christianity have to do with the questions of any pure science? So that there can be no suspense, I shall give the answer immediately. The answer is, "Nothing, absolutely nothing." There can no more be a Christian science of economics than there can be a Christian science of mathematics.[63]

This is, of course, not to say that it is impermissible to make moral judgments with regard to someone's use of his wealth. We may rightly express moral disapproval of someone who squanders his wealth when his dependents rely on him. We may criticize someone for his lack of generosity with his accumulated wealth. When we say that economics must be value free, we are speaking only of economic analysis; we are not saying that no one may ever render a value judgment about someone's use of his own economic resources.

Criticism of *Wertfreiheit* in economics also reveals an unfortunate lack of acquaintance with the medieval university system, and in particular the way in which the medievals studied natural philosophy. At the University of Paris, for instance, the thirteenth century saw a clear distinction being made between natural philosophy (essentially the physical sciences) on the one hand and theology on the other; and the arts masters at Paris successfully managed to win autonomy for their discipline.[64] According to Edward Grant, one of the great historians of medieval science, "Although theology masters who wrote treatises on natural philosophy could have imported theology into their natural philosophy, they rarely did, choosing instead to relegate theological issues to theological treatises."[65] Natural philosophers in the arts faculties "were expected to refrain from introducing theology and matters of faith into natural philosophy."[66] These were considered separate disciplines, and practitioners of the two disciplines were expected to observe this separation. This arrangement was not generally condemned as "compartmentalization."

Consider the case of Albertus Magnus, St. Thomas' great teacher, who was asked by his Dominican brothers to "compose a book on physics for them of such a sort that in it they might be able to understand in a competent way the books of Aristotle." Lest they expect him in this book to intermingle theological ideas with natural philosophy, Albertus explicitly rejected that idea, since such matters "can in no way be known by means of arguments derived from nature." He explained:

> Pursuing what we have in mind, we take what must be termed "physics" more as what accords with the opinion of Peripatetics than as anything we might wish to introduce from our own knowledge . . . for if, perchance, we should have any opinion of our own, *this would be proffered by us (God willing) in theological works rather than in those on physics.*[67]

Asked toward the end of his life why he had not more frequently inserted matters of faith into his treatment of natural theology, St. Thomas replied, "I do not see what one's interpretation of the text of Aristotle has to do with the teaching of the faith." According to Vernon Bourke, St. Thomas did not consider himself "required to make Aristotle speak like a Christian," and he surely "thought that a scholarly commentary on Aristotle was a job by itself, *not to be confused with apologetics or theology.*"[68]

Surely economics, too, is a job by itself. And just as masters in medieval universities were capable of distinguishing between natural philosophy on the one hand and theology on the other, it should likewise be possible, if economics possesses the integrity of a science in its own right, to conceive of economics as a study equally distinct from theology. Such a distinction, having been made within the medieval university in its separation of natural philosophy from theology, is obviously not the nefarious creation of an anti-Catholic liberalism. St. Thomas made a famous distinction between knowledge attainable by reason alone, knowledge attainable by reason and also known by faith, and knowledge attainable only through faith (e.g., supernatural mysteries such as the Holy Trinity). Economics and its laws belong to the category of knowledge that is attainable by reason alone.

Having explained and defended the foundations and value-free nature of economic science, we can now turn to the discussion of specific economic issues.

NOTES

1. Stanley L. Jaki, *Science and Creation: From Eternal Cycles to an Oscillating Universe* (Edinburgh, Scotland: Scottish Academic Press, 1986), 150. Jaki continues: "The coupling of the reasonability of the Creator and the constancy of nature is worth noting because it is there that lie the beginnings of the idea of the autonomy of nature and of its laws." Cf. Ps. 8:4, 19:3–7, 104:9, 19, 148:3, 6; Jer. 5:24, 31:35.

2. Ludwig von Mises, "Social Science and Natural Science," in *Money, Method, and the Market Process: Essays by Ludwig von Mises*, ed. Richard M. Ebeling (Boston: Kluwer, 1990).

3. Roy Porter, *The Creation of the Modern World: The Untold Story of the British Enlightenment* (New York: W. W. Norton, 2000), 387.

4. Ludwig von Mises, *Human Action: A Treatise on Economics*, Scholar's edition (Auburn, Ala.: Ludwig von Mises Institute, 1998), 240. The book was originally published by Yale University Press in 1949.

5. Frédéric Bastiat, *Economic Harmonies*, ed. George B. de Huszar (Irvington-on-Hudson, N.Y.: Foundation for Economic Education, 1997). Emphasis in original. I owe this reference to Jeffrey Herbener.

6. David Gordon, *The Philosophical Origins of Austrian Economics* (Auburn, Ala.: Ludwig von Mises Institute, 1993), 8.

7. Ludwig von Mises, *The Historical Setting of the Austrian School of Economics* (1969; repr., Auburn, Ala.: Ludwig von Mises Institute, 1984); see also Gordon, *Philosophical Origins*.

8. See Ludwig von Mises, *The Ultimate Foundation of Economic Science: An Essay on Method* (Princeton, N.J.: D. Van Nostrand, 1962); idem, *Epistemological Problems of Economics*, trans. George Reisman (Auburn, Ala.: Ludwig von Mises Institute, 2003 [1960]).

9. Jörg Guido Hülsmann, "Facts and Counterfactuals in Economic Law," *Journal of Libertarian Studies* 17 (Winter 2003): 86.

10. Murray N. Rothbard, "In Defense of 'Extreme Apriorism,'" *Southern Economic Journal* 3 (January 1957): 314–20.

11. Mises, *Human Action*, p. 97.

12. After discussing human action, Professor Gabriel Zanotti proposes that "the metaphysics and anthropology of St. Thomas are the most appropriate philosophical bases for providing a foundation for the description of human action just established." Gabriel J. Zanotti, "Fundamentos Filosóficos Epistemológicos de la Praxeología," *Libertas*, no. 13 (October 1990). Translation mine.

13. St. Thomas Aquinas, *Summa Contra Gentiles*, Book 3, Part 1, trans. Vernon J. Bourke (Notre Dame, Ind.: University of Notre Dame Press, 1975), 34–40; quotations on 34, 37, 38. See also Gabriel J. Zanotti, "Misesian Praxeology and Christian Philosophy," *Journal of Markets and Morality* 1 (March 1998).

14. Zanotti, "Fundamentos Filosóficos y Epistemológicos de la Praxeología." Translation mine.

15. It would take us too far afield to consider in much depth the claim of the critics of praxeology that Mises' point here is a mere tautology—i.e., we choose to perform

the action at the top of our ranking, and the action at the top of our ranking is what we choose to perform. Let us simply note that even if Mises' statement were tautological (and I do not believe it is), that would hardly be a decisive argument against it, since tautologies can themselves be useful in clarifying our understanding. Thus, for instance, some philosophers argue that all of mathematics constitutes one great tautology, since the answers to all problems are essentially implied once more elementary concepts are understood. But surely no one would say that mathematics is not useful, or that it does not contribute to our understanding. Cf. Mises, *Human Action*, 38.

16. Murray N. Rothbard, *Man, Economy, and State: A Treatise on Economic Principles* (Auburn, Ala.: Ludwig von Mises Institute, 1993 [1962]), 270.

17. Mises, *Human Action*, 125–27.

18. Thomas C. Taylor, *An Introduction to Austrian Economics* (Auburn, Ala.: Ludwig von Mises Institute, 1980).

19. Mises, *Ultimate Foundation of Economic Science*, 41; cited in Lawrence H. White, "The Methodology of the Austrian School Economists," available at <http://www.mises.org/mofase.asp> (July 8, 2004). This statement may appear to contradict Rothbard's justification of the action axiom as broadly empirical. But the two positions can be reconciled. Rothbard is arguing that the central praxeological truth of the existence of human action can be derived from experience. But he would join Mises in rejecting the idea that experience could somehow contradict or falsify a praxeological law.

20. Hans-Hermann Hoppe, *Democracy, The God that Failed: The Economics and Politics of Monarchy, Democracy, and Natural Order* (New Brunswick, N.J.: Transaction, 2001), xv.

21. Mises, *Human Action*, 32.

22. John Sharpe, "Liberal Economics vs. Catholic Truth," SeattleCatholic.com, November 3, 2002 <http://www.seattlecatholic.com/article_20021103_Liberal_Economics_vs_Catholic_Truth.html> (November 4, 2002).

23. Although not central to my argument, it should be pointed out for the sake of clarification that the Austrian definition of profit differs from that used in common parlance, the one I have employed in my discussion of socialist calculation. To the Austrian, profit exists only when a firm's return exceeds the return he could have earned from the going rate of interest. Such superabundant returns are only ephemeral, since they encourage expansion in the profitable industry by newcomers until the phenomenon of profit once again approaches zero.

24. As Jeffrey Herbener puts it, "These prices make the different units of the factors [of production] commensurate, and therefore permit entrepreneurs to efficiently allocate factors across the production of consumer goods." Jeffrey M. Herbener, "Calculation and the Question of Arithmetic," *Review of Austrian Economics* 9, 1 (1996): 154.

25. Ludwig von Mises, *Economic Calculation in the Socialist Commonwealth* (Auburn, Ala.: Ludwig von Mises Institute, 1990 [1920]).

26. Herbener, "Calculation and the Question of Arithmetic," p. 153.

27. Murray N. Rothbard, "The End of Socialism and the Calculation Debate Revisited," *Review of Austrian Economics* 5, 2 (1991): 66. Emphasis in original.

28. Joseph T. Salerno, "Postscript," in Mises, *Economic Calculation in the Socialist Commonwealth*, 53.

29. Mises, *Human Action*, 676. Emphasis in original.

30. See, for example, Celestine N. Bittle, O.F.M.Cap., *Reality and the Mind: Epistemology* (New York: Bruce Publishing Co., 1936), 61.

31. Ludwig von Mises, *Socialism: An Economic and Sociological Analysis* (Indianapolis, Ind.: Liberty Classics, 1981 [1922]), 74.

32. Mises, *Socialism*, 75.

33. Mises, *Socialism*, p. 90; see also Jeffrey A. Tucker and Llewellyn H. Rockwell, Jr., "The Cultural Thought of Ludwig von Mises," *Journal of Libertarian Studies* 10 (Fall 1991): 23–52.

34. Mises, *Socialism*, 87.

35. See Murray N. Rothbard, "The Myth of Efficiency," in *Time, Uncertainty, and Disequilibrium*, ed. Mario Rizzo (Lexington, Mass.: Lexington Books, 1979), 90–95; reprinted in Murray N. Rothbard, *The Logic of Action One: Method, Money, and the Austrian School* (Gloucester, UK: Edward Elgar, 1997), 266–73. The article also appeared in a French translation in 1991. The pagination in these notes is taken from *The Logic of Action*. For more on Rothbard, efficiency, and the Austrians, see E. C. Pasour, Jr., "Economic Efficiency and Public Policy," in *Man, Economy, and Liberty: Essays in Honor of Murray N. Rothbard*, eds. Walter Block and Llewellyn H. Rockwell, Jr. (Auburn, Ala.: Ludwig von Mises Institute, 1988), 110–24.

36. Murray N. Rothbard, *The Ethics of Liberty* (Atlantic Highlands, N.J.: Humanities Press, 1982), 201–13.

37. The seminal article is Ronald Coase, "The Problem of Social Cost," *Journal of Law and Economics* 3 (October 1960): 1–44. The argument is somewhat more involved than this, but it would make little sense to devote much more space to what is really a tangential point in my overall argument. In essence, though, this is indeed the Chicago position.

38. Rothbard made this point years before Coase's article had been written. See Murray N. Rothbard, "Toward a Reconstruction of Utility and Welfare Economics," in *On Freedom and Free Enterprise: Essays in Honor of Ludwig von Mises*, ed. Mary Sennholz (Princeton, N.J.: D. Van Nostrand, 1956), 224–62; see also Edward Stringham, "Kaldor-Hicks Efficiency and the Problem of Central Planning," *Quarterly Journal of Austrian Economics* 4 (Summer 2001): 41–50.

39. Coase, "The Problem of Social Cost," 19.

40. Gary North, "Undermining Property Rights: Coase and Becker," *Journal of Libertarian Studies* 16 (Fall 2002): 75–100, esp. 84–85; Walter Block, "Coase and Demsetz on Private Property Rights," *Journal of Libertarian Studies* 1 (Spring 1977): 114.

41. Murray N. Rothbard, "Law, Property Rights, and Air Pollution," *Cato Journal* 2 (Spring 1982): 55–99; reprinted in idem, *The Logic of Action Two: Applications and Criticism from the Austrian School* (Gloucester, UK: Edward Elgar, 1997), 121–70. On the distinction between the Austrian and Chicago schools on this point, the debate between Harold Demsetz (Chicago) and Walter Block (Austrian) is useful and interesting: Block, "Coase and Demsetz on Private Property Rights," 111–15; Harold

Demsetz, "Ethics and Efficiency in Property Rights Systems," in Rizzo, ed., *Time, Uncertainty, and Disequilibrium*, 97–125; Walter Block, "Ethics, Efficiency, Coasian Property Rights, and Psychic Income: A Reply to Demsetz," *Review of Austrian Economics* 8, 2 (1995): 61–125; Harold Demsetz, "Block's Erroneous Interpretations," *Review of Austrian Economics* 10, 2 (1997): 101–9; Walter Block, "Private-Property Rights, Erroneous Interpretations, Morality, and Economics: Reply to Demsetz," *Quarterly Journal of Austrian Economics* 3 (Spring 2000): 63–78.

42. Block, "Coase and Demsetz on Private Property Rights," 115.

43. Coase, "The Problem of Social Cost," 2.

44. Demsetz, "Ethics and Efficiency in Property Rights Systems," 109.

45. See Rothbard, "Law, Property Rights, and Air Pollution," 145ff.

46. Rothbard, "The Myth of Efficiency," 273. Emphasis in original.

47. Sharpe, "Liberal Economics vs. Catholic Truth." Emphasis in original.

48. Gordon, *Philosophical Origins*, 32–33. Emphasis added.

49. The German Historical School, Bostaph writes, "was primarily informed by Humean nominalism, while Carl Menger is best understood in the context of nineteenth-century Aristotelian/neo-scholasticism." Samuel Bostaph, "The *Methodenstreit*," in *The Elgar Companion to Austrian Economics*, ed. Peter J. Boettke (Cheltenham, UK: Edward Elgar, 1994), 460.

50. As David Gordon concludes, "Austrian economics and a realistic philosophy seem made for each other." Gordon, *Philosophical Origins*, 41.

51. Richard M. Weaver, "Conservatism and Libertarianism: The Common Ground," in *In Defense of Tradition: The Shorter Essays of Richard M. Weaver*, ed. Ted J. Smith III (Indianapolis, Ind.: Liberty Fund, 2000), 480.

52. Mises, *Human Action*, 67.

53. Hülsmann, "Facts and Counterfactuals in Economic Law," 72–73, 76–78. In these latter cases we speak of tendencies (or, to use a Misesian term adapted by Hülsmann, "case-probable" laws) rather than of exact laws. For example, whether a higher supply of a good would lead to a lower price for the good than otherwise depends on the value scales of individuals. Yet because the amount of the higher supply is dedicated to less urgently valued ends, there is a strong tendency for the price to decrease, since people will typically be willing to satisfy their less-valued ends only at lower prices.

54. Sharpe, "Liberal Economics vs. Catholic Truth."

55. For example, T. J. Flaherty, "Economics without Ethics," *America* (January 14, 1922): 300; Sharpe, "Liberal Economics vs. Catholic Truth."

56. Lucía Santa Cruz, "Etica y Capitalismo: Entrevista a James Sadowsky, S.J.," *El Mercurio*, November 22, 1987. Translation mine.

57. Rothbard, "The Myth of Efficiency," 273.

58. Murray N. Rothbard, "Mises and the Role of the Economist in Public Policy," in *The Meaning of Ludwig von Mises: Contributions in Economics, Sociology, Epistemology, and Political Philosophy*, ed. Jeffrey M. Herbener (Boston: Kluwer, 1993), 207.

59. Gary North, *An Introduction to Christian Economics* (Nutley, N.J.: Craig Press, 1976), xi–xii.

60. Rothbard, *The Logic of Action One*, 80.

61. This claim was advanced, for example, in private correspondence with David E. Rockett, author of the lengthy booklet *Modern Capitalism: A Christian-Agrarian Critique* (2000), and by John Sharpe in an article that appeared on SeattleCatholic.com.

62. Shawn Ritenour, "Praxeology as Christian Economics" (paper presented at the Baylor University conference "Christianity and Economics," November 7–9, 2002).

63. Benjamin Rogge, *Can Capitalism Survive?* (Indianapolis, Ind.: Liberty Fund, 1979). Fr. Sadowsky points out that there is "nothing in the deposit of faith, nothing in the content of revelation" that explains how poverty should best be addressed. "There is no revealed solution to the problem of poverty any more than there is a revealed cure for cancer. Just as there is no revealed medicine, so there is no revealed economics." James Sadowsky, S.J., *The Christian Response to Poverty* (London: The Social Affairs Unit, 1985), 3.

64. Edward Grant, *The Foundations of Modern Science in the Middle Ages: Their Religious, Institutional, and Intellectual Contexts* (Cambridge, UK: Cambridge University Press, 1996), 73–74.

65. Edward Grant, *God and Reason in the Middle Ages* (Cambridge, UK: Cambridge University Press, 2001), 186.

66. Grant, *God and Reason in the Middle Ages*, 184.

67. Grant, *God and Reason in the Middle Ages*, 192. Emphasis added. Albertus' view that theology should intrude as little as possible into natural philosophy is apparent in a great many statements of his. Speaking about whether the heaven was ungenerable and incorruptible, he says, "Another opinion was that of Plato who says that the heaven was derived from the first cause by creation from nothing, and this opinion is also the opinion of the three laws, namely of the Jews, Christians, and Saracens. And thus they say that the heaven is generated, but not from something. But with regard to this opinion, *it is not relevant for us to treat it here.*" Grant, *God and Reason in the Middle Ages*, 192; emphasis added.

68. Grant, *God and Reason in the Middle Ages*, 196–97. Emphasis added.

Chapter Two

Prices, Wages, and Labor

Having seen something of the character of economic law and its ultimate derivation, we are in a better position to develop our principal arguments. Many good and orthodox thinkers have argued for some time now that in order for Catholic social teaching to achieve its stated goals, it must make room for the indispensable testimony of economic science. By the time of *Rerum Novarum*, explains James Sadowsky, S.J., the "important treatises on classical economics had already been completed, and the age of Austrian economics had begun with the publication of Menger's *Principles* in 1871. Yet *Rerum Novarum* betrays no significant amount of attention to any of the writings of the great economists—though if one wishes to understand the workings of the market, that is exactly what one has to do."[1]

This unfortunate lack of knowledge of the operation of the market economy has been noted by a wide array of observers. Daniel Villey contended decades ago that "very few Roman Catholic theologians really know what [economic] liberalism is or understand the working of a market economy."[2] A. M. C. Waterman speaks of "the lack of understanding of the market economy evinced by *Rerum Novarum*" and "an insulation of official doctrine from economic science that persists to this day in the public utterances of the hierarchy."[3]

For well over a century, this lack of knowledge has led to public statements by Catholic spokesmen that can only alienate those familiar with the principles of economics. A number of scholars have chronicled the influence of the economically confused Vicomte Alban de Villeneuve-Bargemont on the development of the social teaching. At a time when real income per head in France was growing at 1.4 percent per year (which meant a doubling of the command over goods and services every fifty years), as it was from 1800 to

1900, Villeneuve attacked industralization on the grounds that "the accumulation and concentration of capital [and] the universal use of machinery . . . would indefinitely multiply the number of the poor." This standard fallacy amounts to saying that all railroads should be demolished, since the use of such machinery causes unemployment and impoverishment for those who had previously hauled freight by carrying it on their backs. In reality, of course, the use of machinery to perform these tasks (and with much greater effectiveness and efficiency) means that the labor that had once been devoted to them is now released into the economy to provide other services or produce other goods that people desire but could not have had before the introduction of machinery released the necessary labor.

One scholar describes the consequences of Villeneuve's lack of acquaintance with economics:

> Villeneuve's immediate and pressing concern was relief of the thousands of paupers under his jurisdiction as Prefect of the department of Nord. *Lacking an analytical framework* within which to investigate the relation between capital accumulation, technical progress and economic growth, he was deceived by appearances into mistaking a correlation between industrialization and pauperism (which he investigated extensively and comparatively) for a causal relation.[4]

It is precisely this missing analytical framework, which Austrian economics provides so elegantly, that has unfortunately led to so much fallacious economic reasoning within Catholic circles.

Implied in the praxeological framework is Frédéric Bastiat's central insight (which Henry Hazlitt made the centerpiece of his classic *Economics in One Lesson* [1946]): economic reasoning involves considering the long-run effects on the entire economy that a given measure is likely to have rather than on its obvious and visible short-run effects on a particular sector. Virtually every economic fallacy results from neglect of this principle—as Bastiat would say, on devoting too much attention to "what is seen" and little if any attention to "what is not seen." We see the jobs created by government make-work projects, for instance; we do not see the jobs that never come into existence because government make-work has robbed the private sector of the necessary capital. We see the people who receive higher wages that a state decree makes possible; we do not see (because they are not so earmarked) the people driven out of work by the same decree—not to mention still other destructive consequences, discussed below.

As with the German Historical School that Ludwig von Mises opposed, proponents of Catholic social teaching tend in practice to deny the very existence of economic law. Their position therefore neglects altogether the role that reason must play in assessing the consequences of seemingly "progressive" economic policies, as well as in apprehending the order and harmony that can exist within complex (in this case market) phenomena. This attitude runs directly counter to the entire Catholic intellectual tradition, according to which man is to conform his actions to reality, rather than embarking on the hopeless task of forcing the world to conform to him and to his desires.

Thus, for example, that every man should earn a "family wage" that allows his family to live in reasonable comfort is a desirable social goal. The strong implication of some Catholic social thinkers that such an outcome can be brought into existence by decree, however, that man's will can establish such a state of affairs by his ipse dixit, and that no recourse to any so-called economic law can be of any help in ascertaining the probable outcome of such measures, is no more intellectually defensible than the suggestion that man's desire to fly renders superfluous any need to take into account the law of gravity.

Such a posture, in addition to the damage it does to the existing stock of wealth and to social comity itself, is thoroughly uncharacteristic of the Catholic Church, an institution that has always emphasized the mind's ability to *perceive* the orderliness of God's creation and to *conform itself* to it. Truth, say Catholic catechisms, consists of *the conformity of mind to reality*. All too many Catholic commentators, on the other hand, demand that man allow mere desire and sentiment to form his judgment in economic matters, rather than assessing the consequences of economic measures with the aid of economic law, and rather than looking in the economic realm for the order and regularity to which the Church points in so many other areas as reflections of the orderliness of God himself.

THE SPANISH SCHOLASTICS

There was nothing inevitable about the direction that Catholic social thought has taken over the past century. As we saw in the introduction, among the great advances in the study of the history of economic thought that took place in the twentieth century was the rediscovery of the fairly voluminous economic insights of the late Scholastic theologians, particularly in Spain. Much of what these sixteenth-century Catholic thinkers taught in the economic realm revealed a considerable understanding of and appreciation for the functioning of the market, including the role of entrepreneurship, the nature of exchange, and the justice of prices and wages determined by the free interplay of supply and demand. Well before Adam Smith, therefore, a whole host of thinkers not only anticipated many of his insights regarding the free market but even avoided some of the errors (the labor theory of value chief among them) that would arise in Smith's work.

To be sure, the Spanish Scholastics did not possess a self-conscious or explicitly elaborated conception of the market as an intrinsically harmonious and self-regulating system analogous to the self-regulating physical universe of Isaac Newton, and it would be anachronistic to expect such a conception. They were, moreover, interested more in the moral dimension of economics than in a descriptive elaboration of how various economic mechanisms functioned. Still, a recognition of the binding nature of economic law is obviously taken for granted in a great many of their contentions. The Scholastics derived certain economic relationships, such as the quantity theory of money, in the process of reaching moral conclusions, and thereby demonstrated their fundamental if at times inchoate recognition that the economy functioned in certain definite ways and that it would be foolish for human whim to attempt to defy them. Thus consider this summary of the Scholastic critique of price regulation:

> Regulation of prices by the authorities or by guilds sooner or later produces incorrect prices and a distorted market. Because the prices of goods are internally related, it serves no purpose to regulate the prices of the end-products only. This thesis is illustrated by means of an example. If the authorities wish to regulate the prices of bread and shoes, the prices of wheat and leather must also be kept under control. If not, then distorted growth takes place in the production line or between this and the distribution line.[5]

Likewise, Juan de Mariana, S.J. (1536–1624) warned of the consequences of state interference with market phenomena:

> Only a fool would try to separate these values in such a way that the legal price should differ from the natural. Foolish, nay, wicked the ruler who orders that a thing the common people value, let us say, at five should be sold for ten. Men are guided in this matter by common estimation founded on considerations of the quality of things, and their abundance or scarcity. It would be vain for a Prince to seek to undermine these principles of commerce. 'Tis best to leave them intact instead of assailing them by force to the public detriment.[6]

In addition to the rediscovery of the importance of the late Scholastics in general, another important recent accomplishment in the history of economic thought was Raymond de Roover's crucial revision of our understanding of what the late Scholastics meant by the "just price." For a long time, it was assumed that the so-called just price was a price distinct from the price reached on the free market, and reflected either the cost of production or the good's alleged intrinsic value. In fact, the just price was the market price, the price established by the "common estimation" of buyers and sellers. The one proviso in this position was that in unusual cases—some kind of emergency, for instance—the public authorities possessed the right to impose a fair price, and in these cases the Scholastics generally agreed that the state-imposed price was the just price.[7] But this was the exception. In 1554, Luís Saravia de la Calle Veroñese summarized the Scholastics' position by noting that the just price "arises from the abundance or scarcity of goods, merchants, and money, as has been said, and not from costs, labor and risk. If we had to consider labor and risk in order to assess the just price, no merchant would ever suffer loss, nor would abundance or scarcity of goods and money enter into the question."[8]

An exception to this consensus was Heinrich von Langenstein the Elder (or Henry of Hesse). Langenstein actually favored government price fixing in order to establish a "just price." One good purpose that would be served by such price-fixing, he contended, was that each seller would thereby be able to maintain his station in life. Anyone attempting to charge a price that could advance him beyond his station would be guilty of avarice. This position had been explicitly rejected by St. Thomas Aquinas, and indeed Langenstein was the only scholastic to advance it.

However, an excessive emphasis on Langenstein's view served for a long time to distort the scholastics' views of the just price. As Murray Rothbard observed in his history of economic thought:

Von Langenstein was scarcely important in his own or at a later day; his great importance is solely that he was plucked out of well-deserved obscurity by late nineteenth century socialist and state corporatist historians, who used his station in life fatuity to conjure up a totally distorted vision of the Catholic Middle Ages. That era, so the myth ran, was solely governed by the view that each man can only charge the just price to maintain him in his presumably divinely appointed station in life. In that way, these historians glorified a non-existent society of status in which each person and group found himself in a harmonious hierarchical structure, undisturbed by market relations or capitalist greed.[9]

And who promoted this view?

This nonsensical view of the Middle Ages and of scholastic doctrine was first propounded by German socialist and state corporatist historians Wilhelm Roscher and Werner Sombart in the late nineteenth century, and it was then seized upon by such influential writers as the Anglican socialist Richard Henry Tawney and the Catholic corporatist scholar and politician Amintore Fanfani. Finally, this view, based only on the doctrines of one obscure and heterodox scholastic, was enshrined in conventional histories of economic thought, where it was seconded by the free market but fanatically anti-Catholic economist Frank Knight and his followers in the now highly influential Chicago School.[10]

So much for Langenstein. Yet although the late Scholastics did demonstrate a profound appreciation for the mechanisms of the market, the exception they allowed for state-imposed prices is a glaring one. There appears to have been little if any Scholastic analysis of the implications of state-imposed prices. When those implications are examined, I believe the Scholastic proviso about state-imposed prices loses its strength, and we are compelled to universalize their view that the market price is the just price.

THE JUST PRICE

A Days Inn on Long Island was fined on December 26, 2001 for having engaged in "price gouging" following the September 11 terrorist attacks. With the nation's airports closed, stranded passengers created a sudden and unexpected rise in demand for lodging. Under these circumstances, the Hicksville hotel raised its room rates by 185 percent—an "unconscionable" increase, according to state officials.

The Days Inn case, although not extraordinarily significant in its own right, presents an opportunity to consider what exactly happens when a businessman engages in so-called price gouging—and what happens when he is forbidden by the state to do so.

According to a press release issued shortly after the attacks, New York State law actually prohibits price gouging during declared states of emergency: "State law prohibits charging unconscionably excessive prices for consumer goods and services that are vital and necessary for the health, safety, and welfare of consumers during any abnormal disruption of the market caused by strikes, power failures, severe shortages or other extraordinary adverse circumstances."

The "adverse circumstances" to which the state law refers would, in fact, constitute the worst time at which to prohibit such price hikes. When, say, a natural disaster hits, there is sudden and severe pressure on current stocks of certain essential goods. Interference with the market's effort to adjust to the new state of affairs can only lead to the kind of shortages that we associate with any attempt at price control.

Let us take a slightly silly but nevertheless instructive example. Suppose it begins raining in a small and more or less isolated town. Suppose further that the rain continues day after day, with no end in sight. It is altogether likely that the price of umbrellas will increase, even dramatically, in the short run. The price increase reflects the fact that new supplies of umbrellas have not magically appeared since the outbreak of the storm. Whatever supplies currently exist will have to suffice for the present crisis.

The higher prices that often accompany such disasters serve a salutary purpose: they encourage people to economize on those items that are in greatest demand at the time. Had the umbrella price been forced by law to remain fixed, a household of six may have purchased six umbrellas. But if the price is allowed to rise—even dramatically—in the wake of these sudden and unexpected circumstances, the family is much more likely to economize: to purchase, say, three umbrellas, covering two heads each. The three they end up not purchasing are now available for another household to acquire.

This is how a market economy encourages sharing and cooperation during crises: not by central planning, reeducation camps, and slavery, but by a price system that is free to fluctuate in response to changing conditions.

The same holds for hotel space. Suppose again that some disaster has struck. At the standard room rate, a family of four seeking short-term lodging may well prefer two rooms: one for Mom and Dad and another for the kids. But if the room rate rises, the family may well decide to settle for a single room for all of them. Thanks to "unconscionable" price gouging, the family in question economizes on hotel space, and the extra room they might have used under normal circumstances is now available for another family during the emergency. (Would it have been compassionate and humane for the second family not to be able to find any lodging at all?)

The fact is, scarce resources must be rationed somehow. A market economy with freely fluctuating prices constitutes one form of rationing. Those who condemn the "greed" of those who charge what the market will bear appear to believe that the rationing that price controls bring is somehow morally superior.[11] But price controls simply reward those who, in effect, can run fast. Put that way, how can such a system be considered morally superior to its market alternative? Why, from a moral point of view, should the limber and sprightly win out over the slow or handicapped? Price controls not only decrease the quantity of a good that producers are willing to sell, but without the discipline imposed by higher prices, the limited supply of goods will be acquired only by those who arrive first—and these buyers will have no incentive to economize on them.

Similarly, price controls favor those who have the leisure time to wait in long lines, and those who are most capable of doing so are not likely to be the poor and disadvantaged in whose name "social justice" advocates call for price controls. An envy-driven egalitarianism almost certainly accounts for some of the impetus behind price controls, the idea being that rich and poor alike will have to wait in the same lines and suffer the same inconveniences. But John D. Rockefeller can always get one of his servants to stand in line.

So-called price gouging cannot, of course, go on forever. Generally speaking, the disaster in question eventually subsides, new supplies become available, and the like. But if the market is shackled during the critical transition period from crisis to normalcy, the potentially catastrophic shortages of critical goods and services that may result will only add to the misery of those already adversely affected.

Allowing the market to function has the additional benefit of providing incentives whereby the shortage may be alleviated. Suppose a hurricane does serious damage to homes in Florida. The price of lumber rises immediately, to reflect the scarcities brought into effect by the sudden, overwhelming rise in demand. Seizing upon this opportunity for profit, lumber suppliers from across the country rush to make their products available to Floridians in need. This pressure on lumber supplies in the rest of the country raises lumber prices there as well (although not as severely). These price increases encourage all Americans to economize on lumber, thereby releasing additional supplies for use in Florida. A man in Cincinnati intending to build a doghouse, finding the price of lumber unexpectedly high, may well decide not to build one at all, or at least to forego the project for now. The unfettered ability to bid up prices thus allows Floridians to draw lumber supplies away from less urgent uses throughout the country and toward the more urgent uses of those who have lost their homes in the disaster.[12]

During the oil crisis of the 1970s, price controls led to a host of perverse outcomes that basic economic literacy would have avoided. Because of their inability to express in the marketplace the urgency of their need for oil, truck drivers were increasingly reluctant to transport *food shipments* to southern Florida, out of fear that they would be unable to acquire the necessary fuel for the return trip up the peninsula. Even the continuing functioning of *oil rigs themselves* off the Louisiana coast was jeopardized because of an inability to acquire various oil products they needed.[13] Here are price controls in all their absurdity, interfering with the production of the very good whose scarcity was said to justify price controls in the first place. As one economist explains, "[I]n a free market the more important employments of oil would have outbid the less important ones, and the reduction in the supply of oil would have been taken out exclusively at the expense of the marginal employments of oil—that is, at the expense of the least important employments for which the previously larger supply of oil had sufficed."[14]

Finally and most perversely of all, the price controls made it unprofitable for other oil suppliers to enter the American market and alleviate the shortage. Higher prices would have attracted these new sources and helped to bring the crisis to an end; the lower prices mandated by the controls gave no one any financial incentive to supply America with additional oil, and guaranteed that the crisis would go on indefinitely.

Price controls also replace the harmony of mutual interests between buyer and seller with mutual antagonism and bitterness. An anecdote from the days of the oil shortage in the 1970s illustrates the point. As part of the inevitable rationing that occurred under the price controls, people with license plates ending with even numbers could purchase gasoline on one day and those with odd numbers the next. This alternating occurred day after day. A New Jersey gas station attendant, speaking of customers unaware of the new rationing rules, was quoted as saying, "If he's that stupid, he waits in line an hour and doesn't know the rules, I let him get to the pump—and then I break his heart."[15] Overwhelmed with customers desperate to acquire a product that price controls have rendered artificially scarce, gas stations—or any other business in a similar situation—can get away with treating the customer with contempt, since there are always plenty more where he came from.

A better example, however, since it involves a situation that has existed far longer than the oil shortage ever did, is rent control—that is, price controls on rental housing. Rent control, naturally, leads to housing shortages (as a greater number of willing consumers chase a declining number of willing sellers), though once again, people shut out of the housing market are unlikely to be aware of the role of rent control in their woes. Since the landlord may well find that he can no longer earn a decent profit (if indeed he can earn any at all), he has little incentive to be attentive to the needs or complaints of his tenants. An artificially long line of potential occupants is always available, so he need not concern himself too much with tenant satisfaction. Repairs will go undone. The building will deteriorate, since at the rents he is forced to charge, the landlord has little incentive to engage in normal upkeep. And given their awareness that they may not be able to find another rental unit in the city, tenants who loathe their landlords and consider themselves engaged in a low-level war with them will nevertheless remain. As Hazlitt explained, rent-control laws "create ill feeling between landlords who are forced to take minimum returns or even losses, and tenants who resent the landlord's failure to make adequate repairs."[16]

Let us return to the Days Inn. No one argues that individual businessmen are infallible. It is by no means uncommon for a businessman to make an inaccurate appraisal of market conditions. An Oklahoma gas station, for example, made national news when it raised the price of gasoline to five dollars per gallon following the attacks of September 11. That particular appraisal of market conditions proved absurd and laughable, and the proprietor doubtless lost business as a result. The market has a way of punishing false appraisals.

This may well have happened in the case of the Days Inn. The proprietor is not infallible and was responding to conditions as he perceived them. After receiving complaints from consumers about the increased rates in Hicksville, the company's central office, Days Inn Worldwide Inc., suggested to him both that he refund the money of travelers who were overcharged and that he make free rooms available to members of the military and the USO as well as workers from the Red Cross.

Thus private forces were already being brought to bear against the proprietor in question, and indeed ordinary market forces more than suffice to penalize the maverick vendor who jumps the gun following some unexpected event or disaster. The problem is that state officials doubtless considered this case a victory for the general principle that "price gouging" is a vicious and antisocial offense, and one that ought to be prohibited, especially during emergency conditions.

The truth, however, is just the opposite: prohibiting such activity across the board only handicaps the market in its effort to make current stocks of goods last during the crucial days following a disaster. The sixteenth-century thinker Martin de Azpilcueta, better known as Doctor Navarrus, summarized the matter well when he observed that price fixing was unnecessary in times of abundance and ineffective during times of scarcity. He also joined other late Scholastics in being skeptical of claims that the public authority possessed any particular economic insight that qualified it in certain circumstances to proclaim a "just price."[17]

It would be to stretch the idea of morality beyond all recognition to claim that a measure that creates ill will between buyers and sellers, provides no incentive to economize on the rationed good (or to subordinate less urgent uses to more urgent ones), and actively prevents the *alleviation* of a shortage could in any way be described as morally superior to the free market, whose price system possesses none of these disadvantages. To the contrary, the foregoing analysis points to one conclusion only: that the demands of morality can be satisfied only by means of the price that is reached through the voluntary agreements between buyer and seller. The market price, therefore, may with good reason be viewed as the *only* just price.

WAGES

A proper understanding of the late Scholastic theory of the just price, which viewed the market price as just, sheds considerable light upon the late Scholastic theory of wages, which was "perfectly consistent with their price theory."[18] That is, the just wage was that which was reached by means of the common estimation of the market. Luis de Molina taught that the owner was "only obliged to pay [the laborer] the just wage for his services considering all the attendant circumstances, not what is sufficient for his sustenance and much less for the maintenance of his children and family."[19] Domingo de Soto stated the matter even more concisely, concluding that "if they freely accepted this salary for their job, it must be just." He held that "no injury is done to those who gave their consent," and suggested to laborers: "[I]f you do not want to serve for that salary, leave!"[20] The same view of wage determination was also held by two earlier figures, whom Raymond de Roover describes as the two great economic thinkers of the Middle Ages: San Bernardino of Siena and Sant'Antonio of Florence.[21] Chafuen points out that while this teaching is easily misunderstood as a case of callous disregard for the well-being of workers, it was no such thing:

> Their condemnation of monopolies, frauds, force and high taxes are all directed toward the protection and benefit of the working people. Nonetheless, they never proposed the determination of a minimum wage sufficient to maintain the laborer and his family. In the belief that fixing a wage above the common estimation level would only cause unemployment, they recommended other means.
> Reason allows us to distinguish between goals and means. One of the goals of the Schoolmen's economic policy recommendations, as of any other school of thought, is the betterment of the worker's condition. Nonetheless, they understood that tampering with the market would be inconsistent with their goals. These reasons, and not a lack of charity, were the basis of their proposals. Those who criticize Late Scholastic wage theory for a so-called "lack of compassion" demonstrate their lack of understanding of the market.[22]

This defense of the fundamental justice of the free market, although not altogether abandoned (the popes certainly do not advocate socialism), was somewhat eclipsed in modern papal pronouncements, beginning most obviously with *Rerum Novarum*, clearly the seminal Church document on the question of capital and labor. In the face of labor agitation and unrest throughout the West, Pope Leo XIII decided to issue a pronouncement on what was then referred to as the social question. The encyclical discusses at some length the justice and necessity of private property, and for that reason utterly rejects socialism as a legitimate economic system. This was an especially courageous move, flying as it did in the face of intellectual fashion.

The socialists, Leo explains, "hold that by thus transferring property from private individuals to the community, the present mischievous state of things will be set to rights, inasmuch as each citizen will then get his fair share of whatever there is to enjoy." Such proposals are "emphatically unjust," and would "rob the lawful possessor, distort the functions of the State, and create utter confusion in the community."[23] Indeed "the remedy they propose is manifestly against justice. For, every man has by nature the right to possess property as his own." This right to property derives from man's very nature

since he, unlike the animals, possesses the faculty of reason. Lacking this faculty, animals acquire goods only for their immediate use. On this account, "it
must be within [man's] right to possess things not merely for temporary and
momentary use, as other living things do, but to have and to hold them in sta-
ble and permanent possession; he must have not only things that perish in the
use, but those also which, though they have been reduced into use, continue
for further use in after time."[24]

The Pope makes a Lockean argument for the right to private property:

> Here, again, we have further proof that private ownership is in accordance with
> the law of nature. Truly, that which is required for the preservation of life, and
> for life's well-being, is produced in great abundance from the soil, but not until
> man has brought it into cultivation and expended upon it his solicitude and skill.
> Now, when man thus turns the activity of his mind and the strength of his body
> toward procuring the fruits of nature, by such act he makes his own that portion
> of nature's field which he cultivates–that portion on which he leaves, as it were,
> the impress of his personality; and it cannot but be just that he should possess
> that portion as his very own, and have a right to hold it without any one being
> justified in violating that right.[25]

In a socialist society in which the rights of private property are not honored, the Pope explains, "no one would have any interest in exerting his talents or his industry; and that ideal equality about which they entertain pleasant dreams would be in reality the levelling down of all to a like condition of
misery and degradation." Socialism must therefore "be utterly rejected, since
it only injures those whom it would seem meant to benefit, is directly contrary to the natural rights of mankind, and would introduce confusion and dis-
order into the commonweal. The first and most fundamental principle, therefore, if one would undertake to alleviate the condition of the masses, must be
the inviolability of private property."[26]

In this respect, *Rerum Novarum* built upon an earlier Leonine encyclical,
Quod Apostolici Muneris (1878), against socialism. There Leo had also taught
that the Church "holds that the right of property and of ownership, which
springs from nature itself, must not be touched and stands inviolate. For she
knows that stealing and robbery were forbidden in so special a manner by God,
the Author and Defender of right, that He would not allow man even to desire
what belonged to another."[27] The socialists, on the other hand, "strive to seize
and hold in common whatever has been acquired either by title of lawful inheritance, or by labor of brain and hands, or by thrift in one's mode of life."[28]
Leo spoke of "the plague of socialism" and of "uprooting the evil growth of
socialism."[29] (In a similar vein, Pope Pius XI would declare in 1931 that "no
one can be at the same time a good Catholic and a true socialist."[30])

Leo was joined in his opposition to socialism by the practically unanimous agreement of Catholic priests and bishops at the turn of the century. Socialists often appealed to the example of Christ and of various early Christian communities in support of their position, but Catholic commentators were quick to point out that Christ nowhere enjoined poverty on his followers as a universally binding commandment. His instruction to the young man to sell all his goods if he wished to be perfect was referred to by the Church as an evangelical counsel or a "counsel of perfection," a supererogatory work not only not necessary for salvation, but also positively harmful to the common good if implemented by force. Socialism, in trying to impose on an entire society a system that Christ had urged only on those to whom he had given a special grace, made demands on society and on human nature that could only lead to antagonism and confusion in the state.[31]

Some Catholic writers combined natural-law arguments with ones from utility or efficiency—e.g., that socialism could not deliver what it promised, that it invited economic chaos, and so on. Others pointed out what they saw as a not incidental link between socialism and materialism—and, what they considered the same thing, a connection between socialism and atheism.[32] It was not without reason that the Church feared socialist prejudice against religion and against Catholicism in particular; socialists in general made little effort to conceal their contempt for the very idea of the supernatural. The hundreds of articles on the link between socialism and atheism notwithstanding, Catholics were more than prepared to refute socialists on their own terms. A considerable minority of Catholics warned that to dismiss socialism simply as an atheistic system—even if true—was unwise; it might, for example, be perceived as an evasion of the economic issues at stake.[33] Such arguments in themselves proved nothing, since it was at least possible to conceive of a form of socialism that did not reject revealed religion. The most common strategy among Catholic intellectuals in countering socialism remained, therefore, the appeal to natural law.

While the Pope condemned socialism per se in *Rerum Novarum*, he did not condemn capitalism per se, since it was, after all, a system based ultimately on the very principle of private property that Leo defended against the socialists. What he did criticize were certain aspects of capitalism that he thought should be corrected. As we shall see, he spoke of the need for a "just wage" and for various protections for workingmen. At the same time, the Pope was not especially sympathetic to the use of the strike, and advocated that government intervene in order to settle such disputes between employer and employed in order that the "grave inconvenience" of such work stoppages be vitiated.

To be sure, the popes have consistently rejected the Marxist position whereby labor and capital are by necessity locked in unavoidable conflict and struggle. They contend that no such inherent conflict exists in society, and that the capital-labor relationship, far from being necessarily antagonistic, ought naturally to be mutually agreeable and harmonious.[34] But having said that, they at times appear to take for granted that intervention by public authority is indispensable for obtaining justice in the economic realm. Recall the consensus among the late Scholastics that just wages were established in the same way as just prices, namely by the common estimation of the market and the free consent of individuals. *Rerum Novarum*, on the other hand, flatly declares it a falsehood to conceive of wages as "regulated by free consent, and [that] therefore the employer, when he pays what was agreed upon, has done his part and seemingly is not called upon to do anything beyond."[35] To be sure, workers and employers may enter into agreements pertaining to wages, but

> there underlies a dictate of natural justice more imperious and ancient than any bargain between man and man, namely, that wages ought not to be insufficient to support a frugal and well-behaved wage-earner. If through necessity or fear of a worse evil the workman accept harder conditions because an employer or contractor will afford him no better, he is made the victim of force and injustice.[36]

Leo XIII later speaks of the importance of wages "sufficient to enable [the laborer] comfortably to support himself, his wife, and his children."[37]

Among the principal themes that Leo XIII introduces into Catholic discourse with *Rerum Novarum* is the idea of a "third way" between socialism and pure laissez-faire. The operation of the market, Leo suggests, had in some cases led to intolerable outcomes that public authority ought to rectify. Moreover, *Rerum Novarum* enshrines the critical and fateful idea that the wage rates established by market processes could be held up to moral critique by outside observers on the basis of their adequacy in meeting workers' material needs.

Pope Pius XI's *Quadragesimo Anno* (1931) is another critical document within the corpus of Catholic social thought. An encyclical commemorating the fortieth anniversary of *Rerum Novarum*, *Quadragesimo* was released during the Great Depression, a fact that may account for the more polemical and hostile tone it adopts towards businessmen and the market. Toward the beginning of the document, Pius laments the allegedly appalling conditions that afflicted the vast majority of workers. He goes on to praise the passage of laws on behalf of worker safety and well-being in the wake of Leo's encyclical. "These laws," Pius observes, "undertake the protection of life, health, strength, family, homes, workshops, wages and labor hazards, in fine, everything which pertains to the condition of wage workers." Having helped to inspire such measures, Pius concludes, it was *Rerum Novarum* "to which great credit must be given for whatever improvement has been achieved in the workers' condition."[38]

To the casual observer this statement is innocuous enough. But there is a hidden assumption here, which is central to the rest of the document as well as to nearly all of late-nineteenth- and twentieth-century Catholic criticism of the market order, and upon which practically the entire edifice of recent Catholic social thought has been built. Thus if this assumption, rarely if ever stated explicitly, should turn out to be erroneous, the entire structure on which it rests must be considered a legitimate matter for honest debate among Catholics of good will.

That assumption is that the wage rates and the working conditions that come into existence through the unhampered market process do not necessarily reflect fundamental economic realities. These wages and conditions, the assumption continues, may be improved upon through wise state intervention. Closely related to this fundamental assumption is the implicit claim that such intervention can be purely benign, and Pareto superior from the workers' point of view—that is, the process of making some better off will make no one worse off. To the extent that the architects of Catholic social teaching acknowledge the ill effects of such intervention at all, they must believe these effects to be outweighed by the benefits allegedly conferred by intervention, though how such a reckoning of costs and benefits could be arrived at in a nonarbitrary way is not clear.[39]

This assumption regarding wage rate determination may seem so obvious to many people as not even to require proof, but if churchmen are going to presume to establish moral principles on the basis of the consequences that follow from this assumption, then *some* demonstration of its truth must be attempted. For if this assumption is wrong, then the counsel that churchmen have offered in economic matters may in fact have the opposite outcome from that intended, and the accusations of injustice and immorality that have been leveled against certain employers and the economic system as a whole may turn out to be unjustified.

Consider *Quadragesimo Anno*'s renewal of *Rerum Novarum*'s call for a "living wage": "In the first place, the worker must be paid a wage sufficient to support him and his family." This demand is followed later in the same paragraph by a qualifying statement: "But if this cannot always be done under existing circumstances, social justice demands that changes be introduced as soon as possible whereby such a wage will be assured to every adult workingman."[40] Thus Pius XI concedes, without elaborating on the point, that paying a worker a so-called family wage "cannot always be done under existing circumstances." Might it not be able to be done because the productivity of labor is not sufficiently high to make such wages possible? *Quadragesimo* does not provide an answer. The document then demands that "changes be introduced as soon as possible" to make such wages feasible, but it is unclear about what kind of changes are necessary.

"In determining the amount of the wage," the Pope goes on, "the condition of a business and of the one carrying it on must also be taken into account; for it would be unjust to demand excessive wages which a business cannot stand without its ruin and consequent calamity to the workers." Pius XI does recognize, then, that wage rates are obviously subject to some upper bound beyond which they cannot go. He concludes: "Hence it is contrary to social justice when, for the sake of personal gain and without regard for the common good, wages and salaries are excessively lowered or raised; and this same social justice demands that wages and salaries be so managed, through agreement of plans and wills, in so far as can be done, as to offer to the greatest possible number the opportunity of getting work and obtaining suitable means of livelihood." Such statements help to underscore why the late Scholastics favored leaving wage determination to the "common estimation" of the market, since any other method is inherently arbitrary and leads to endless complications. Thus *Quadragesimo* acknowledges that there is a limit to the wage level the market can bear, but offers only an appeal to "agreement of plans and wills" in order to determine what that limit was. Pius rejects out of hand the fundamental posture of liberal economics according to which the market left to itself "would have a principle of self direction which governs it much more perfectly than would the intervention of any created intellect."[41] That the unhampered market is *not* the way to provide employment "to the greatest possible number" is not a self-evident principle, and presumably the mechanics of maximizing employment and wage rates would appear to be an area for legitimate disagreement among Catholics. Again, no alternative method for maximizing employment opportunities is provided.

In more recent years the popes have begun to demand, in addition to a "living wage," various additional benefits for workers. Thus Pope John Paul II declares in *Laborem Exercens*: "The expenses involved in health care, especially in the case of accidents at work, demand that medical assistance should be easily available for workers, and that as far as possible it should be cheap or even free of charge. Another sector regarding benefits is the sector associated with the *right to rest*. In the first place this involves a regular weekly rest comprising at least Sunday, and also a longer period of rest, namely the holiday or vacation taken once a year or possibly in several shorter periods during the year. A third sector concerns the right to a pension and to insurance for old age and in case of accidents at work."[42]

There are philosophical difficulties with speaking of a pension as a *human right* fundamental to man's nature when its enjoyment is not possible at all times and in all places, and cannot be exercised simultaneously and in the same way by all men (how would two men on a desert island enforce their "right to a pension" upon one another, apart from fruitlessly barking commands at each other and attempting to reduce each other to slavery?[43]), but for our purposes we shall leave them aside. More important from an economic point of view is that this kind of analysis, doubtless well intentioned and undertaken with human welfare in mind, needs at the very least to be supplemented by the kind of proviso that Pius XI included in *Quadragesimo*, where he warned that indiscriminate attempts to increase the welfare of certain workers could do more harm than good by placing impossible burdens on employers. Making medical assistance "cheap or even free of charge" makes it more costly to hire workers in the first place, and thus guarantees higher unemployment. It would be one thing if we were presented with a trade-off between "free" health care on the one hand and increased unemployment and impoverishment on the other. The problem is that all too often, no such difficulty is raised or even acknowledged. Employee compensation is implicitly conceived of as something more or less arbitrary, from which it is concluded that we can actually make certain compensation packages morally obligatory without taking into account any need to make provision for inevitable drawbacks. But surely this is a factor with which moral analysis should concern itself.

The possibility that the determination of wage rates could involve something more than mere employer whim is scarcely even raised, let alone cogently addressed, within the main documents that are said to constitute Catholic social thought, and the concept of economic law, when it is mentioned at all, is typically ridiculed and dismissed as a rationalization of greed. This impression only increases when one considers the position of Msgr. John A. Ryan, perhaps the best-known American Catholic writer on economic issues in the early twentieth century. Ryan, a professor of political science and moral theology who taught at Minnesota's St. Paul's Seminary and the Catholic University of America, founded and edited the *Catholic Charities Review* and directed the Department of Social Action of the National Catholic Welfare Conference. In his famous book *A Living Wage* (1906), Ryan points out that according to the logic of the classical economists, wages freely bargained for would ipso facto be just wages. Wondering whence they derived such a theory, he goes on to discuss the teaching of Adam Smith, failing to make any mention of the late Scholastics, who of course held precisely the view that Ryan holds up to ridicule and contempt.[44]

Not surprisingly, Ryan rejects the idea that a wage decided upon through free bargaining between laborer and employer is inherently just (a position that he was probably unaware had been held by so many venerable sixteenth-century Catholic thinkers) and argues instead that it is morally obligatory upon employers to pay wages that would allow workers and their families to live in reasonable comfort. A contemporary Catholic reviewer of *A Living Wage* tried without success to point out to Ryan that a business is not a charitable foundation but an enterprise devoted to producing some good or service at the lowest cost to the consumer. Ryan's critic concluded: "As an individual or as head of a family, the laborer produces the same amount of work; how then could the employer as such be obliged in strict justice to take into account a condition which is of no advantage to him?"[45]

Like others before him, Ryan inserts into his moral argument an occasional qualifying clause that he does nothing to explain or clarify. "When the employer cannot pay a Living Wage," he concedes, "he is for the time being freed from actual obligation, as no one is morally bound to do the impossible."[46] Thus Ryan himself admits the existence of limitations on what employers can be expected to pay, but having already dismissed the suggestion that on the market wages tend to approximate the worker's discounted marginal value product (DMVP)—that is, the market value of the goods whose production the employment of a particular laborer makes possible, discounted by the going rate of interest—he provides no rational or objective substitute in its place for wage determination other than an "ability to pay" principle that he himself admits is vague and unhelpful.[47] Adding to the confusion is Ryan's later admission: "If, however, it be maintained that there is no obligation to pay the laborer *more* than the value of his product because there is no possibility of doing so, no objection can be offered."[48] But if this is true, then how can state authorities be sure, when imposing "living wage" legislation, that they are not forcing men out of work by decreeing a wage beyond what their product is worth?

Ryan rejects the idea that the level of wages has anything to do with the productivity of labor, which he argues is impossible to measure: "Do the skilled workers in an automobile factory produce more than the common laborers who pave streets? There is no third term by which the two products can as such be compared."[49] But of course there is a third term: *money*. The institutions of money and private property are what make economic calculation possible.[50] It is because we can reckon all goods and services in the economy in terms of a common unit that entrepreneurs can calculate profit and loss, and in the first place can decide among the limitless production possibilities (that is, what kinds of technology to use, how capital or labor intensive to be, where to locate one's physical plant, what combination of factors to employ, and so on) which is the most efficient and least wasteful in terms of foregone opportunities to which the inputs he uses might have been put. Ryan seems completely unaware of this aspect of money prices and wages.

More importantly, Ryan fails to understand the true relationship that exists between the productivity of labor and the purchasing power of wages. The relationship is an indirect one, which may help to explain why Ryan failed to uncover it. In *Capitalism*, George Reisman elegantly describes what Ryan missed—what Reisman calls "the productivity theory of wages." Reisman provides an algebraic derivation of the theory in his book, so I shall confine myself simply to describing it and demonstrating its fruitfulness in the study of economic history.

First, Reisman cautions against the idea that a rising standard of living implies a situation in which workers consistently earn more *money*. Because we currently live under a monetary regime in which the money supply is increased year after year by the Federal Reserve, we have grown accustomed to seeing wages and salaries also rise, in nominal (or money) terms. But under a system of sound money, an important point that is obscured under a regime of fiat money becomes much more obvious. In an economy with what Reisman calls an "invariable money" (essentially an unchanged quantity of money), it is technically impossible for *everyone* to earn more money over time. The fundamental way in which people's standard of living rises, then, is not that they earn more money but that the money they do earn comes to command greater purchasing power.

This greater purchasing power comes into existence as a result of increases in the productivity of labor—the amount of output per worker. The more output the economy is capable of producing, the greater purchasing power will a worker's wage command. According to Reisman, "it is the productivity of labor that determines the supply of consumers' goods relative to the supply of labor, and thus the prices of consumers' goods relative to wage rates."[51] In other words, the more production per capita, the lower will prices be in relation to wages, and the more those wages will buy.

Think of it this way. The American economy in the 1870s possessed a dramatically smaller productive capacity than the American economy of 2005. The productivity of labor was drastically lower than it is today. As a result, it was *physically incapable* of producing the sheer volume of products per capita of which our present economy is capable—and, of course, a whole host of goods that we take for granted simply did not exist at all, not having been invented yet.[52]

Although once again it should be borne in mind that by historical standards people living in nineteenth-century England and the United States enjoyed a far higher standard of living than Europe had ever known, we understandably look back on their standard of living with revulsion. Such people lived in a society in which, from our point of view, all goods were extremely scarce. Few if any goods could be produced in the fantastic abundance of which our present economy is capable.

Leaving emotion aside, however, consider from the point of view of economic science the inevitable constraints on people's standard of living that exist as a result of this scarcity (a scarcity, it can hardly be overemphasized, that is ultimately caused by a low productivity of labor, which the expansion of capitalism necessarily works to raise). Suppose some catastrophe should occur today that very significantly lowers the productivity of labor. All automobiles are destroyed, and with them the knowledge to create new ones. Thus, our entire transportation system reverts to railroads and the horse and buggy. In addition, fax machines, cellular and standard telephones, e-mail, and the Internet all vanish, as do radio and television, and our communications infrastructure is reduced to the telegraph. Likewise, all other capital equipment invented and developed over the course of the past 150 years is wiped out. Many conveniences we take for granted no longer exist at all, and the vast majority of the remainder must be made either by hand or with what from our point of view are the clumsiest and most inefficient machines. Needless to say, this economy is capable of far, far less production than it was before the catastrophe.

Does it not stand to reason that under these drastically changed circumstances, we would all have to work much longer and harder in order to maintain even a minimally acceptable standard of living? In such a situation, the goods we need would all be unusually scarce, and would all command what from our point of view today would be very high prices indeed, in terms of the hours and minutes of our labor that we would have to expend to be able to earn the money to buy them. A great many consumers chasing relatively few goods inevitably means high prices. Since the relative lack of capital equipment means a low productivity of labor—again, understood as low output per worker—as a matter of simple logic it is unavoidable that workers throughout the economy will have to toil long and hard to produce the amount of consumer goods people believe they need. If in our obstinacy we all determined to maintain a 40-hour work week even in the face of such changed conditions and such dramatically reduced output per worker, we would not produce anything approaching the amount of consumer goods that most of us need, and the result would be still greater impoverishment and destitution. It is this simple fact of reality, rather than any sinister machinations of greedy businessmen, that would account for our low standard of living in such a case.

In effect, this is something like the situation that people faced in England during the early Industrial Revolution, and to a lesser but still considerable extent the economy in which American workers lived in the latter nineteenth century, the period in which it is routinely alleged that they were unconscionably "exploited" by greedy businessmen. Apparently, it has never occurred to critics of the market that the reason people back then could afford far fewer and considerably lower quality consumer goods than we do today might have something to do with the fact that the country's productive capacity could not have produced any more. The working assumption among such critics appears to be that feeding, clothing, and housing more and more people over time, and making possible a steadily rising life expectancy, is nothing too impressive (despite the fact that it had never been done in such a sustained and remarkable way anywhere in the world until the eighteenth century). No, these critics also expect the increased population that capitalism makes possible to enjoy, right away, spacious and commodious homes, fine cuisine, and ample leisure time, and if they lack these things the only explanation can be that greedy businessmen are wickedly depriving the workers of them. That these things might not even exist in any great numbers is not even considered.

What, specifically, can be done to improve this situation? If goods could be provided in greater abundance, they would be less dear and more within reach of the ordinary consumer. How can goods be provided in greater abundance? By increasing the productivity of labor—again, the amount of output per worker. And that can be done by means of technological innovation and investment in capital goods. When capitalists reinvest their profits, they make possible the purchase of steam shovels instead of regular shovels, computers rather than typewriters, copy machines rather than the labor of scribes. They can equip warehouses with forklifts, thereby allowing a single worker to perform tasks that might well have required the labor of ten workers.

As a result of such investment, productivity and therefore output in the economy are increased considerably. The whole process is driven by the profit motive, which leads businessmen continually to search for new and improved products and to cut costs in order to earn premium profits. Competition then serves to pass on the quality improvements and cost cuts on to the consumers, who obtain progressively more and better products at lower and lower real prices.

Depending on consumer demand for goods in industries where productivity increases, the result can be that a larger or a smaller number of workers is employed in that industry. In the case of automobiles, for example, where improvements in productivity and consequent cost and price reductions opened up a mass market, the result was a vast increase in the number of workers employed. In the case of agriculture, where improvements in productivity were accompanied by far less than proportionate increases in food consumption, the result was a great diminution in the number of workers employed. In this and all other cases in which the increase in productivity means fewer workers are needed in a particular area of production, labor is released for employment elsewhere in the economy, producing goods that consumers want but in the past could not have had because the requisite labor was simply not available. The rise in the productivity of labor is how wealth is created—and how real wages rise.

This entire process is apparently beyond most of the people who consider themselves qualified to teach it. From the fourth-grade social studies teacher who doesn't know any better to the college professor who very well should, the implicit judgment is that the condition of workers in the late eighteenth and nineteenth centuries called for government intervention in the form of massive wealth redistribution from the capitalists to the workers. One problem with such a plan, says Reisman, is that

> there was virtually nothing to redistribute. The workers of the early nineteenth century did not lack automobiles and television sets because the capitalists were keeping the whole supply to themselves. There simply were no automobiles or television sets—for anyone. Nor did the workers of those days lack sufficient housing, clothing, and meat because the capitalists had too much of these goods. Very little of such goods could be produced when they had to be produced almost entirely by hand. If the limited supplies of such goods that the capitalists had could have been redistributed, the improvement in the conditions of the workers would hardly have been noticeable. If one person in a thousand, say, is a wealthy capitalist, and eats twice as much and has twenty times the clothing and furniture as an average person, hardly any noticeable improvement for the average person could come from dividing the capitalists' greater-than-average consumption by 999 and redistributing it. At the very best, a redistribution of wealth or income would have been useless as a means of alleviating the poverty of the past.[53]

In fact, Reisman goes on, such wealth redistribution, in addition to being ludicrously inadequate for fulfilling the expectations of its supporters, directly harms the long-term interests of the workers themselves, as well as those of society as a whole. If businessmen wish to stay in business, they must reinvest the vast bulk of their profits in still further additions to their capital stock—which in turn further increase the productivity of labor, thereby increasing the supply of goods that the economy is capable of producing. These increases in the productivity of labor, by increasing the overall amount of output and thereby increasing the ratio of consumers' goods to the supply of labor, make prices lower relative to wage rates and thereby raise real wages. The cost of the wealth redistribution advocated by the political left includes the investment in capital equipment that business must now forego, and the lowered incentive to engage in such investment in the future, since its fruits will be taxed away. "The truth is," says Reisman, "that what made possible the rise in real wages and the average standard of living over the last two hundred years is precisely the fact that for the first time in history the redistributors were beaten back long enough and far enough to make large-scale capital accumulation and innovation possible."[54]

Politicians naturally want to take credit for the economic progress and rising standard of living we have enjoyed for the past two centuries, and virtually all textbook treatments of these issues dutifully parrot the government line: were it not for the power of the state, people would still be toiling 80 hours per week and children would be working in mines. Again contrary to what the overwhelming majority of people have been led to believe, it is logically inescapable that such desirable social outcomes as reduced working hours and the elimination of child labor were brought about precisely by the *extension* of capitalism. It is beyond tiresome to listen to a modern-day professor's moral outrage at the fact that nineteenth-century workers often worked 60, 70, or even more hours per week. If only people had been more "socially conscious," goes the typical argument, these laborers might have been spared having to work such exhausting hours.

There is no doubt that by today's standards, people in the nineteenth century did indeed work an exhausting schedule. But, again, when output per worker is miserably low, then a supply of consumer goods that most people consider adequate requires people to work correspondingly long hours to produce them all. As the productivity of labor increases, and with it the level of real wages, people begin to opt for additional leisure rather than continue to work the long hours of the past. Without the need for any legislation whatever, a situation will eventually arise in which employers find offering correspondingly fewer hours to be in their own economic interest, and will offer them without the need for government coercion. If someone who once worked 80 hours per week now wishes to work only 60 (that is, three-fourths as many hours), and is willing to accept a wage less than three-fourths that of his previous wage as a premium on the leisure he will now enjoy, it makes perfect sense for his employer to offer these terms.[55]

To the extent that maximum-hours legislation corresponded with people's desire to work fewer hours, it was superfluous, since such an outcome would have come about by means of the process just described. But to the extent that such legislation was economically premature, forcing fewer hours on workers who needed the wages of their longer hours in order to maintain what they considered an adequate standard of living, it harmed the very people it was allegedly intended to help.

The same can be said for legislation to improve working conditions, which was praised by Pius XI in *Quadragesimo*. As Reisman explains, improvements in working conditions that pay for themselves in terms of less workplace damage and disruption will of course be readily adopted by any profit-seeking enterprise. But even improvements that do not pay for themselves will still be adopted in cases in which the wage premium that would have to be offered to attract workers in the absence of the improvement would be higher than the cost of simply introducing the improvement.

When air conditioning was first invented, it would have been absurd to demand as a legal requirement that all workplaces be air conditioned. Hardly anyone would have been able to afford it, and the result would have been economic devastation and mass unemployment. (The same would have been true for automobile consumers if all automobiles had been required to have air conditioners—the result would not have been to provide everyone with an air-conditioned car, but to ensure that only the rich owned cars.) But at what pace, in what quantity and in what workplaces would it gradually begin to make sense for air conditioning to be introduced? As the socialist calculation problem teaches us, without some market test based on prices in the real world, there is no nonarbitrary way of making this determination.

The only nonarbitrary way of introducing such improvements, therefore, and the only way of doing so that does not price workers out of jobs entirely or impoverish society out of proportion to the satisfaction derived by workers now enjoying air-conditioned facilities, is by paying attention to the market. Everyone knows that certain lines of work, because of their difficulty or because of undesirable or unpleasant aspects of the labor involved, carry a wage premium to attract sufficient workers by compensating them for these negative factors. As time goes on and more and more places become air conditioned, the wage premium for non-air-conditioned workplaces will rise. The wage differential that the non-air-conditioned workplace must pay in order to attract workers away from employers with air-conditioned facilities may eventually reach a level at which it would be less expensive for the firm simply to install the air conditioning rather than to go on paying higher wages than their competitors who provide air conditioning. These market signals allow for rational allocation of resources, and help to ensure that improvements in workplace conditions—which, after all, have no logical limit: who would not want five-hour lunch breaks, the services of a masseuse, and an office with a view of Niagara Falls?—do not come at the expense of other goods that workers and consumers value more. There is no such thing as a free lunch, economists sometimes say, and any improvement in working conditions must come at the expense of something else that must now be foregone.

There is no way, in isolation from market exchange, that improvements in working conditions can be rationally compared with these foregone opportunities.

Workers, like anyone else, are faced with choices, and with economic tradeoffs. They can take a job that offers higher pay but poorer working conditions, or a job that offers lower pay but better working conditions. Which of these an individual worker will choose is based on his value judgments. Employing this kind of analysis, Reisman describes the situation of American workers in the 1990s:

> Just as they can afford along with automobiles and television sets such things as air conditioners and flush toilets in their homes, they can also afford things of comparable benefit to them in their places of work, such as, once again, air conditioners and flush toilets. For even if, as well may be the case, such things as air conditioners and flush toilets in work places do not directly pay for themselves through improved efficiency on the part of the workers, it is almost certainly true that the immense majority of workers in the present-day United States is prepared to accept wage rates that are lower in establishments that offer such amenities by far more than the cost to employers of installing and maintaining such amenities, or, what is equivalent, to demand wage rates in workplaces that do not offer such amenities that are higher by far more than the cost of providing such amenities.
>
> Thus, for example, while the cost of providing air conditioning in the summer heat may amount to, say, $5 per worker per week, the cost in the premium wage rates to attract workers to work without such air conditioning might well be $20 per worker per week. Obviously, in such circumstances, offering air conditioning is the profitable thing for employers to do.[56]

The same analysis here applied to amenities like air conditioning is equally valid for safety devices and procedures. "A free market," Reisman writes, "strikes a proper balance in the pursuit of safety in the workplace—a balance that takes into account the real incomes of wage earners, which it constantly operates to increase, together with the importance that they attach at any given time to greater safety relative to other uses of their incomes. All this is conveyed in the extent to which workers are ready to respond to different combinations of safety and take-home wages." As with maximum-hours legislation, to the extent that safety regulation corresponded to what this market process was bringing about anyway, it was superfluous. To the extent that it went beyond that point, it was positively harmful. As a result of the increased costs of employing workers, unemployment will certainly result, as well as higher prices and lower take-home pay (as deductions are made to support the unemployed) for those fortunate enough to keep their jobs.[57] This is why it is dangerous to draw sweeping policy conclusions from certain isolated statements in the corpus of Catholic social teaching.

A similar analysis can also shed light on the problem of child labor. Far from a product of the Industrial Revolution, child labor has existed since the beginning of time. When the productivity of labor is hopelessly low, parents naturally think of children as economic actors who can contribute to the well-being of their families. Without their children's participation in the family's work, the entire household could suffer terrible privation. This is a fact of life in poor, low-productivity societies that no "progressive" legislation can wish away. As Anna Krueger writes, "The issue of child labor is vexing: there are legitimate issues of intolerable working conditions, but employment of children may provide food that prevents a family from starving. In some instances, also, it may provide girls with an alternative to forced early marriages."[58] Even the International Labor Organization conceded in a 1997 report, "Poverty, however, emerges as the most compelling reason why children work. Poor households need the money, and children commonly contribute around 20 to 25 percent of family income. Since by definition poor households spend the bulk of their income on food, it is clear that the income provided by working children is critical to their survival."[59]

To say that legislation can bring about an end to child labor is akin to saying that a man's fever can be cured by dousing his thermometer in ice. The only way child labor can come to a genuine end is when the need for it has dwindled or disappeared. In societies where the productivity of labor has risen sufficiently—in other words, when the labor of fewer people is now necessary to perform the same amount of work as before—the contribution of children to the productive process no longer carries the same urgency. In wealthy societies like these, parents have the luxury of keeping their children at home, and in our own case, even providing them with over twelve years of formal education by age 18. Again, this outcome could not have been wished into existence. It had to be brought about through a dramatic increase in the productivity of labor—in other words, by the capital investment that occurs on the unhampered market.

Those who, out of a combination of legitimate humanitarian concern and unfortunate economic ignorance, attempt to accelerate this process by means of legislation prohibiting child labor only add to the very misery they claim to be alleviating. It is only because such humanitarians have spent their lives in the fantastically wealthy capitalist societies of the West that they could have failed to realize that dire poverty, which makes child labor inevitable, has been the lot of the entire human race for the great majority of its history. The fact is, legislation or no legislation, the typical family in a very poor country still needs the income the child's work brings. If the law prevents their children from being employed legally, then—supposing they do not want to starve—they are likely to employ their children illegally, where conditions are almost certain to be far worse. In fact, in exceedingly poor societies where liberal humanitarians have prohibited child labor, it is not uncommon to find that the children wind up in prostitution—hardly an improvement in their welfare, to say the least. In fact, Oxfam, the British charity, recently reported that when factory owners in Bangladesh gave in to pressure to fire child laborers, thousands starved or went into prostitution.[60]

Reisman does not hesitate to draw the obvious if all-too-rare conclusion from all this: it is the capitalists, routinely portrayed as devilish villains, who are alone responsible for the dramatically higher standard of living that American workers enjoy today. The typical American worker enjoys luxuries and abundance that people of previous ages could scarcely have imagined. These luxuries and abundance are due primarily not to the physical effort of ordinary laborers, important as their contribution is, but to the scientific genius of those who invent the machines and implements with which laborers can multiply many times over what they could have produced by the strength of their bare hands, and by the organizational genius of businessmen who make the critical decisions involved in overseeing the process of production and who put machines and implements into the hands of their workers.

Reisman's demonstration puts to rest once and for all the old morality play in which the greedy businessman wickedly deprives his workers of an adequate standard of living. As Reisman shows, it is precisely in his capacity as a capitalist that he does the most to increase everyone's standard of living—far more than any puerile "redistribution" of wealth could accomplish. Surely Reisman's discussion is indispensable to anyone attempting a moral analysis of the free market, yet Msgr. Ryan, who seems to be unaware of these ideas as elaborated by Mises and other predecessors of Reisman, feels free to condemn those who disagree with his heavily interventionist point of view.

In light of our discussion of wages and how they are increased, we are in a better position to evaluate Pius XI's statement in *Quadragesimo Anno* that all men must be paid a wage sufficient to support their families in reasonable comfort, and that where this is not possible "social justice demands that changes be introduced as soon as possible whereby such a wage will be assured to every adult workingman."[61] According to our analysis of wages, when *Quadragesimo* instructs us to introduce changes in order to make a living wage available to workingmen, we should remove as many obstacles to investment as possible, and eliminate taxes on capital, "excess profits," and the like. Unfortunately, these are the very sorts of things that students of Catholic social teaching call for in order to redistribute wealth. It is certainly admirable to want to improve the lot of the worker, but before deciding on a course of action it is indispensable, practically and morally, to know the causes and cures of what ails him.

It can come as little surprise that Msgr. Ryan dismisses the idea that economic law acts as a constraint on the "lasting modification in the rates of
wages by human action."[62] "A strong Labor Union," he declares, "might meet
the objection of the employer, that efforts to get more pay must prove futile,
since wages are fixed by economic law, with the declaration: 'Yes, but we
will help to make the law.'"[63] Our previous discussion has helped to demonstrate just how destructive such an attitude is.

More hostile still to the idea of economic law is Heinrich Pesch, S.J.
(1854–1926), the founder of Solidarism, a kind of corporatism on which
Quadragesimo Anno is said to have modeled its own approach.[64] (While
Pesch died five years before the publication of *Quadragesimo*, his intellectual
circle, especially Oswald von Nell-Breunig, S.J., was frequently consulted
during its drafting.)[65] According to Pesch, advocates of the idea of economic
law assume that man always acts with purely economic motives in mind. This
was a common Catholic criticism, and one that persists: John Paul II, in *Laborem Exercens*, criticizes "economism" as a mode of thought that "directly
or indirectly includes a conviction of the primacy and superiority of the material, and directly or indirectly places the spiritual and the personal (man's
activity, moral values and such matters) in a position of subordination to material reality."[66] Pesch suggests that economic law would hold only if this assumption of man's exclusively "economic" behavior and outlook were true.
Since this assumption is demonstrably false, Pesch believes he has thereby refuted the case for economic law. Pesch even purports to provide an example
of how it can actually be a virtue to flout so-called economic law: "If in bad
times many 'hands' present themselves for employment, so that the 'exchange value of their labor power' falls below their reproduction value—the
subsistence costs of the workers—then the owner of the factory is still empowered to pay a higher wage than the actual exchange value and 'the market price of labor power' indicates. He is not mocking the 'natural law' of liberal economism, and perhaps many will deem his conduct as very rational and
noble."[67]

In fact, Pesch's example is not especially enlightening. The question is not
whether some employer for some limited time might possess the means to exercise charity. The question is whether wages as a whole can be permanently
increased through mere good will, voluntary or otherwise, rather than through
the increases in productivity made possible by increased capital investment.
During the Great Depression, Herbert Hoover repeatedly urged employers to
keep wages high (despite falling prices), and the pressure he brought to bear
had its influence. Wages remained high throughout the Great Depression. But
this disproved no economic law—to the contrary, it demonstrated the re-
silience of economic law. Some workers benefited by these higher wages, but

surely there is room somewhere in our moral calculus for those who were thereby not able to find a job at all. The unemployment rate averaged a whopping 18 percent from 1933 to 1940. There were doubtless many who deemed Hoover's conduct "very rational and noble," but there is no record indicating the degree of consolation this afforded workers who were priced out of the market by the federal government's wage policy.[68]

Pesch ridicules the pretensions of economists to scientific exactitude and mathematical precision, and he is correct to do so, but for some reason he concludes from this that any kind of universal, unchangeable economic law per se cannot exist.[69] The Austrian school of economics, on the other hand, maintains that laws of economics, of a qualitative rather than a quantitative nature, can be derived deductively through praxeology, the general theory of human action. Why it should be impossible for human reason to establish such qualitative economic laws, even if the mathematical exactitude of quantitative laws must elude the social sciences, Pesch leaves unexplained. Indeed Pesch makes no serious attempt to reckon with the methodological work of such economists as J. B. Say, John Cairnes, and Nassau Senior (the latter two of whom Murray Rothbard described as "proto-praxeologists"),[70] confining himself to triumphantly unmasking the "economic man" canard. Say insisted that the method of economics was one of deduction from first principles, and not analogous to the hard sciences with either their empirical testing or their mathematical precision. Say and Senior both made provision for immaterial satisfactions and thereby expressly avoided any assumption about man's behavior being driven by exclusively material concerns.[71] Thus Pesch's criticisms do not apply to these thinkers, with whom he ought to have been familiar.

Neither do they apply to Ludwig von Mises, whose methodological work appeared after Pesch was writing. Readers will recall from the previous chapter Mises' critique of the ideological and epistemological positions of the so-called German Historical School, which denied the very idea of universally valid economic law. It can hardly be a surprise to learn that Heinrich Pesch (as well as other architects of Catholic social teaching) was himself sympathetic to the German Historical School. Doubtless the proponents of such a position thought they were thereby striking a blow for traditional Catholicism at the expense of liberalism and the Enlightenment, but the result of this line of thought was a decidedly un-Catholic denigration of the powers of reason.[72]

Mises proved that it was quite possible to insist that economic laws did exist and did place constraints on what was possible in the economic sphere without also endorsing any nonsense about mathematical precision or purely "economic" motives exhausting man's reasons for acting. Mises pointed out what should have been obvious: namely, that "this doctrine of [emphasizing only] the 'economic' side of human action utterly misrepresents the teachings of the classical economists."[73] Economics, he wrote, deals with "the actions of real men. Its theorems refer neither to ideal nor to perfect men, neither to the phantom of a fabulous economic man (homo oeconomicus) nor to the statistical notion of an average man (homme moyen). Man with all his weaknesses and limitations, every man as he lives and acts, is the subject matter of catallactics. Every human action is a theme of praxeology."[74] At no point does praxeology assume that man always chooses with purely economic self-interest in mind; nor does it have anything to say about what goals man should choose. It is concerned simply with the logic of choice itself and the implications that follow from it.

And praxeology can tell us a great deal about the consequences of intervention in the labor market. The price of a given type of labor is determined by the interplay of the forces of supply and demand, which can be depicted graphically on the basis of the praxeological derivation we performed in chapter 1. Faced with the reality of scarcity, entrepreneurs must bid for labor, since, *as with any other factor of production*, the competitive bidding on the part of other businesses prevents them from arbitrarily deciding upon whatever wage rate pleases them. Labor is indeed scarce relative to nature-given factors; if this were not so, there would be no unused, submarginal land. If labor were superabundant, or at least abundant in relation to land, all land would be brought into use. The fact that some land and some resources remain untapped reflects the scarcity of labor—that is, labor is too dear to be wasted on extracting resources or using land whose returns would be lower than in some other area, in which scarce labor is more urgently needed.[75] Moreover, as Reisman notes, many of us would be happy to have the services of cooks, gardeners, personal secretaries, and the like, but are frustrated in this desire precisely because of the scarcity of labor. Most of us cannot command the funds necessary to divert scarce labor away from other sectors of the economy and toward the fulfillment of domestic labor and personal services for ourselves as individuals. In addition, while it is possible for any given person to desire a supply of goods that could be produced only by the labor of many individuals, *on average* a person can of course never acquire more than the products of just one other person. And "when the very young and the sick and infirm are allowed for, who can only be supported by the labor of others, it turns out that for each person who consumes there is, on average, substantially less than the labor of one person available to produce." Reisman provides much more evidence of the ineradicable scarcity of labor, including the fact that as workers grow wealthier and more comfortable, they begin to desire more and more leisure—and thereby wish to supply less and less labor.[76]

We have already seen that the real purchasing power of the average nominal wage depends on the productivity of labor. Here we simply wish to add that the precise determination of the level of that nominal wage in this or that industry is determined by means of the supply of and demand for labor, as employers compete with each other to acquire the services of this most scarce of resources. The usual objection to this argument rests on the alleged "inability to wait" on the part of workers: since workers need employment to survive, and since they do not possess a substantial stock of goods on which to subsist while they seek work, they are forced to accept work at wages that do not adequately reflect their productivity. This argument, however, is long on assertion and short on proof. It is especially implausible given the unprecedented mobility of labor in the modern world, with affordable modes of transportation that past centuries could scarcely have imagined. Employers, on the other hand, possessing enormous investments in fixed plant and other capital, generally lack such mobility, and therefore may themselves be said to possess a certain inability to wait.[77] Moreover, nowhere in this argument is there any acknowledgment that employers must *compete* for scarce labor, in the same way that they compete for any scarce resource, and that workers are faced with a variety of employers, all of whom must compete for their labor services. As Reisman helpfully points out, *it makes no difference to the wage rate he actually receives* that a worker may theoretically be willing to work for a subsistence wage. A man may be so frustrated with maintaining and finding parking for an automobile in New York City, for instance, that he would theoretically be willing to pay someone to take it off his hands, but this psychological fact has absolutely no bearing on the selling price he is able to command for the car, a price which is determined by supply and demand and not by what in a state of existential despair he might be willing to accept.[78]

The claim that wage rates are set by the arbitrary decision of the employer also fails to explain why, under a regime of government-mandated wage and price controls, employers begin offering fringe benefits in order to elude the wage controls and *attract workers* with more generous overall compensation packages than competing businesses were offering. During World War II, for instance, health care benefits started to become a common feature of employment. Is this not a clear case of employers *bidding workers away from competitors* through offers of greater compensation?

AN INCREASED STANDARD OF LIVING

It is, therefore, both disappointing and rather surprising that facts such as these, which contradict the suggestion that employers can arbitrarily depress

wage rates, appear to have attracted no prolonged attention in papal documents, or even a curiosity about how market mechanisms may have made this
kind of progress possible. Instead, the central if sometimes unstated contention
of the major twentieth-century statements of the Church's social teaching has
consistently remained that at least in some areas the market is arbitrary and unfair, and that human intervention can rectify these alleged injustices. More
specifically, *Rerum Novarum*, *Quadragesimo Anno*, and other pertinent documents simply take for granted that wage rates are determined by the more or
less arbitrary fiat of employers (a statement of fact on which men of good will
may disagree). Leo XIII speaks of the workingmen of his age as having been
"surrendered, isolated and helpless, to the hardheartedness of employers and
the greed of unchecked competition." The result, he claims, was that "a small
number of very rich men have been able to lay upon the teeming masses of the
laboring poor a yoke little better than that of slavery itself."[79] Pius XI sets forth
this thesis in *Quadragesimo Anno*: "Property, that is, 'capital,' has undoubtedly
long been able to appropriate too much to itself. Whatever was produced,
whatever returns accrued, capital claimed for itself, hardly leaving to the
worker enough to restore and renew his strength."[80] Such a statement, as we
have seen, is in effect the very opposite of the truth. Likewise, in *Laborem Exercens* Pope John Paul II suggests that wage rate determination is more or less
arbitrary when he remarks that during the early days of industrialization, entrepreneurs, following "the principle of maximum profit," attempted "to establish the lowest possible wages for the work done by the employees."[81]

Little or no acknowledgment is made of the enormous increase in living
standards that became evident among the great mass of the population from
the Industrial Revolution to the present, or the substantial increase in the purchasing power of wages that occurred throughout the nineteenth century, the
century of laissez-faire. This is surely one of the most outstanding features of
modern European economic history, yet for some reason it features not at all
in the social encyclicals. To the contrary, the social encyclicals routinely
speak as if the workers' condition had actually stagnated or even deteriorated
(as indeed popular opinion continues to believe). William Luckey writes that
it is "hard to excuse Leo XIII" for his statements to this effect. "Using life expectancy figures, which ought to have been available to Leo, it is clear that at
the dawn of the nineteenth century life expectancy in England was about 37
years, but after 1871–1875, about 20 years prior to *Rerum Novarum*, there is
an acceleration in life expectancy with no setbacks, so that by 1900 English
life expectancy is about 50. Real per capita income begins to soar immediately after 1800 in all of Europe."[82]

Luckey argues that one of the reasons for the strange reluctance on the part
of both the popes and a number of prominent Catholic economic theorists to

acknowledge what should have been evident was that they adopted "an economic theory that is its own predictor." Especially influential in this regard was William Emmanuel, Baron von Ketteler, who was appointed Bishop of Mainz in 1850 and who played such an influential role in the development of the social teaching. In *The Labor Problem and Christianity* (1864), von Ketteler maintained that "the wage rate in our time is determined by subsistence in the strictest sense of the word, i.e., the minimum food, clothing, and shelter that a person needs to sustain a bare physical subsistence."[83]

Thus von Ketteler adopted a theory of wages that possesses a superficial plausibility but which is completely at odds with reality, as the productivity theory of wages reveals. "Without consulting the factual reality," Professor Luckey observes, "the iron law of wages 'predicts' that capitalism automatically results in the pauperization of the workers, from which they cannot extricate themselves." On this basis is the state's taxation of the capitalist justified, for in no other way can justice be done to the workers than by forcing the capitalist to yield what he has wrongfully confiscated from his exploited workers. If this view of wages is accepted, then it becomes philosophically plausible to argue that state aggression against the property of the capitalist is justified, and is not mere thievery.[84] And if this view of wages is accepted, the stance that the popes have taken in certain key documents logically follows.

The question that is hardly ever asked, but should be, is why the obligation of charity should fall entirely upon the shoulders of the employer. Fr. James Sadowsky explains that the very fact that an employee has accepted employment is an indication that he expects to be made better off than he would have been had he attempted to go into business for himself. Thus in the case of a worker in dire need, while "certainly from a Christian point of view we ought to help him meet his needs," the question that *ought* to arise is this: "Why, however, should it be precisely the *employer* on whom this obligation falls, if in fact the employer is not worsening but bettering the condition of his employee?"[85] Advocates of the minimum wage, living wage, and family wage never even raise this fairly critical question. As two other scholars recently put it, "If you want to give money to poor people, why not just go ahead and do it?"[86]

LABOR UNIONS

What about labor unions? It is all very well to claim to favor voluntary workers' associations, and that nothing in Catholic social teaching obligates anyone to support every decision or tactic used by a particular union. That is certainly true. What I want to suggest, however, is that in order for a labor union to accomplish its stated goal of improving the welfare of its members, the logic of the economy is such that this can be accomplished only by the use of some kind of compulsion, and that the notion of the purely voluntary union in practice turns out all too often to be a mere chimera.

The judicious use of reason and an unbiased examination of the evidence reveal that labor unions operate clearly and manifestly in opposition to the welfare of labor taken as a whole. Any suggestion that support for labor unions is somehow morally obligatory upon a Catholic must, therefore, be false, since the premise on which it rests is fallacious. A Catholic obviously cannot be forced to support a particular labor policy devised in the name of helping workers when he knows very well that it will do no such thing.

One caveat should be noted before proceeding. Although I have suggested that a purely voluntary union possesses a great tendency toward coercive behavior, it is possible to imagine a union that operates on a truly voluntary basis. Henry Hazlitt, who was very much an opponent of labor unions, even acknowledged that a noncoercive strike could serve the salutary purpose of alerting the employer to the fact that he is offering a wage rate below the prevailing market wage and must therefore adjust it if he wishes to continue employing the same number of workers as before.[87] Pope Leo XIII wrote in 1895 that "whilst it is proper and desirable to assert and secure the rights of the many, yet this is not to be done by a violation of duty; and that these are very important duties; not to touch what belongs to another; to allow every one to be free in the management of his own affairs; not to hinder any one to dispose of his services when he please and where he please."[88] Those are precisely the principles of voluntary rather than coercive unionism.

The old craft guilds were quite candid about their restrictionist policies; they deliberately limited the number of people who could enter a given craft, often by imposing very high standards for membership. Since modern labor unions appear to welcome all comers, their restrictionist aspect is easily missed. "The crucial point," Murray Rothbard explains, "is that the unions insist on a minimum wage rate higher than what would be achieved for the given labor factor without the union. By doing so . . . they necessarily cut the number of men whom the employer can hire."[89] This conclusion cannot be escaped, as a simple supply and demand-curve analysis reveals.[90] Thus their policy has the effect of restricting the supply of labor in the given area.

In the case of an industry that is especially profitable, as the result of increased consumer demand or the introduction of some cost-cutting measure, and which would therefore be on the verge of expansion, the existence of union wage rates would not necessarily create any unemployment among workers in that industry. What it would do, however, is hamper or prevent altogether the expansion of the industry, and thus the creation of additional jobs. Production that in the absence of union coercion would have certainly taken place never does, and instead production is diverted to less urgently desired fields. This is yet another example of the importance of bearing in mind what is seen and what is not seen, since this case of union coercion is no less destructive than any other, even if the jobs lost are only potential jobs (which of course are not seen, and therefore easily neglected in a careless analysis).[91]

How the union achieves these artificially high wage rates is largely by means of the strike threat, as well as through various legal privileges it has been accorded by the government. Edward Chamberlin describes these privileges:

> If A is bargaining with B over the sale of his house, and if A were given the privileges of a modern labor union, he would be able (1) to conspire with all other owners of houses not to make any alternative offer to B, using violence or the threat of violence if necessary to prevent them, (2) to deprive B himself of access to any alternative offers, (3) to surround the house of B and cut off all deliveries, including food (except by parcel post), (4) to stop all movement from B's house, so that if he were for instance a doctor he could not sell his services and make a living, and (5) to institute a boycott of B's business. All of these privileges, if he were capable of carrying them out, would no doubt strengthen A's position. But they would not be regarded by anyone as part of "bargaining"—unless A were a labor union.[92]

In practice, during strikes the police have typically stood aside and done nothing in the face of union intimidation and even violence against nonunion workers or those who simply wish to continue working. By means of this kind of coercion, labor unions are able to deprive employers of labor if they do not accede to union demands. The result of union activity, therefore, is to raise the money wages of their members, while at the same time relegating many workers, driven out of this line of work by the decreased quantity of labor demanded there, to other lines of work, whose money wages must decrease as a result of the greater supply of workers now forced to compete for them.

The net result of all of this must be negative—that is, the gains to certain workers must be more than offset by the disabilities inflicted upon other workers. The reason is not difficult to see. When union activity reduces the number of people who can be profitably employed in skilled trades, it correspondingly increases the number of skilled laborers forced to find work in fields requiring only unskilled labor. This is why labor economist Morgan Reynolds could conclude that "unions divert labor from more productive to less productive activities, thereby impoverishing the common man."[93] The outcome of this displacement of skilled labor is no different from a situation in which laborers never possessed these skills in the first place. If union privilege prevents some workers from putting their skills to their proper use, the effect is the same as if they had never gone to the trouble to acquire them at all. Once again, union activity has an impoverishing effect upon society. No society can become wealthier by doing the equivalent of reducing the skills and productivity of its workers.

Reynolds has identified seven distinct ways in which labor unionism imposes substantial costs on the economy, all of which tend to be ignored in standard calculations of the economic burden of unions:

1. The redistribution of income (rent) from the general community to union bureaucracies and their members.
2. The unemployment effects of unions.
3. The consequences of union wage inflexibilities over the business cycle.
4. The cost of union work rules.
5. The dynamic impact of unions in discouraging research and development, investment, and entrepreneurship.
6. The direct costs of strikes, strike threats, negotiating costs, labor consultants, National Labor Relations Board elections, bureaucratic costs, grievance costs, and related expenses.
7. The political role of unions in increasing inflation, international trade barriers, government spending, and related forms of discoordination sustained by political action.[94]

It is, therefore, rather difficult to calculate the precise burdens that labor unions have imposed upon the economy. But in a study published jointly in late 2002 by the National Legal and Policy Center and the John M. Olin Institute for Employment Practice and Policy, economists Richard Vedder and Lowell Gallaway of Ohio University calculated that labor unions have cost the American economy an incredible $50 trillion over the past 50 years alone.

How could the figure be so high? "The deadweight economic losses are not one-shot impacts on the economy," the study explains. "What our simulations reveal is the powerful effect of the compounding over more than half a century of what appears at first to be small annual effects."

While the study found that unionized labor does indeed earn wages 15 percent higher than those of their nonunion counterparts—as is to be expected, of course, given the logic of labor unionism—wages in general suffer dramatically as a result of an economy that is 30 to 40 percent smaller than it would have been in the absence of labor unionism.[95] This constitutes a staggering destruction of wealth.

Migration patterns among the states are also highly suggestive. According to Vedder and Gallaway, the eleven states with the lowest unionization rates from 1990 to 1999 "had net in-migration of 3,530,108, which is more than one thousand persons a day, every day, for nine years." Conversely, the eleven most highly unionized states suffered a drain of population amounting to some 2,984,007 people.

Likewise, recent research reveals that between 1970 and 2000, states with so-called "right-to-work" laws (which prevent workers from being compelled to join a union as a condition of employment) created jobs at nearly twice the rate of states without such laws. In fact, the average family in a right-to-work state boasts $2,800 more in purchasing power annually. None of the seven states in which the poverty rate has increased over the past thirty years had right-to-work legislation.[96]

The condition of the American manufacturing base is the source of much hand wringing and concern, but it turns out that here, too, unionism is a likely culprit. While right-to-work states created 1.43 million manufacturing jobs over the past three decades, states without such laws lost 2.18 million manufacturing jobs.[97]

We have already seen quite a number of reasons that such an outcome is to be expected, but let us say a bit more about union work rules. Labor unions are notorious for opposing the introduction of labor-saving machinery, since they believe (sometimes rightly) that it will lead to the unemployment of some of their members. But such machinery—in the steel industry, let us say—allows the same amount of output to be produced by fewer hands, thereby releasing into the economy a supply of labor that can now be applied to the production of goods that we could not have had before because the requisite labor had been tied up in the production of steel. This is an example of how wealth is created. The additional goods produced by the additional labor have the happy result of raising real wages, since (as we have seen) an increase in the supply of goods available will increase real wages by endowing all real incomes with greater purchasing power. Thus by opposing the introduction of labor-saving machinery, labor unions *directly sabotage the very mechanism by which real wages are raised.*[98]

Labor unionism is all the more pernicious because its negative effects go essentially unnoticed, while its beneficiaries are clear and identifiable. Not equipped with the tools of sound economic analysis, the general public is hardly likely to come to spontaneous realization of the causes of the unemployment that unionism has brought about. To the contrary, workers who have been displaced from unionized sectors of the economy and have been forced into less remunerative work are likely to conclude that unionism is the solution to their lower wages. And the process continues.

The unimportance of labor unionism is empirically evident as well: at a time when unionism was numerically negligible and federal regulation all but nonexistent, American workers were much better off than their much more heavily unionized counterparts in Europe. Real wages in manufacturing climbed an incredible 50 percent in the United States from 1860 to 1890, and another 37 percent from 1890 to 1914.[99]

It turns out, therefore, that the testimony provided both by reason and by overwhelming empirical evidence leads inexorably to the conclusion that labor unions are in fact harmful, rather than beneficial, to the cause of labor, and the relatively anemic growth that characterizes heavily unionized economies tends to make unionism deleterious even to unionized workers themselves in the long run.[100] Since the support for labor unionism that permeates Catholic social teaching describes it as something necessary for the economic well-being of workers who would otherwise find themselves impoverished, and since the exact opposite is in fact the case, it would at the very least be unreasonable for labor union sympathy to be portrayed as morally binding on Catholics, especially on those who know very well the profound destruction and harm that such policies have created. To be sure, the popes themselves have never claimed that a favorable attitude toward coercive labor unionism constitutes an infallible moral teaching, but it is easy to come away from much popular exposition of Catholic social teaching with that impression.

No appeal to reason is made within recent Catholic social thought to explain why those who believe in the productivity theory of wages are in fact mistaken, or why it is factually incorrect to insist that artificially imposed wage increases will lead to unemployment, or why the benefits accruing to those select workers who may enjoy the higher wages must morally outweigh the damage done to other workers who are thereby forced to find work in lower paying fields or who find no work at all. This latter question certainly does contain moral implications: is it morally acceptable to favor policies that all but guarantee unemployment for some workers? But since the possibility that interventionist wage policies might create unemployment is essentially not raised, this important moral question is never addressed.

And this, ultimately, is what Catholic social teaching has not fully engaged. Suppose that the description of wage rate determination sketched earlier is in fact correct. In that case, coercive attempts to enforce a wage rate higher than that reached on the free market must lead to unemployment (or at least to more unemployment than would have existed in the absence of such attempts), as employers substitute capital for artificially overpriced labor. There is no reason to doubt the sincerity of the popes who thought they were defending the integrity of the family, the very cell of human society, when they advocated the payment of wages sufficient to provide for a man and his family in reasonable comfort. But if material comfort is the desired outcome and decent wages the means of achieving it, the question of *how* wages can be increased across the board inevitably arises—a question whose answer requires that we have recourse to the sober reflection of human reason. Simply assuming that because higher wages are desirable they can be brought into effect by legislative decree, and then rendering a moral judgment on employers who do not meet these requirements, does no good to those workers now priced out of the market by the enforced payment of higher wages. The popes are obviously not incorrect to identify the well being of the family as an important and desirable end, but what are we to say about policies whose inevitable outcome is the unemployment of many heads of households, with countless more relegated to less remunerative or desirable fields than those from which artificial wage increases have shut them out of the market? The only certain method for raising wage rates permanently and across the board is to increase the productivity of the workers who earn those wages. Nothing can change this fundamental fact. These issues and questions do not receive anything like the attention they deserve in the literature of Catholic social thought, and yet they touch the heart of the whole problem of the improvement of the standard of living of the average laborer.

By any definition, it lay well beyond the competence of the Magisterium to presume to describe the workings of economic relationships. The Magisterium itself can no more tell us what makes wages rise than it can tell us how to build a skyscraper. Catholics who make this point are routinely accused of denying the Church's right to make moral statements pertaining to economic activity. This criticism is completely baseless, and only serves to distract attention from the substantive issues at stake. Of course the Magisterium may instruct Catholics on the moral demands of the marketplace, since how one ought to conduct oneself in the market involves the application of moral principle—an area, unlike economics per se, in which the Church can indeed claim expertise. Thus the Church has properly emphasized the justice and indispensability of the institution of private property; she has likewise condemned fraud, dishonesty, and theft, all of which derogate from the moral order upon which the market economy is based. This is all to the good, and well within the province of magisterial pronouncement. But the attempt to elevate such principles as the "just wage" to the level of binding doctrine is something altogether different, and indeed is fraught with error. To maintain that private property is just, or that people ought to be upright and honest in their economic activities, requires nothing more than simple reflection on the teaching of Christ, the Fathers, and natural law itself. The same cannot be said for exhortations to employers that they pay a "just wage," for embedded within such counsel is a set of unproven assumptions about how economic relationships work, and the belief that all that stands between the world today and the great society of tomorrow is wise legislation, rather than the capital investment which is alone capable of increasing the overall stock of wealth. "What was wrong with Catholic social thought in the nineteenth century," writes Fr. Sadowsky, "was not so much its ethics as its lack of understanding of how the free market can work. The concern for the worker was entirely legitimate, but concern can accomplish little unless we know the causes and the cures for the disease."[101]

NOTES

1. James A. Sadowsky, "Capitalism, Ethics, and Classical Catholic Social Doctrine," *This World*, Fall 1983, 116.

2. Daniel Villey, "The Market Economy and Roman Catholic Thought," *International Economic Papers* 9 (1959): 94.

3. A. M. C. Waterman, "The Intellectual Context of *Rerum Novarum*," *Review of Social Economy* 49 (Winter 1991): 476.

4. Waterman, "The Intellectual Context of *Rerum Novarum*," 473. Emphasis added.

5. Louis Baeck, "Spanish Economic Thought: The School of Salamanca and the *Arbitristas*," *History of Political Economy* 20 (Autumn 1988): 385. Baeck concludes: "By emphasizing the economic mechanisms that influence the determination of value and the formation of prices, the schoolmen of Salamanca finally put the Franciscan nominalism of the late Middle Ages to rest." Such statements constitute a welcome corrective to the perhaps exaggerated claim of de Roover that "[t]o compare the economic system to a clockwork or to the human body and to study how it functions or operates is an idea which did not occur to the medieval Schoolmen and which was entirely alien to their way of thinking . . . . The question asked was never: how does it work or why does it change? The scholastics were preoccupied with another set of problems: what is just or unjust, licit or illicit?" Raymond de Roover, *San Bernardino of Siena and Sant'Antonio of Florence: The Two Great Economic Thinkers of the Middle Ages* (Boston: Baker Library, 1967), 7–8. Again, in the process of determining where justice lay, the Scholastics certainly did, if only incidentally, describe the mechanics of economic relationships.

6. Quoted in Murray N. Rothbard, *An Austrian Perspective on the History of Economic Thought*, vol. 1, *Economic Thought before Adam Smith* (Hants, England: Edward Elgar, 1995), 120.

7. Raymond de Roover, "The Concept of the Just Price: Theory and Economic Policy," *Journal of Economic History* 18 (1958): 421.

8. Quoted in Rothbard, *Economic Thought before Adam Smith*, 110.

9. Rothbard, *Economic Thought before Adam Smith*, 78.

10. Rothbard, *Economic Thought before Adam Smith*, 78.

11. In addition, we might raise this question. A person having difficulty purchasing an expensive yet important good may well be in need of charity. But what is the

moral justification for placing the entire burden of this charity on the seller of the good? I owe this point to James Sadowsky, S.J.

12. Cf. Walter Williams, "The Role of Profits," townhall.com, June 26, 2002 <http://www.townhall.com/columnists/walterwilliams/ww20020626.shtml> (October 28, 2002).

13. George Reisman, *Capitalism* (Ottawa, Ill.: Jameson Books, 1996), p. 211.

14. Reisman, *Capitalism*, 211.

15. Reisman, *Capitalism*, 240.

16. Henry Hazlitt, *Economics in One Lesson* (New York: Crown, 1979 [1946]). 127–33; Reisman, *Capitalism*, 240–41.

17. Raymond de Roover, "Joseph A. Schumpeter and Scholastic Economics," *Kyklos* 10 (1957): 139.

18. Alejandro Chafuen, *Christians for Freedom: Late Scholastic Economics* (San Francisco: Ignatius, 1986), 124.

19. Chafuen, *Christians for Freedom*, 125.

20. Chafuen, *Christians for Freedom*, 126, 127.

21. De Roover, *San Bernardino of Siena and Sant'Antonio of Florence*, 23–27.

22. Chafuen, *Christians for Freedom*, 130–31.

23. Leo XIII, *Rerum Novarum* 4.

24. Leo XIII, *Rerum Novarum* 6.

25. Leo XIII, *Rerum Novarum* 9.

26. Leo XIII, *Rerum Novarum* 15.

27. Leo XIII, *Quod Apostolici Muneris* 9.

28. Leo XIII, *Quod Apostolici Muneris* 1.

29. Leo XIII, *Quod Apostolici Muneris* 4, 10.

30. Pius XI, *Quadragesimo Anno* 120.

31. George M. Searle, C.S.P., "Why the Catholic Church Cannot Accept Socialism," *Catholic World* (July 1913): 449–50.

32. *America* magazine was at the forefront of warning Catholics both of the explicit hostility toward religion that existed among many socialists, and of the inherent danger to revealed religion present in the materialist philosophy undergirding socialism. See, for example, Joseph Husslein, S.J., "Wage System in the Gospel," *America* 7 (August 10, 1912): 415; idem, "The Economic Fetish," *America* 14 (October 23, 1915): 46–47; idem, "Varieties of American Socialism," *America* 9 (September 20, 1913): 557–58; idem, "The Christ of Socialism," *America* 6 (April 6, 1912); idem, "Christian Socialism," *America* 6 (March 30, 1912): 582–84; H.J. Maeckel, S.J., "Socialism and Christian Marriage," *America* 6 (February 24, 1912): 464–65; idem, "Socialism and Religion," *America* 6 (January 20, 1912): 345–47; "Socialists and the Eucharistic Congress," *America* 7 (September 14, 1912): 543; Richard Dana Skinner, "Socialism and Present-Day Indifference," *America* 7 (May 4, 1912): 79–80.

33. See William J. Kerby, "Atheism and Socialism," *Catholic University Bulletin* 11 (July 1905): 315–26; [John J. Burke], "With Our Readers," *Catholic World* (September 1914): 861–62; see also the discussion in Patrick Bernard Lavey, "William J. Kerby, John A. Ryan, and the Awakening of the Twentieth-Century American

Catholic Social Conscience, 1899–1919" (Ph.D. diss., University of Illinois, Urbana-Champaign, 1986), 90–139.

34. "The great mistake made in regard to the matter now under consideration is to take up with the notion that class is naturally hostile to class, and that the wealthy and the working men are intended by nature to live in mutual conflict. So irrational and so false is this view that the direct contrary is the truth. Just as the symmetry of the human frame is the result of the suitable arrangement of the different parts of the body, so in a State is it ordained by nature that these two classes should dwell in harmony and agreement, so as to maintain the balance of the body politic. Each needs the other: capital cannot do without labor, nor labor without capital. Mutual agreement results in the beauty of good order, while perpetual conflict necessarily produces confusion and savage barbarity." Leo XIII, *Rerum Novarum* 19.

35. Leo XIII, *Rerum Novarum* 43.

36. Leo XIII, *Rerum Novarum* 45.

37. Leo XIII, *Rerum Novarum* 46. At the same time, the Pope, defending the right to private property and the benefits that derive from private ownership, warns that these benefits "can be reckoned on only provided that a man's means be not drained and exhausted by excessive taxation," and that the state "be unjust and cruel if under the name of taxation it were to deprive the private owner of more than is fair." *Rerum Novarum* 67. See also *Rerum Novarum* 14, in which the Pope lays down still further limits on the authority of the state.

38. Pius XI, *Quadragesimo Anno* 28.

39. Inasmuch as regulation of working conditions has the same economic effect as a forced wage increase in that it makes hiring labor (rather than substituting inanimate capital) relatively more costly, for the duration of the discussion the question of working conditions will be subsumed under the general question of wages.

40. Pius XI, *Quadragesimo Anno* 71.

41. Pius XI, *Quadragesimo Anno* 88.

42. John Paul II, *Laborem Exercens* 19.

43. Cf. Frank van Dun, "Human Dignity: Reason or Desire? Natural Rights versus Human Rights," *Journal of Libertarian Studies* 15 (Fall 2001): 10.

44. John A. Ryan, *A Living Wage: Its Ethical and Economic Aspects* (New York: Macmillan, 1906), 13–15.

45. George M. Sauvage, review of *A Living Wage*, by John A. Ryan, in *Catholic University Bulletin* 13 (July 1907): 470–75; quotation on 474.

46. Ryan, *A Living Wage*, 249.

47. Ryan, *A Living Wage*, 250.

48. Ryan, *A Living Wage*, 244. Emphasis in original.

49. Ryan, *A Living Wage*, 245; see also 244–46, 261.

50. The seminal essay is Ludwig von Mises, *Economic Calculation in the Socialist Commonwealth* (Auburn, Ala.: Ludwig von Mises Institute, 1990 [1920]); the calculation issue is discussed in chapter 1.

51. Reisman, *Capitalism*, 621.

52. Msgr. Ryan conceded the importance of increased output for raising workers' standard of living, though he failed to draw the logical conclusions from this point

that Reisman correctly draws in *Capitalism*. Labor had learned, said Ryan, that it must "become more interested in the efficiency of industry and the increase of the social product. For the betterment of the condition of the masses is very largely a question of having a larger product to distribute." Joseph M. McShane, S.J., *"Sufficiently Radical": Catholicism, Progressivism, and the Bishops' Program of 1919* (Washington, D.C.: Catholic University of America Press, 1986), 151.

53. Reisman, *Capitalism*, 653.

54. Reisman, *Capitalism*, 653.

55. Reisman, *Capitalism*, 660–61.

56. George Reisman, "The Free Market and Job Safety," Mises.org, January 22, 2003 <http://www.mises.org/fullarticle.asp?control=1143&id=70> (January 23, 2003).

57. Reisman, *Capitalism*, 662–63.

58. Cited in Jim Rose, "Child Labor, Family Income, and the Uruguay Round," *Quarterly Journal of Austrian Economics* 1 (Winter 1998): 78.

59. Cited in Rose, "Child Labor, Family Income, and the Uruguay Round."

60. David R. Henderson, "The Case for Sweatshops," Hoover Institution Weekly Essays, February 7, 2000 <http://www-hoover.stanford.edu/pubaffairs/we/current henderson_0200.html> (October 10, 2003).

61. Pius XI, *Quadragesimo Anno* 71.

62. Ryan, *A Living Wage*, 7.

63. Ryan, *A Living Wage*, 9.

64. Mises himself discusses the work of Pesch and the Solidarists: "It denies—without, however, arguing this more closely or bringing to light ideas not put forward before by the socialists, especially the non-Marxists—that merely acting for one's own property-interests within a legal order guaranteeing liberty and property ensures an interaction of the individual economic actions corresponding to the ends of social cooperation." A similarity with Catholic social teaching in general is apparent: Solidarism denies that a liberal economic order brings about economic harmony—"without, however, arguing this more closely." According to Solidarism, various forms of pressure, whether legal or through the Christian conscience, should be brought to bear in the form of "obligations on the possessors in favour of the poorer people and in favour of the public welfare." Thus Solidarism is "but a single step" from Socialism, says Mises, for "it places above the owner an authority—indifferent whether Law and its creator, the State, or conscience and its counsellor, the Church—which is to see that the owner uses his property correctly." Ludwig von Mises, *Socialism: An Economic and Sociological Analysis*, trans. J. Kahane (Indianapolis, Ind.: Liberty Fund, 1981 [1922]), 233–36. Thanks to David Gordon for this reference.

65. Thomas C. Kohler, "Quadragesimo Anno," in *A Century of Catholic Social Thought: Essays on 'Rerum Novarum' and Nine Other Key Documents*, ed. George Weigel and Robert Royal (Washington, D.C.: Ethics and Public Policy Center, 1991), 32.

66. John Paul II, *Laborem Exercens* 13.

67. Heinrich Pesch, *Liberalism, Socialism and Christian Social Order*, book 1: *The Philosophical Roots of Economic Liberalism*, trans. Rupert J. Ederer (Lewiston, N.Y.: Edwin Mellen Press, 2000), 131.

68. Richard K. Vedder and Lowell E. Gallaway, *Out of Work: Unemployment and Government in Twentieth-Century America* (New York: Holmes & Meier, 1993), 89ff.; Murray N. Rothbard, *America's Great Depression*, 4th ed. (New York: Richardson & Snyder, 1983), 187ff.

69. Pesch also makes a great deal of Carl Menger's reference to "exact" laws of economics, apparently misunderstanding what Menger meant by the term. Pesch, *Philosophical Roots*, 142, 259.

70. Murray N. Rothbard, *Individualism and the Philosophy of the Social Sciences* (San Francisco: Cato Institute, 1978), 49.

71. Rothbard, *Individualism and the Philosophy of the Social Sciences*, 50; on all this, see 45–56.

72. William R. Luckey, "The Intellectual Origins of Modern Catholic Social Teaching on Economics: An Extension of a Theme of Jesús Huerta de Soto" (paper presented at the Austrian Scholars Conference, Ludwig von Mises Institue, March 23–25, 2000); see also Pesch, *Philosophical Roots*, ch. 13, in which Pesch reveals his sympathy toward the German Historical School. At the same time, Pesch does acknowledge the extremism of the Historical School as well as the contributions of the Austrians: "That the representatives of the Austrian School by and large rendered some not insignificant services to economic research, even those who do not share their scientific position will have to acknowledge. The incisive investigation into value and interest theory, the opposition to a one-sided empiricism and exclusive historicism, the introduction of abstraction which no science can do without: those are the contributions of the Austrian School and its representatives—Karl [sic] Menger, Eugen v. Böhm-Bawerk, Emil Sax, among others, who must not be overlooked despite all other shortcomings." Pesch, *Philosophical Roots*, 260–61.

73. Ludwig von Mises, *Human Action: A Treatise on Economics*, Scholar's edition (Auburn, Ala.: Ludwig von Mises Institute, 1998 [1949]), 63.

74. Mises, *Human Action*, 646–47. Elsewhere, Mises observes that the general theory of choice and preference that informed his work and that of any complete and mature economics involved "much more than merely a theory of the 'economic side' of human endeavors and of man's striving for commodities and an improvement in his material well-being. It is the science of every kind of human action. . . . In making his choice man chooses not only between various material things and services. All human values are offered for option. All ends and all means, both material and ideal issues, the sublime and the base, the noble and the ignoble, are ranged in a single row and subjected to a decision which picks out one thing and sets aside another. Nothing that men aim at or want to avoid remains outside of this arrangement into a unique scale of gradation and preference." Mises, *Human Action*, 3. Likewise, Rothbard explains that "the truths of economic theory involve the formal relations between ends and means, and not their specific contents. A man's ends may be 'egoistic' or 'altruistic,' 'refined' or 'vulgar.' They may emphasize the enjoyment of 'material goods' and comforts, or they may stress the ascetic life. Economics is not concerned with their content, and its laws apply regardless of the nature of these ends." Murray N. Rothbard, *Man, Economy and State: A Treatise on Economic Principles* (Auburn, Ala.: Ludwig von Mises Institute, 1993 [1962]), 63.

75. Rothbard, *Man, Economy and State*, 390–91; Mises, *Human Action*, 589–95.

76. Reisman, *Capitalism*, 60.

77. Cf. Hans F. Sennholz, *The Politics of Unemployment* (Spring Mills, Pa.: Libertarian Press, 1987), 149–50.

78. Reisman, *Capitalism*, 614–15.

79. Leo XIII, *Rerum Novarum* 3.

80. Pius XI, *Quadragesimo Anno* 54.

81. John Paul II, *Laborem Exercens* 11. For an overview of John Paul II's thought on such matters, see Samuel Gregg, *Challenging the Modern World: Karol Wojtyla/John Paul II and the Development of Catholic Social Teaching* (Lanham, Md.: Lexington Books, 1999), esp. ch. 5, "Industrial Relations: Protecting the Person."

82. Luckey, "Intellectual Origins of Modern Catholic Social Teaching on Economics."

83. See Luckey, "Intellectual Origins of Modern Catholic Social Teaching on Economics"; see also *The Social Teachings of Wilhelm Emmanuel von Ketteler, Bishop of Mainz (1811–1877)*, ed. Rupert J. Ederer (Washington, D.C.: University Press of America, 1981), 321.

84. Luckey, "Intellectual Origins of Modern Catholic Social Teaching on Economics."

85. Sadowsky, "Capitalism, Ethics, and Classical Catholic Social Doctrine," 124. Emphasis in original.

86. Walter Block and William Barnett II, "The Living Wage: What's Wrong?" *Ideas on Liberty*, December 2002, 23.

87. Hazlitt, *Economics in One Lesson*, 141.

88. Leo XIII, *Longinqua* 17.

89. Rothbard, *Man, Economy, and State*, 623.

90. Supply and demand curves were logically (if briefly) derived by means of praxeological reasoning in chapter 1.

91. Rothbard, *Man, Economy, and State*, 624–25.

92. Edward H. Chamberlin, *The Economic Analysis of Labor Union Power* (Washington, D.C.: American Enterprise Association, 1958), 41–42.

93. Morgan O. Reynolds, *Making America Poorer: The Cost of Labor Law* (Washington, D.C.: Cato Institute, 1987), 46.

94. Reynolds, *Making America Poorer*, 82.

95. See Lawrence W. Reed, "Labor Freedom Makes Sense," *Ideas on Liberty*, February 2003, 14–15. The Vedder and Gallaway study, entitled "Do Unions Help the Economy? The Economic Effects of Labor Unions Revisited," is available as of this printing at <http://www.nlpc.org/olap/lrev/economy.pdf> (July 8, 2004).

96. Reed, "Labor Freedom Makes Sense," 15. I present these data only to reinforce the economic case against labor unionism, not to endorse right-to-work legislation, which itself constitutes unwarranted state intervention into the contractual agreements of private parties and amounts to fighting one intervention with another intervention.

97. Reed, "Labor Freedom Makes Sense," 15.

98. Cf. Reisman, *Capitalism*, 658.

99. George Brown Tindall and David Emory Shi, *America: A Narrative History*, vol. II, brief 5th ed. (New York: W. W. Norton, 2000), 692. See also Sylvester Petro, *The Labor Policy of the Free Society* (New York: Ronald Press, 1957), 101–2.

100. On the effects of labor unionism, see also W. H. Hutt, *The Strike Threat System* (New York: Arlington House, 1973).

101. Sadowsky, "Capitalism, Ethics, and Classical Catholic Social Doctrine," 125.

Chapter Three

Money and Banking

No discussion of economics would be complete without an overview of money and banking. The topic is particularly important for our purposes not only because money is obviously at the heart of any economy that has advanced beyond the most primitive stage, but also because so much confusion exists on the subject even among reasonably educated people. Although the late scholastic theologians possessed a fairly sound grasp of money and inflation, certain more recent Catholic writers, admired to this day by some traditional Catholics, offered suggestions for monetary reform that would have had terrible consequences if implemented. It is very likely that more crank theories have been advanced regarding money than about any other economic topic.

No state intervention or central direction is necessary for the introduction of money. Money comes into existence thanks to the use of man's reason, by which he is able to perceive the benefits that accrue to him when a highly marketable commodity becomes a medium of exchange, thereby dramatically reducing the barriers to mutually beneficial trade that exist under a system of barter and facilitating a far smoother acquisition of the various goods he needs.

The difficulties and limits of a barter economy—that is, an economy in which goods and services are traded directly, rather than by means of a medium of exchange—are well known. In order for any transaction to take place under a barter system, there must exist what economists refer to as a double coincidence of wants. A man seeking two scrambled eggs but able to trade only a Frisbee in exchange must seek out someone who not only possesses two scrambled eggs but who also wishes to exchange them for a Frisbee.

In addition, many transactions simply cannot take place at all under barter. Someone whose sole possession is a splendid castle will find it difficult to purchase a loaf of bread unless he finds a baker willing to accept one ten millionth of a castle in return.

It is not long before people living under barter begin to realize that they can facilitate transactions by means of one or more intermediate goods. If Person A knows that Person B, who has what A wants, would accept something that A can get in trade, A can exchange for this intermediate good, and then obtain what he wants.

It is by means of such thinking that a common medium of exchange eventually emerges. Economic actors realize that by identifying a commodity that is desired by just about everyone in society, they can carry out their transactions with much more efficiency and success. Suppose that some community should settle upon seashells as that commodity. Now, instead of a gloveless man with fifty pencils fruitlessly searching for a man who not only possesses a pair of gloves but who also wishes to exchange them for fifty pencils, he will now instead acquire seashells with the pencils and then use the seashells to acquire the gloves.

What commodity will acquire the character of money depends to some degree on circumstances. It is relatively well known that in prisoner-of-war camps, cigarettes have frequently come into spontaneous use as money, since under those conditions they satisfy the requirements for a medium of exchange. In this case, it is dramatically obvious that no state imposed the currency; it came into use as a result of the prisoners' rational apprehension of a mechanism that would advance their material well being.

In the Western world, it was silver and gold that came to serve as money.[1] These metals possess the qualities indispensable to a medium of exchange: they are durable, portable, relatively valuable per unit weight (unlike, say, dirt or toothpicks), and divisible. They are also highly desired throughout the population.

The term *commodity money* refers to a medium of exchange that either is a commercial commodity or represents title to such a commodity. Thus if paper currency is used in such an economy, it is convertible on demand into the commodity on which the currency is based—e.g., gold—and simply acts as a more convenient substitute for the commodity itself. This is an important conceptual point: the paper currency is not itself money, but rather a substitute for money. Fiat money, on the other hand, refers to a medium of exchange that is not a commodity or a producer or consumer good of any kind, and which does not represent title to a commodity.[2] It is simply irredeemable paper. (This, of course, is the system we have now.)

Once a particular commodity—we shall use gold here—has acquired the character of money, the institution of banking is not far behind. Excellent analyses of banking from an Austrian perspective have already been written, so my presentation here will be relatively brief.[3]

BANKING

People will inevitably wish to store some portion of their money for safe-keeping. For the sake of analysis, let us think of the bank as originally a money warehouse, brought into being for the purpose of storing people's money. The depositor places his gold with the banker, and in turn receives a receipt, or bank note, which he is entitled to redeem at any time for the gold he has stored at the bank. As time goes on, people typically begin to find it convenient to use the bank notes themselves as currency, rather than redeeming them for gold every time they wish to make a purchase. These notes are as good as gold, so to speak, and as long as people have confidence in the financial soundness of the issuing bank, the notes will circulate as money. (It is conceptually the same thing if the bank, instead of issuing notes to a depositor, opens up a checking account for him. The depositor then writes checks on the basis of his holdings at the bank.[4]) These depositors do not earn interest on these accounts. To the contrary, they pay the banker a storage fee.

The kind of bank we have just described is entirely solvent. It is able to meet all of its obligations on demand. If all depositors wished to withdraw their gold from the bank at the same time, the bank would encounter no difficulty in accommodating them.

The situation changes with the introduction of a practice known as fractional-reserve banking.[5] Once people begin using the bank notes as money, it becomes all too easy for bankers to attempt to earn illicit profits by printing out bank notes with no gold backing behind them and lending them out, earning a profit when these loans are repaid with interest. Of course, such banks have more outstanding liabilities than they have units of gold on reserve in order to satisfy any demands for redemption that may occur, but such bankers consider it unlikely that all depositors will demand their gold simultaneously. They keep a fraction of gold in reserve in order to meet the modest demands for redemption that seem to characterize normal business conditions.

In a system of free and competitive banking, the amount of profit that a bank can earn this way is very limited. Suppose Bank A engages in fractional-reserve banking, issuing more notes than it can redeem with the quantity of gold in its vaults. Among the bank's own clientele, Bank A's notes circulate freely as money (as long as its clientele retains confidence in Bank A's fundamental soundness). But as soon as a client of Bank A makes a purchase from a client of another bank, Bank A is in potential difficulty. When this recipient of a bank note from Bank A deposits it in his own bank, Bank B, his bank (having little use for a slip of paper from Bank A) will go to Bank A and demand redemption of the note into specie (hard currency—i.e., the precious metal). The more this happens, the more Bank A's gold reserves begin to dwindle, and the more restrained it will have to be in its note issue. As soon as Bank A is unable to redeem one of its notes into gold, it must go out of business. This is why, without some kind of government prop to support it, a system of fractional-reserve banking cannot become too widespread–constant demands for redemption, coupled with fears of being unable to meet them, will discourage a bank's attempt to inflate its note issue.

This is where central banking enters the picture. Previously, as we have seen, individual banks engaging in fractional reserves had to contend both with the problem of a possible loss of confidence among the bank, leading to massive claims for redemption (a "bank run") as well as with the demands that occur on a regular basis by other banks and their clients for redemption of notes into specie. "To overcome this obstacle," explains Hans-Hermann Hoppe, "in the next step the state must monopolize the banking system or force the competing banks into a cartel under the tutelage of its own state-operated central bank. Once it is in command of a monopolized or cartelized banking system, the state can put the coordinated and joint counterfeiting process of the entire banking system into effect that avoids this risk."[6]

The central bank typically enjoys a monopoly of the note issue: no other institution may any longer circulate bank notes. Under a regime of central banking, then, individual banks are not allowed to increase the money supply by issuing their own notes. What they can still do, however, is increase the money supply by making loans in the form of checking accounts on which borrowers can write checks. Thus the banks, engaging in fractional reserves, typically make loans not in the form of cash issued to the lender but in the form of checking accounts that the banks can create at will. In keeping with the principle of fractional-reserve banking, a *fraction* of these checking deposits is covered by the Federal Reserve notes (i.e., cash) that the bank possesses in its own account with the Federal Reserve, but the vast bulk of them are created out of thin air.

Under such a system there is no problem of one bank demanding redemption of another bank's notes, since no individual bank is allowed to issue notes in the first place. But there nevertheless *appears* to be the analogous problem of one bank demanding that another bank's check be converted into cash. (There is no problem if a client of Bank A writes a check and gives it to another client of Bank A, since when this latter person deposits the check, Bank

A simply adjusts the two clients' accounts accordingly.) If a client of Bank A writes a check on his checking account, and the recipient of that check deposits it in Bank B, this latter bank will naturally present the check to Bank A and demand its redemption in cash. (It does Bank B no good to keep a check from Bank A lying around.) If this happens often enough, Bank A is in trouble.

To see how a system of central banking essentially eliminates this problem, we must first understand something about how the Federal Reserve and its member banks interact with one another. All commercial banks are required by law to be members of the Federal Reserve. Today, with no precious metal backing our currency any longer, the relationship between the Federal Reserve and individual banks works as follows. Since an individual bank is not allowed to print cash, when faced with large demands for redemption of checking deposits into cash a bank must go to the Federal Reserve to obtain it, and to do so it must dip into its own account balance there.[7] (Small demands for cash can be met out of the cash on hand in the bank's vault.) In addition, the Federal Reserve sets reserve requirements for the banks, thereby establishing a minimum percentage of Federal Reserve notes that the banks must keep on hand to meet depositors' demands for cash. Thus if the reserve ratio is 10 percent, a bank must have at least one dollar in its account at the Federal Reserve for every ten dollars of liabilities it issues in the form of checking deposits. The reserve requirement helps determine the rate at which the banks will all inflate, since their desire for profit will generally keep them loaned up to the permissible limit, keeping no more in reserve than is required by the Federal Reserve.

Now let us return to Banks A and B, and explain why the presence of the central bank essentially eliminates the problem of one bank interfering with the inflationary policy of another by demanding redemption of its checks into cash. The central bank, by pumping money into the economy (more on which below), permits the entire banking system to inflate together, using Federal Reserve notes as their reserves. As Rothbard explains:

> In a free-banking system, inflation by any one bank would soon lead to demands for redemption by the other banks, since the clientele of any one bank is severely limited. But the central bank, by pumping reserves into all the banks, can make sure that they can all expand together, and at a uniform rate. If all banks are expanding, then there is no redemption problem of one bank upon another, and each bank finds that its clientele is really the whole country. In short, the limits on bank expansion are immeasurably widened, from the clientele of each bank to that of the whole banking system.[8]

How does this process eliminate the problem of one bank demanding redemption from another? With all banks finding their reserves increased as a result of the Federal Reserve's pumping money into the economy, they will all inflate on top of this new money at the same rate (as determined by the Federal Reserve's reserve requirement).* As a result, the various redemptions will tend, on net, to cancel each other out. This is one reason that a central bank is so insidious: it removes the constraints that would exist on a free market against substantial credit inflation by the banks.

This means that no bank can long inflate *beyond* the rate that the Federal Reserve wants, of course, though help is available even in this case in the form of the federal funds market. Banks facing short-term difficulties can borrow from banks possessing surplus reserves. In extreme cases (particularly with big banks), the Federal Reserve will even step in and act as the so-called "lender of last resort," providing the troubled bank with reserves either by lending it reserves or by buying some of its assets.[9]

The final question to consider is how the Federal Reserve increases the money supply in the first place. It does so not by printing cash and putting it into circulation but primarily through what are called open-market operations, in which the Federal Reserve purchases assets, usually government bonds. The process works as follows. The Federal Reserve purchases, say, $1 billion in government bonds from a bond dealer, such as Goldman, Sachs. The bond dealer, now in possession of a $1 billion check from the Federal Reserve, deposits this check in its bank. (Individuals and firms other than banks cannot have accounts at the Federal Reserve itself, so the Federal Reserve's check must be deposited in some commercial bank.)

Since in the present monetary regime the banks can profit legally and securely by fractional-reserve banking, the bank receiving the check from Goldman, Sachs—Bank A, let us say—will not simply hold on to the money. It will deposit the check at the Fed, where its account there now goes up by $1 billion. The banks typically keep no more cash in reserve than the Federal Reserve's reserve ratio requires, so Bank A, with this fresh injection of reserves, will likely now have more in reserve than Federal Reserve requirements demand. The bank will therefore use this new $1 billion of reserves as a base on which to inflate still further.

---

*It is important to understand that a bank in receipt of a check from the Federal Reserve does not immediately extend credit to the extent permitted by the reserve requirement. Thus if the reserve ratio is 20 percent, the recipient bank does not immediately turn $1 billion in reserves into $5 billion in new loans (which would amount to keeping 20 percent of the new money on reserve). Instead of expanding by 500 percent, as in this case, the banks instead expand by 1 minus the reserve requirement, or in this case, 80 percent. The aggregate result, however, once this additional credit works its way through the banking system and subsequent banks lend out 80 percent of *their* new reserves, is that the initial injection of $1 billion winds up expanding credit by $5 billion. By the end of the process, moreover, the banks have worked their way back down to the 20 percent in reserves that is required by law, as redemptions in the amount of 80 percent of the new money lent are honored from bank to bank to bank over the course of the expansion. For more on this process, see Murray N. Rothbard, *The Mystery of Banking* (New York: Richardson & Snyder, 1983), 163–71.

And where does the Federal Reserve get the money to purchase the $1 billion in loans in the first place? *It creates the money out of thin air.* It simply writes a check on itself and spends it.[10] In this way, central banks are money producers, and thus analogous to gold miners rather than banks in the strict sense.

The Federal Reserve, therefore, is in every sense a legally privileged counterfeiter, and a monopolistic one at that. And it has behaved just as our knowledge of human nature would lead us to expect from an institution endowed with a monopoly counterfeiting privilege: it has printed a staggering amount of money. Since the establishment of the Federal Reserve in 1913, the dollar has lost about 95 percent of its value. Yet the Federal Reserve still manages to persuade people that it is a great inflation-fighting institution, when in fact, through its vast increases in the money supply, the Federal Reserve is itself the source of the erosion of the value of the dollar. This is why Austrian economists favor both a gold standard and the complete abolition of the Federal Reserve system. It is also why so many Austrians favor a 100 percent-reserve banking system, in which banks would be legally required to back all demand deposits, dollar for dollar, with specie in their vaults. Banks that violated this basic principle of honesty would be forced to declare bankruptcy as soon as they were unable to meet a legitimate claim for redemption—just as would a dry cleaner who could not produce his customers' clothing on demand, or a warehouse operator who could not produce the items that people had stored in his care.

One more point must be introduced as we consider the economic and moral aspects of various monetary regimes. One of Mises' great innovations in monetary theory was his so-called regression theorem. (I have confined the theorem itself, which some may find rather technical, to the notes.[11]) What deserves notice in this context are its implications, since Mises' regression theorem holds important implications for the introduction of fiat currency. One of the major ideas implied by the theorem is that in order for some commodity to come into circulation as money, it *must* first possess *use value*. That is, apart from its value as a medium of exchange (that is, its *exchange value*), it must be valued in itself. (The great scholastic theologian Jean Buridan had anticipated this point in the fourteenth century, arguing that money must originate as a useful commodity on the market, valued originally for non-monetary purposes.[12]) Menger had showed how money could develop from a commodity (our earlier analysis of this process in fact borrowed from Menger), but Mises proved that it had to develop this way.

The conclusion that follows from these statements is a dramatic one: fiat currency cannot come into existence voluntarily, in a truly free market. To the contrary, it must be introduced by coercion, with a massive act of state confiscation of people's stocks of the commodity for which the paper had served as a substitute. And indeed, the fiat currency that has existed in the United States since Franklin Roosevelt's abandonment of the gold standard in 1933 was carried out by precisely the kind of confiscation that the regression theorem implies. By that time, in carrying out ordinary transactions people had grown accustomed to the convenience of using paper money as substitutes for gold, and which could be converted into gold at any time. People therefore accepted the paper not for its use value, which was nil, but because of its exchange value—it was, literally, as good as gold.

Once paper money has come into circulation as a convertible substitute for gold and people have become habituated to its use, the stage is set for the state to confiscate the people's gold, leaving only fiat paper—which continues to circulate out of habit but which as valueless paper could never have originated as a medium of exchange.[13] This is what happened in 1933, when people were forced to hand over their gold. Their paper currency would henceforth be convertible into nothing.

FIAT CURRENCY AND CENTRAL BANKING: MORAL PROBLEMS

To the immorality of the vast-scale seizure of private property involved in introducing a fiat currency must be added the moral difficulties associated with inflation. Inflation, wrongly described by many people as rising prices (an *effect* of inflation), refers to an increase in the amount of money in circulation not matched by an increase of the money commodity. (Under a commodity money, inflation refers to an increase in bank notes not backed by specie; under a fiat currency, which does not possess a specie backing, inflation refers to an increase in the amount of paper currency in circulation.) A commodity money provides an inherent check against monetary expansion. The ever-present demand by depositors for redemption of notes in gold prevents any sustained inflation of the money supply. But if deposits are redeemable in nothing but worthless paper, a crucial check against monetary expansion has been removed. Gold possesses the advantage of being finite in quantity and impossible to counterfeit. There is, on the other hand, practically no limit to the amount of paper that can be printed and stamped as money.

Often overlooked in non-Austrian analyses are the *distribution effects* (sometimes referred to as "Cantillon effects," after the eighteenth-century economist Richard Cantillon) of inflation. It is generally conceded that inflation of the money supply leads to rising prices (or, at the very least, to prices that are higher than they would have been in the absence of the inflation). But the price increases associated with inflation do not occur all at the same time, reaching all goods across the entire economy. The new money does not enter the economy in a uniform way, affecting everyone to the same degree and at the same time. Some get the new money earlier than others. Those who receive the new money first are able to spend it in an economy in which prices have not yet risen. Those who receive the new money from its first recipients, in turn, find themselves at an advantage vis-à-vis those who have not yet received it, since prices have likely not yet risen to a level commensurate with the new quantity of money.

As the new money works its way through the economy, it raises the prices of the goods on which its recipients spend it. Those who receive the new money last, after it has worked its way throughout the economy, suffer the brunt of the distribution effect, since all this time, without having come into possession of any of the new money, they have had to pay the higher prices that the new money has brought about. We now see that the distribution gains of the first possessors of the new money have come at the expense of those who received the money only much later. (In our example above, involving Fed purchases of government debt from Goldman, Sachs, it is Goldman, Sachs who receives the new money first, thereby benefiting from Fed activity at the expense of everyone else.) If there is a principle of Catholic morality according to which such insidious wealth redistribution is acceptable, it is not known to the present writer.

Inflation also hurts those on fixed incomes, or those who rely for their sustenance on accumulated savings. In either case, the same nominal amount of money possesses less real purchasing power as a result of the government's increase of the money supply, and practically everyone—particularly the most economically vulnerable—thereby become the victims of indirect theft.

Creditors are also hurt by inflation, since the dollars they are repaid are worth less than the dollars they originally lent. Lest those too overcome by class envy to appreciate basic justice should actually favor such an outcome, Mises reminds people that practically all of them are creditors:

> Does inflation touch only businessmen and financiers? Nothing of the sort. You who read these lines are certainly a creditor. Every person who has a legal claim to deferred payments of any kind is a creditor. If you have a savings account with a bank, if you own bonds, if you are entitled to a pension, if you have paid for an insurance policy, you are a creditor, and are, hence, directly hit by inflation.
>
> Professional men, civil servants, commissioned officers of the armed forces, teachers, most white-collar workers, salaried employees, skilled specialists, mechanics, and engineers normally provide for their own old age and for their dependents in ways that make them creditors, that is through savings, insurance,

pensions, and annuities. . . . They will collect the number of dollars to which they are entitled—but each of those dollars will be thinner than it used to be, capable of providing less food, clothing, and shelter.[14]

Inflation also throws business calculation into chaos. Under an inflationary regime, businesses find it difficult to distinguish between genuine and illusory profits. Basing themselves on nominal expenditure and revenue figures, they tend to overestimate profits, mistaking the consequences of an inflated money supply for an increase in real profits. It is standard accounting practice for an asset's cost to be reckoned as the amount of money spent to purchase it. But when inflation occurs, the price of replacing that asset when it wears out rises. This is why inflation can cause business to overstate its profits (not properly taking into account the now higher replacement costs of their assets), and even to spend and invest money that it actually needs just to maintain its capital stock. In other words, by misleading business into a false sense of prosperity, inflation can cause businessmen to engage in inadvertent capital consumption.[15] Commodity monies, on the other hand, can actually facilitate economic calculation, since their quantities tend to change so slowly. According to Hans Sennholz, "This kept changes in their purchasing power at rates that could be disregarded by business accounting and bookkeeping."[16]

Inflation's interference with business calculation is not insubstantial. As the distribution effects of inflation work their way through the economy, business firms may see the prices of the goods they produce begin to rise. If entrepreneurs believe that these price rises represent a permanent phenomenon, they are liable to expand production, investing in additional capital and labor. If, on the other hand, they believe that these price increases are caused simply by inflation and are not likely to be long lasting, they will refrain from rearranging resource allocation in line with the rising prices. The trouble is, they have no way of knowing whether given price increases are caused by genuine increases in demand or by inflation. They have no way of knowing the specific path of the inflation as it works its way throughout the economy, and whether their own firms are part of that path. "For Austrians," writes Steven Horwitz, "inflation is a major drag on economic growth because it unnecessarily complicates the entrepreneur's job and leads to error and wasted resources."[17]

Inflation also undermines conservative values. "The millions who see themselves deprived of security and well-being become desperate," explains Mises. "The realization that they have lost all or most all of what they had set aside for a rainy day radicalizes their entire outlook. They tend to fall easy prey to adventurers aiming at dictatorship, and to charlatans offering patent-medicine solutions." These effects are "especially strong among the youth.

They learn to live in the present *and scorn those who try to teach them 'old-fashioned' morality and thrift*."[18]

Moreover, lurking behind any inflation is the ever-present possibility of a degeneration into what economists call hyperinflation. Hyperinflation refers to an inflation of the money supply so enormous as to render the currency utterly worthless and create an overall monetary collapse. This is what occurred in Germany in 1923, when it took 4.2 trillion German marks to equal a single American dollar. (Not coincidentally, 1923 also witnessed Adolf Hitler's first attempt to seize power.)

State manipulation of a fiat currency is not conceptually distinct from simple counterfeiting, and thus a fundamental dishonesty permeates a monetary system that lacks a commodity backing. It is for this reason that supporters of the gold standard have historically argued that only gold is sound, honest money.[19] Under a pure gold standard, in which banks are required to maintain a 100 percent gold reserve for all their demand deposits and in which any paper money in use is immediately redeemable in gold at par, the massive counterfeiting by the state's privileged central bank that occurs as a matter of routine under a fiat currency would not occur. This reason alone constitutes a prima facie case in favor of gold from a moral point of view.

Juan de Mariana, S.J., considered the moral implications of monetary debasement in his *Treatise on the Alteration of Money*. He begins by strenuously denying that the king is the owner of his subjects' goods. The king has not been given the power to "fall upon their houses and lands, and to seize and set aside what he will. . . . [N]either the power conferred upon the leader in time of war nor the authority to govern subjects, grants the authorization to take possession of the goods of individuals."[20]

The great Jesuit goes on to argue that the king also has no right to demand tribute from his people without their consent.

> What I said above confirms this point: The private goods of citizens are not at the disposal of the king. Thus, he must not take all or part of them without the approval of those who have the right to them. This is the pronouncement of legal experts: The king does not have the power to make a decision that results in loss of private goods unless the owners agree, nor may he seize any part of their property by planning and imposing a new tax.[21]

Having established these points, Mariana considers whether the king has the right to enrich himself by debasing the currency and keeping the difference for himself. Since this is but a species of royal actions that Mariana has already condemned, it comes as little surprise that he rejects this idea as well. The king, he says, may not "take away arbitrarily any part of [the people's] possessions for this or any other reason or any ploy. Such seizure occurs whenever money is debased: For what is declared to be more is worth less." Since currency debasement is merely another form of confiscating the people's property, it cannot be allowed: "But if a prince is not empowered to levy taxes on unwilling subjects and cannot set up monopolies for merchandise, he is not empowered to make fresh profit from debased money. These strategies aim at the same thing: cleaning out the pockets of the people and piling up money in the provincial treasury."[22]

Mariana was not alone among the great scholastics. Gabriel Biel, for example, a fifteenth-century professor of theology at the University of Tübingen, taught that "if a prince should reject valid money, in order that he may buy it up more cheaply and melt it, and then issue another coinage of less value, attaching the value of the former currency to it, he would be guilty of stealing money and is required to make restitution."[23]

FRACTIONAL-RESERVE BANKING: MORAL IMPLICATIONS

There are also moral implications of fractional-reserve banking, and here again, as we shall see, the late scholastics had a great deal of sound advice. Simply put, the practice of fractional-reserve banking, which is made enormously simpler if the currency is irredeemable paper, amounts to institutionalized fraud. Banks that engage in this practice are inherently bankrupt, since if all their clients simultaneously demanded that their deposits be turned over to them, the bank would be forced to concede its inability to meet its obligations. In many cases, however, governments have granted favors and special privileges to such banks. Very often, fractional-reserve banks, under pressure for redemption by their depositors, have been legally permitted to suspend specie payment—which means they are allowed to continue in operation, demanding that their own debtors meet *their* obligations, while at the same time refusing to provide specie (that is, gold or silver) to depositors requesting it. No other business is allowed to operate on such a basis, and there is no obvious moral difference between banking and any other business enterprise that should entitle it to exemption from this basic standard of morality.

The late scholastics generally took this position as well. In the sixteenth century, such theologians as Luis Saravia de la Calle, Martín de Azpilcueta Navarro, and Tomás de Mercado argued that the demand deposit did not amount contractually to a transfer of property, even for a time, from the depositor to the banker, and that it would be wrong for the banker to attempt to seek profit by lending out deposits that are supposed to be available to depositors on demand. Even in the case of such scholastics as Luis de Molina and Juan de Lugo, whose position was rather confused but which appeared to favor the principle that the depositor forfeited some control over demand deposits to the banker, a modern scholar suggests that they would nevertheless have rejected the fractional-reserve system when presented with all of its implications. Fr. Bernard W. Dempsey has shown that on the basis of their own principles, even these men, faced with the modern system, would have to favor a banking system based on 100 percent reserves, or something very much like it.[24]

Legally, the transaction whereby a client deposited money into a bank was originally treated as a *bailment*—that is, as hiring someone for the safekeeping of valuables.[25] Since *demand deposits* were by definition to be available on demand, the banker could not lend them out in the meantime, since he could not know when they might be demanded by the depositors. Such a principle makes good legal and moral sense. We do not forfeit control of our property when we store it in a warehouse; and there is no reason that we should even for a time forfeit control of our money when we store it in a money warehouse. (The only case in which it would be morally legitimate for a depositor's money to be treated as temporarily not his own would be in the case of a *time deposit*, in which case the depositor would have voluntarily contracted to relinquish control over his money for a set period of time, during which the banker could do with it as he saw fit.)

As time went on, however, banking law gradually began to evolve in the direction of treating deposited money not as a *bailment* but as *debt*. The classic legal case occurred in England, in the House of Lords, as *Foley v. Hill and Others*. Lord Cottenham declared:

> Money, when paid into a bank, ceases altogether to be the money of the principal; it is then the money of the banker, who is bound to an equivalent by paying a similar sum to that deposited with him when he is asked for it. . . . The money placed in the custody of a banker is, to all intents and purposes, the money of the banker, to do with it as he pleases; he is guilty of no breach of trust in employing it; he is not answerable to the principal if he puts it in jeopardy, if he engages in a hazardous speculation; he is not bound to keep it or deal with it as the property of his principal; but he is, of course, answerable for the mount, because he has contracted. . . .

This principle, on which American banking would also be based, served to legitimize the practice of fractional-reserve banking. As Murray Rothbard observed, the banker was thereby authorized to do whatever he wished with the money of his depositors, and "if he cannot meet his contractual obligations he is only a legitimate insolvent instead of an embezzler and a thief who has been caught red-handed."[26]

At this point, let us dispose of a standard misconception. Some people believe that prosperity depends on increases in the money supply, and that the natural increase in the supply of gold will not occur rapidly enough to provide this increase. This argument, according to which an increase in the money stock is socially desirable and beneficial, is, in the words of one expert, "one of the great economic fallacies of our time."[27] It completely misconceives the nature of money. As David Ricardo correctly explained two centuries ago:

> If the quantity of gold or silver in the world employed as money were exceedingly small, or abundantly great . . . the variation in their quantity would have produced no other effect than to make the commodities for which they were exchanged comparatively dear or cheap. The smaller quantity of money would perform the functions of a circulating medium as well as the larger.[28]

Likewise, Frédéric Bastiat remarked in 1849 that "a small quantity of rare metal facilitates transactions as much as a large quantity of abundant metal."[29]

This is one of the great insights of Mises and the Austrian School: above a certain threshold, *any supply of money is optimal*. Claims that we need an increased supply of money, or a "flexible" money supply, or a money supply that expands along with growth in business activity, all reveal a fundamental misconception of the nature and function of money. An increase in the supply of any economic good confers a social benefit in that the overall stock of wealth is increased. But since money serves as a medium of exchange and is not itself consumed, an increase in its supply confers no social benefit, and serves only to dilute the value of each unit of money in existence.

THE BUSINESS CYCLE

In addition to all of these practical and moral disadvantages, fiat money can also lead to the phenomenon known as the business or trade cycle—that is, the boom-bust tendency in the economy—while a commodity money would not. At this point, then, let us consider the Austrian theory of the business cycle, for which economist F. A. Hayek, elaborating on a theory developed by Ludwig von Mises, won the Nobel Prize in economics in 1974.

Rothbard argued that any theory of the business cycle must, at the very least, explain two things. First, it must account for the sudden cluster of entrepreneurial error that occurs on the cusp of a recession or depression. The market possesses a natural tendency to weed out those who make poor entrepreneurial decisions, and systematically favors those who excel at it. Entrepreneurs maintain and expand their economic position by their superior fore-casting abilities and their skill at anticipating consumer demand, while people who do not possess such abilities lose market share or go out of business altogether. It therefore demands explanation why so many businessmen should suddenly and simultaneously make egregious entrepreneurial errors.[30] (According to the Austrian theory, as we shall see, the reason is that a factor common to them all—namely, an artificially low interest rate, brought about by the inflationary policies of a central bank—misleads them into erroneous decisions.)

Second, an adequate theory of the cycle must account for another empirical fact about economic depressions: that they hit capital-goods, or producer-goods, industries much more heavily than they do consumer-goods industries. A great many economists have tried to argue that "underconsumption" accounts for economic depressions; this is the standard explanation for the Great Depression that students are likely to find in their American history textbooks. (This underconsumption theory was vigorously promoted by Msgr. John Ryan, the so-called "Right Reverend New Dealer" discussed in chapter 2 who devoted so much work to elaborating the social teaching.[31]) But this theory is obviously incorrect, since if underconsumption were really the problem, Rothbard asks, "then how is it that retail sales are the last and the least to fall in any depression, and that depression *really* hits such industries as machine tools, capital equipment, and raw materials?" During the boom phase of the cycle, moreover, it is these industries that prosper most spectacularly, and not those catering directly to the consumer. Why the greater intensity of both boom and bust in capital-goods industries?[32]

It was Mises who first proposed the Austrian theory of the business cycle in *The Theory of Money and Credit* (1912), building upon and revising some of the insights of the British Currency School, but basing his argument ultimately upon capital theory that was characteristically Austrian. The Austrian view proceeds as follows. In an unhampered market economy, the interest rate declines when people save more—that is, when they put their money into savings accounts. Banks, in turn, lend these saved funds out to borrowers. (This lending does not rely on fractional reserves; these are not demand deposits but savings accounts, whose funds the bank may justly lend.) The more people save, therefore, the more the banks have available to lend. And the more the banks have available to lend, the lower will the interest rate be. That only stands to reason: as something comes into greater and greater abundance, its price tends to fall lower and lower. In this case, the amount of loanable funds increases, so its price—the price of borrowing, or the interest rate—correspondingly falls.

Another concept central to the Austrian theory of the business cycle is the idea of higher and lower-order stages of production. Higher order stages of production are stages of the production process that are further away from finished consumer goods: things like mining and refining, or the construction of a factory or production facility. These are sometimes called producer goods industries, since they involve things that are produced not for immediate use but are themselves used to produce final consumer goods. Grain production, for instance, is a higher-order stage than is the bakery that sells the final consumption good.

Higher order stages of production tend to be the most sensitive to interest rate fluctuations. Building a new plant or expanding mining capacity might turn a profit only in the relatively distant future. If interest rates are high, this means higher costs year after year. But if the interest rate should come down, projects that once looked unprofitable suddenly become potentially profitable.

In an unhampered market with a commodity money, everything works out smoothly. By saving more of their money, consumers have indicated that they are prepared to spend less in the present. Investors see this signal in the lower interest rate. They tend to begin investing in more time-consuming stages of production that they can now afford thanks to the lower interest rate, and thanks to the fact that consumers have indicated a relatively decreased desire to consume in the present. (In effect, they are willing to wait.)

But consider what happens when the central bank (in our case, the Federal Reserve) intervenes in the economy. The Fed has a variety of mechanisms at its disposal to increase the availability of credit and lower interest rates. Whether the rate is lowered by voluntary saving on the part of the public or whether it is lowered by these actions of the Federal Reserve, the result in both cases is that businesses see that interest rates have come down. So they tend to borrow more, and this borrowing tends to be concentrated in higher order stages of production, which are more interest-rate sensitive.

In this case, though, there is a problem. This time, the lower interest rate does not reflect an increased willingness on the part of consumers to defer purchases and consume less in the present. This time, the lower interest rate is created by entirely artificial means. Investors are thus misled into directing resources into higher order, time-consuming stages of production, while in the meantime consumers continue to follow their old consumption patterns.

Now we can either have more investment and less consumption in the present, or less investment and more consumption in the present. But the Fed-generated boom attempts to do both simultaneously—more investment and more consumption at the same time. Something has to give. The economy is being pushed in two mutually exclusive directions at once. As Hayek would put it, the economy has been pushed beyond its "production possibilities frontier" (which he depicted graphically on his so-called "Hayekian triangle"). In a genuine boom, fueled by additional savings, people's abstention from consumption makes resources available to investors. The Fed-driven boom, on the other hand, makes no additional resources available. People's time preferences have not changed. "[I]n the absence of an actual change in time preferences," explains Roger Garrison, "no additional resources for sustaining the policy-induced boom are freed up. In fact, facing a lower interest rate, people will save less and spend more on current consumables. The central bank's credit expansion, then, results in an incompatible mix of market forces."[33]

The Fed's intervention has therefore created systematic discoordination throughout the economy. Resources have been *malinvested*—that is to say, resources have been invested not in accordance with consumer desires, but in response to false signals. Resources have been wasted. Some of them can be recovered, since some building and equipment can be transferred to lines of production more in conformity with consumer desires, but even this transition process takes time and resources to accomplish.

When lower interest rates are caused by increased saving on the part of the public rather than by Fed manipulation, then the boom is sustainable. People's deferred consumption provides the means for investors to engage in long-term projects far removed from the immediate production of consumer goods—plant and equipment, raw materials, steel mills, etc. The interest rate coordinates investment in accordance with people's time preferences. When people save more, the interest rate goes down, signaling to investors that the requisite funds are available, and that people are willing to defer their purchases to this degree.

But when the lower interest rate is the result of Fed manipulation, the boom is built on sand. It is built not on authentic savings, the only sound source of investment funds, but on artificial credit creation. "With seemingly favorable credit conditions," a leading expert on the theory explains, "long-term investment projects are being initiated at the same time that the resources needed to see them through to completion are being consumed. As the market guides these projects into their intermediate and late stages, the underlying economic realities become increasingly clear: Not all of the investment undertakings can be profitably completed."[34] The bust is therefore inevitable.[35]

At this point, capital goods that are complementary to those production processes still unfinished are in unexpectedly short supply, with investors enticed by cheap credit now competing for resources with established firms, and competitive entrepreneurial bidding for them begins to drive up their prices. These increased prices, largely unanticipated by the investors who embarked on these projects in the first place, naturally lead to a greater demand for credit to cover them, which in turn raises interest rates back up. It now becomes clear that the boom has been built on sand, and that enough resources do not exist in the economy for all of these investment projects to be completed.[36] Some portion of the invested capital is irretrievably lost, and provides physical evidence of the waste and destruction of wealth caused by the artificial boom. While the price system works at this point to bid resources away from earlier stages of production and toward later ones, this process is not without difficulties. "Some capital goods attracted to the earlier stages of production by the monetary expansion may not be retrievable," two scholars of the subject explain. "As a consequence, many production projects may have to be abandoned; many others can be completed but only with a great delay and/or at a much higher cost than could have been anticipated."[37]

Thanks to the Austrian theory, it becomes possible to understand both the sudden cluster of entrepreneurial error and its concentration in the capital-goods industries. The cluster occurs because entrepreneurs are misled by a distorted signal to which any substantial economic actor must be attentive: the interest rate. The concentration of this error in capital-goods industries, and particularly in the higher-order stages of production, can be explained with reference to the same fact. The further away in time a particular stage of production is from finished consumer goods, the more sensitive will it be to fluctuations in the interest rate.[38] Thus the malinvestment will tend to be concentrated in higher-order capital goods, and the inevitable liquidation will of necessity be concentrated there.

There are at least two good reasons for engaging in what to some readers may have seemed a rather technical discussion of the Austrian theory of the business cycle. First, it reinforces the moral claim of a pure gold standard, since if all money were convertible into gold on demand, no central bank (which should not exist in any case) would be able to engage in the kind of credit manipulation and stimulus that leads to the business cycle in the first place. Surely if a particular monetary system can avoid the impoverishment and dislocation of recessions and depressions, this factor alone should speak volumes in its favor.[39]

Second, the Austrian theory also contains critically important insights for proper moral analysis, and shows why moral judgment is liable to go dreadfully wrong if undertaken in ignorance of the true causes of the business cycle. Countless moralists are to be found during recessions and depressions calling for various state measures intended to alleviate the dislocations associated with the downturn. Since this topic is well covered in the Austrian literature, let us confine ourselves to one typical suggestion: emergency aid, from low-interest loans to outright subsidies, to failing businesses. As the

Austrian analysis makes clear, this is precisely what should *not* be done, since it only perpetuates the credit-induced misallocation of capital into the indefinite future. Liquidation of the malinvesments incurred during the boom must be allowed to continue unimpeded, lest the inevitable liquidation process and its attendant suffering be indefinitely prolonged.

In fact, the policy implications of the Austrian theory are obvious: *the government should do nothing at all*. Any attempt to lend support to malinvested capital only obstructs the recovery, since economically sound firms are forced to continue to compete with these unsound firms for the scarce resources they need. Support for failing businesses thus tends to impoverish those firms that are capable of employing the resources of their less successful counterparts more efficiently and more in line with consumer demands and time preferences but who are impeded from doing so. Government stimulus to consumption, which remains the conventional wisdom despite its repeated failure (as in Japan, which has been in the economic doldrums after more than a decade of consumption-driven policy), is at least as bad an idea, since the business downturn was clearly not caused by insufficient consumption. In a certain sense, the downturn was caused by *too much* consumption, which made long-term investment projects correspondingly unprofitable (since they were out of line with consumer desires to consume in the more immediate future). This is why Rothbard suggests that the most helpful path to pursue at such a time is certainly *not* more consumption, but "more saving, to validate some of the excessive investments of the boom."[40]

The importance of economic knowledge to moral analysis is, therefore, amply reinforced in the case of the business cycle. Without an adequate knowledge of the causes and cures of the cycle, how can someone trained in moral philosophy or theology be sure that he is not in fact recommending a course of action that will only exacerbate the problems he aims to solve?

Consider, on the other hand, the analysis of Fr. James Gillis, C.S.P. (1876–1957), editor of the monthly *Catholic World* from 1922 to 1948. According to Gillis, "At bottom, all questions, even economic questions, are simple." The Pope, he said, solved the problem of the Depression—"supposedly so intricate"—with one word: "greed."[41] This is an excellent example of the unfortunate disparagement of economics as a science on the part of certain Catholic spokesmen. If "greed" is the entire explanation for the business cycle, we may as well discard economic analysis entirely.

Such anti-intellectualism on the part of so influential a churchman—who if he were speaking within the confines of any other discipline would not dream of engaging in so cavalier and careless a mode of argument—not only does the Church no good (and indeed is positively harmful to the Church by making her appear hostile or at least indifferent to reasoned, scientific argument) but also does society no good. The Austrians, with their understanding of the consequences of artificial credit creation, and aware of the long-term effects of intertemporal capital misallocation, possess the intellectual tools necessary to prevent future business cycles. The Gillis view excludes economic analysis altogether. How, exactly, is "greed" to be prevented, and in what way (if any) would such anti-greed measures address the problems of artificial credit creation—which *must* lead to economic downturns—that the Austrians have identified?

INFLATION: OTHER CATHOLIC APPROACHES

The arguments presented thus far make up the case against any system of fiat currency, whether the present system or the alternatives proposed by some well-known Catholics. Quite a number of traditional Catholic commentators have correctly concluded that there is something profoundly wrong with the present monetary system in the United States. When it comes to what they would substitute for it, however, such thinkers have sometimes been less intellectually rigorous.

Fr. Charles Coughlin, for instance, who enjoyed considerable popularity during the 1930s and whose writing is admired by some even today, actually advocated *more* inflation than was occurring under the existing system. Such a proposal would simply have led to all the problems described above, and on a larger scale.

The same type of proposal, by which the government would directly control the money supply rather than through a central bank, was advanced by Fr. Denis Fahey, a figure still more popular among traditionalists. On some topics, Fahey did indeed have valuable contributions to make, but on money it would have been better for all concerned if he had never published his recommendations for a state-issued fiat currency. Nearly all of the arguments in his book *Money Manipulation and Social Order* are fallacious. (Perhaps most unfortunate is that on numerous occasions he cites Gertrude Coogan, a monetary crank if there ever was one.[42])

Coughlin placed altogether too much emphasis on the "private ownership" of the Federal Reserve System, for it is surely an unusual "private" organization whose officers are all appointed by the federal government and which was established by an act of Congress. A far more significant and substantive critique of the Federal Reserve would involve its ability to create money out of thin air, its dilution of the value of our currency, and its responsibility for the business cycle. On these fundamental issues, Fr. Coughlin was in lockstep with the Federal Reserve—he simply wanted the federal government, rather than the Federal Reserve, to do the inflating.[43] This is hardly a sweeping critique.[44]

To their credit, Coughlin and Fahey recognized that something was wrong with fractional-reserve banking, and both would have forbidden the practice.[45] Strangely, Hilaire Belloc, who appears to have had a far sounder grasp of the issues, considered the practice essentially harmless, and even somewhat beneficial, if carried out on not too extensive a scale.[46]

Unlike Coughlin and Fahey, Hilaire Belloc appreciated the dangers of a state-manipulated currency.[47] Frs. Coughlin and Fahey, on the other hand, appalled at the control that central bankers exercised over the money supply, would hand monopolistic control over the money supply directly to the government. Such a proposal, as one economist put it, "would stop one kind of inflation only to inaugurate another."[48] Why the state, an institution as monopolistic as any that has ever existed, could be trusted with such a task these men simply never addressed in any serious way. Indeed both theory and history tell us otherwise. The French revolutionaries, for instance, destroyed their country's currency with months, and the Americans hardly fared any better. As one scholar put it, "Here is the question we must ask every monetary reformer: *What, legally and economically, will keep the government from printing too much paper money or issuing too much credit?* The honesty of the politicians? The good judgment of the bureaucrats in charge of printing money?"[49]

Coughlin's answer, such as it is, reveals little if any grasp of the immensity of the problem. "Those empowered to issue money would have no incentive to overissue money," he writes. "They would not be the beneficiaries of the new purchasing power."[50] Worse than the naïveté of such a statement is its ignorance—the distribution, or Cantillon, effects of the injection of the new money would certainly benefit certain people at the expense of others. Favored firms with which the government does business would get the money first, since Coughlin recommends increasing the money supply through government purchases. These firms would therefore be at an advantage vis-à-vis everyone else in the economy, and would gain at the direct expense of everyone else (for reasons we saw in the discussion of distribution effects, above). It hardly requires much imagination to realize that, contrary to Coughlin's assurances, the politicians would benefit very handsomely from the purchasing power of the new money, insofar as they could simply direct it toward favored sectors and constituents.

Both figures claim, for whatever reason, that money should be issued on the basis of the nation's productive capacity, as measured in estimated national wealth. The fatal flaw in this approach, of course, is that this estimate of the nation's wealth is itself denominated in money. As soon as the money bureaucracy that these men want to establish issues money on the basis of this estimate, the result will be higher prices, and therefore a higher nominal value of the nation's wealth. This higher figure will then be used to justify another infusion of money, and such theorists as these will be heard to complain of yet another "scarcity of money." The process will repeat itself again and again, all the while debasing and destroying the currency.[51] Unlike a 100 percent reserve system, in which banks cannot issue more in notes than they have specie in their vaults, there is no logical limit to the expansion of the un-backed paper money favored by Coughlin and Fahey. Paper, ink, and a print-ing press are all that is required.

The inflationist approach of Coughlin and Fahey would have produced all the negative consequences, described above, of any inflationist scheme. All the injustice toward non-favored segments of the community (who get the new money last), all the confusion and chaos in business calculation, all the incentives to consume and spend rather than save and invest, all the impov-erishment—these would remain.[52] They did not object in principle to the counterfeiting and inflationism of the Federal Reserve; they simply wanted the government itself to engage in these practices directly rather than through what they considered the plutocratic intermediary of an institution like the Federal Reserve. To say the least, it is rather peculiar to hear some present-day Catholics endorsing the monetary policies of these men as if they consti-tuted a radical break with the present system, when in fact on every signifi-cant point they represent no difference at all. Increasing the number of green paper tickets in circulation does absolutely nothing to increase the amount of *wealth* in existence. As we have seen, the creation of wealth occurs when cap-ital investment allows the same amount of goods to be produced with less la-bor, thereby freeing up labor for the production of goods that could not oth-erwise have been produced. This takes real effort and sacrifice, not paper and a printing press.

And on the most fundamental issue of all, namely granting the government a monopoly of the note issue, Coughlin and Fahey again have no fundamen-tal disagreement with the Federal Reserve. Their one divergence from the present system would be that politicians, rather than central bankers, would possess a monopoly of the note issue. The government would possess a mo-nopoly on printing paper currency that would be backed by nothing. Individ-ual banks, on the other hand, would be prohibited from issuing notes backed 100 percent by reserves in their vaults. "This," writes Gary North, "is anti-economics with a vengeance."[53]

In the midst of all this theorizing, Coughlin and Fahey never really exam-ine the 100 percent gold alternative in any serious way. (Fahey stacks the deck in advance by conceiving of a gold standard as a system in which the

Bank of England prints more notes than it has gold in its vaults—not exactly a genuine gold standard![54]) Both are convinced that the economic well-being of a nation is intimately connected to how many green paper tickets are in circulation.[55] And both would convert the central bank monopoly into a direct government monopoly. In their ideal world, each government would be one great counterfeiter.

What a shame that such men possessed so much contempt for and so little comprehension of a genuine gold standard—a monetary system based on simple honesty and in which counterfeiting by anyone, including the government, would be impossible. Any other system must lead not only to inflation, but also to corruption, influence peddling, impoverishment, and economic instability—just what Coughlin and Fahey sought to minimize or abolish.

USURY

The subject of money and a morally acceptable monetary regime inevitably raises the controversial question of usury. Although today the term is used to describe the charging of high rates of interest, the original usury prohibition applied to the taking of *any* interest on a loan. Interestingly, no one in the ancient world, neither the Greeks nor the Chinese, Indians, or Mesopotamians, prohibited the charging of interest. The one exception was the Hebrews, who permitted the charging of interest to non-Jews but forbade the practice among Jews.[56]

Scriptural support for a complete ban on interest is surprisingly thin. Virtually the only scriptural verse used to support the usury ban appears in Psalm 14: "Lord, who shall dwell in thy tabernacle? . . . He that hath not put out his money to usury. . . ." It was only in the late twelfth century that we begin to see references to a phrase from Luke 6:35—"lend, hoping for nothing thereby."[57] But, as even the 1913 *Catholic Encyclopedia* concedes, while "some persons interpret [this verse] as a condemnation of interest," it is "only an exhortation to general and disinterested benevolence."[58] Others, including the great Dominican Domingo de Soto (1494–1560), had also denied that the verse from Luke had anything to do with lending at interest or that Christ had declared usury to be sinful.[59] In recent centuries, the view that this passage prohibits all gain on a loan has been abandoned.[60]

The *Catholic Encyclopedia* goes on to observe that discussions of usury are rare and very far from systematic in the early centuries of the Church.

> The vehement denunciation of the Fathers of the fourth and fifth centuries were called forth by the moral decadence and avarice of the time, and we cannot find

in them any expression of a general doctrine on this point; nor do the Fathers of the following centuries say anything remarkable on usury; they simply protest against the exploitation of misfortune, and such transactions as, under the pretense of rendering service to the borrower, really threw him into great distress. The question of moderate rates of interest seems scarcely to have presented itself to their minds as a matter of discussion.[61]

Only very gradually did usury, at first classified as a lack of charity, become viewed as a sin against justice.[62] Although it was licit for a man to earn a profit on trade, to earn a profit on a loan for which only the borrower bore the risk was said to be usury. To ask for anything above the exact equivalent of the loan fell under this condemnation.

In the thirteenth century, St. Thomas Aquinas advanced several arguments against usury, with one of them considerably more important than the others. It ran as follows:

[W]e must observe that there are certain things the use of which consists in their consumption: thus we consume wine when we use it for drink, and we consume wheat when we use it for food. Wherefore in such like things the use of the thing must not be reckoned apart from the thing itself, and whoever is granted the use of the thing, is granted the thing itself; and for this reason, to lend things of this kind is to transfer the ownership. Accordingly if a man wanted to sell wine separately from the use of the wine, he would be selling the same thing twice, or he would be selling what does not exist, wherefore he would evidently commit a sin of injustice. In like manner he commits an injustice who lends wine or wheat, and asks for double payment, viz. one, the return of the thing in equal measure, the other, the price of the use, which is called usury.

On the other hand, there are things the use of which does not consist in their consumption: thus to use a house is to dwell in it, not to destroy it. Wherefore in such things both may be granted: for instance, one man may hand over to another the ownership of his house while reserving to himself the use of it for a time, or vice versa, he may grant the use of the house, while retaining the ownership. For this reason a man may lawfully make a charge for the use of his house, and, besides this, revendicate the house from the person to whom he has granted its use, as happens in renting and letting a house.

Now money, according to the Philosopher (*Ethic*. v. 5; *Polit*. i. 3) was invented chiefly for the purpose of exchange: and consequently the proper and principal use of money is its consumption or alienation whereby it is sunk in exchange. Hence it is by its very nature unlawful to take payment for the use of money lent, which payment is known as usury: and just as a man is bound to restore other ill-gotten goods, so is he bound to restore the money which he has taken in usury.[63]

In his *Quaestiones disputatae de malo*, he added:

In those things whose use is their consumption, the use is not other than the thing itself; whence to whomever is conceded the use of such things, is conceded the ownership of those things, and conversely. When therefore, someone lends money under the agreement that the money be integrally restored to him, and further for the use of the money wishes to have a definite price, it is manifest that he sells separately the use of the money and the very substance of money. The use of money, however, as it is said, is not other than its substance: whence either he sells that which is not, or he sells the same thing twice, to wit, the money itself, whose use is its consumption; and this is manifestly against the nature of natural justice.[64]

It is a peculiar argument. St. Thomas argues that some things are consumed in the very act of being used, and that money is one of these. A contrary example, he says, is a house. A house is not consumed in the act of being used, and for this reason it is legitimate to charge rent on a house. But since money is consumed when used, it is not legitimate to charge rent on money, as it were, for this would be charging both for the use of the money and for the money itself. This is surely unjust, says St. Thomas, just as it would be unjust for a man to attempt to sell wine (another good consumed in its use) separately from the use of the wine.

Two immediate objections present themselves. First, St. Thomas observes that it would be unjust for a man to attempt to sell wine separately from the use of the wine, or wheat apart from the use of the wheat. But when in all of human history has such a transaction been seen? Why, on the other hand, is the phenomenon of interest so widespread, across time and across cultures? Might there be a fundamental difference here?

Second, let us suppose that St. Thomas is correct that lending money at interest amounts to "selling the same thing twice." So what? What exactly is wrong with that, particularly since both parties agree to the terms?

More serious intellectual difficulties with St. Thomas' argument become apparent when we consider what he had to say about a medieval form of licit investment in commerce called the *societas*. The *societas* was an arrangement whereby two or more people united their resources (money, skill, and the like) in some common enterprise. These partnerships often consisted of one person who supplied only money and another who supplied only labor. The risks as well as the profits were typically shared.[65]

St. Thomas heartily endorses the *societas*. But what is particularly interesting about his endorsement is that the arguments he uses in its favor tend to undermine his arguments against usury. He writes: "He who commits his money to a merchant or craftsman by means of some kind of partnership does not transfer the ownership of his money to him but it remains his; so that at his risk the merchant trades, or the craftsman works, with it; and therefore he can licitly seek part of the profit thence coming as from his own property."[66] This argument seems sensible enough: someone in a partnership retains ownership of his resources when he puts them at the disposal of his partner, and is therefore entitled to a share of the profit. But here St. Thomas contradicts his earlier claim that use and ownership are inseparable. In his analysis of usury, he had said that the transfer of the use of money also transferred its ownership, but here he argues that although one partner uses the other partner's funds, they remain the property of the latter. For the sake of consistency, then, St. Thomas would appear bound to condemn the *societas* as usury. "But," as John Noonan, author of the authoritative study of the Scholastics' views on usury, puts it, "the common acceptance of the *societas* and the promptings of natural justice are stronger than his theory."[67] And so St. Thomas accepts the *societas*. That he accepts it does not in itself prove that his arguments against usury are incorrect, merely that he has involved himself in a contradiction in attempting to hold both positions simultaneously.

The second point of note involves St. Thomas' connection of risk and ownership. Ownership, St. Thomas says in his above statement, belongs to him who bears the risk of loss. But as Noonan points out, this is simply an *ad hoc* criterion of ownership that nowhere appears in St. Thomas' treatment elsewhere of the rights of private property; nowhere there does he so much as raise the issue of risk, let alone connect it to the idea of ownership. "Faced with an objection, and well aware of the popular tradition on risk, St. Thomas has produced the risk criterion ad hoc to distinguish loans [in which the lender is said to enjoy profits without bearing any risk] from capitalistic partnership . . . . As a practical criterion, it will serve well for two centuries at least. But when finally it comes itself to be questioned by scholastic theologians, no rational basis for it will be found."[68]

Thirdly, St. Thomas here uses risk as a criterion for ownership, but does not attempt to justify profit on the basis of risk. His argument is that (1) where the incidence of risk falls determines the owner of the property, and (2) the owner in turn is entitled to profits deriving from his property. In this case, though, the property in question is money. According to St. Thomas, money itself is sterile, which is why it is unnatural for a lender to seek profit from it.[69] Any surplus value gained from money, he contends, is due to the work of the man who uses it and who therefore is alone entitled to it. But if this is true, then how can St. Thomas consistently argue, as he does, that the capitalist in a *societas*—that is, the man who merely supplies the capital—is entitled to a share of the profits? Shouldn't all the profit go to the man who did the work, the partner whose labor brought forth the excess value from the money?[70]

All of this inconsistency from so staggering an intellect as that of St. Thomas speaks volumes about the logical difficulties involved in the prohibition of interest.

From the thirteenth through the sixteenth centuries, scholastic theologians began developing the Church's teaching on usury, applying reason and logical argument to the issue of interest. These arguments, if taken to their logical conclusions (which they usually were not), tended to undermine the entire interest prohibition. This is an enormously complicated subject about which very lengthy studies have been written, so we shall cover only some of the important turning points here.

By all accounts a significant breach in the prohibition occurred with Cardinal Hostiensis, the thirteenth-century canonist who served as an ambassador under Pope Innocent IV. Hostiensis made provision for *lucrum cessans* (profit ceasing), which permitted the charging of interest as compensation for profit foregone by the lender by virtue of his inability to invest the lent funds himself during the period of the loan. This is, in essence, a recognition of the economic concept of opportunity cost. Hostiensis' argument was of great significance. "For the very first time," Noonan writes, "the honest businessman is given a lawful reason for charging beyond the principal."[71]

Still, Hostiensis permitted this exception only for non-habitual lenders who happened to lend out of charity rather than to professional lenders who lent money for a living. Pierre de Jean Olivi (1248–1298), who agreed with Hostiensis' position on *lucrum cessans*, also limited this allowance to non-habitual lenders.[72]

It was only a matter of time before theologians broadened this and other exceptions afforded by the scholastic analysis into more general permissions. Thus, for example, it was a common opinion among scholastics that a lender could charge a penalty for late repayment, since he was thereby deprived of the use of his money for a period of time. But if being deprived of one's money for a period of time is just grounds for charging a late fee, why may it not also be just grounds for charging interest? After all, the lender is without the use of his money for the entire life of the loan, not just for the duration of time in which payment was late.

The discussion of usury moved in fits and starts over the centuries, with theologians defending this or that rationale for profit on a loan. Often a theologian would criticize the grounds for licit interest offered by his colleagues but would go on to offer some of his own. In general, an overall trend toward the liberalization of the allowance of interest is evident, particularly in the fifteenth and sixteenth centuries. The process was occasionally punctuated by a dramatic assault on the traditional arguments against usury, as in the case of Conrad Summenhart (1465–1511), who held the chair of theology at the University of Tübingen, and to a lesser extent Leonard Lessius (more on whom below), but more typical was the gradual wearing away of traditional arguments and the expansion of exceptions to the interest ban.

In the early sixteenth century, the Franciscan Juan de Medina (1490–1546) became the first scholastic writer to defend the idea that risk assumed by the lender constituted legitimate grounds for charging interest. As Medina put it, exposing one's property "to the risk of being lost, is sellable, and purchasable at a price, nor is it among those things which are to be done gratuitously."[73] A later figure, the Jesuit Cardinal Juan de Lugo (1583–1660), placed considerable emphasis on this point. He stated the matter simply: "Where today is there to be found a debt so placed in safety that in security it equals ready cash?"[74] Thus the argument had come full circle: earlier scholastics had argued against interest because the lender bore none of the risk involved in whatever venture the borrower should invest it, whereas de Lugo argues that in the very act of lending the lender exposes himself to risk.

In his outstanding history of economic thought, Murray Rothbard pointed out another of Medina's important arguments: namely, that by Medina's day, "theologians now admit that someone who guarantees a debtor's loan can licitly charge for that service; but in that case, if the borrower cannot find a guarantor, why cannot the lender charge the borrower for assuming the risk of non-repayment? Is not *his* charge similar to the charge of the guarantor?" That is, if it is morally allowable for a third party to be paid to guarantee the loan, how could it be morally illicit for the borrower himself to pay the lender a similar fee (in the form of interest) if such a guarantor cannot be found?[75]

The Jesuit theologian Leonard Lessius (1554–1623), who held a chair in theology and philosophy at the University of Louvain, also played a significant role in eroding the interest prohibition. For one thing, he pointed out that the relative lack of liquidity that a lender must endure for the duration of a loan was a factor deserving of compensation, since unexpected situations may arise in which the lent funds would have been desirable to have on hand. Those thus deprived of their money, he wrote, "value more the lack of their money for five months than the lack of it for four, and the lack of it for four more than three, and this is partly because they lack the opportunity of gaining with that money, partly because their principal is longer in danger."[76] He also extended the allowance of *lucrum cessans*, which had been subject to considerable restriction, to all loans, including those by professional money-lenders.[77]

By the sixteenth century, Catholic theologians had overturned virtually all of the older arguments against usury—at the very time that Martin Luther was busily attempting to rehabilitate them. As the *Catholic Encyclopedia* explains,

It may be remarked that the best authors have long since recognized the lawfulness of interest to compensate a lender for the risk of losing his capital, or for positive loss, such as the privation of the profit which he might otherwise have made, if he had not advanced the loan. . . . These are what are called extrinsic grounds, admitted without dispute since the end of the sixteenth century, and justifying the stipulation for reasonable interest, proportionate to the risk involved in the loan.[78]

Still further developments had been made by the seventeenth and eighteenth centuries, and in a series of decisions by the Holy Office in the early nineteenth century it was decreed that anyone may accept the interest permitted by law.[79] According to the *Catholic Encyclopedia*, the Church today "permits the general practice of lending at interest, that is to say, she authorizes the impost, without one's having to inquire if, on lending his money, he has suffered a loss or deprived himself of a gain, provided he demand a moderate interest for the money he lends. *This demand is never unjust.* Charity alone, not justice, can oblige anyone to make a gratuitous loan (see the replies of the Penitentiary and of the Holy Office since 1830)."[80]

What had been missing from the debates over usury was the concept of time preference, the basic principle of human action according to which man prefers the enjoyment of a good in the present to the enjoyment of the same good in the future. This natural phenomenon explains, very simply, why goods in the present enjoy a premium over goods in the future, and therefore provides the origin and justification for the payment of interest.

If time preference did not exist, the price of land would have to approach infinity, since there would be no time discounting of the capital value of a productive good such as land. In other words, the price of land would approach the sum of its productive output into the indefinite future. If a particular parcel of land should be estimated to produce, on average, an annual product equivalent to 100 ounces of gold, in the absence of time preference, someone purchasing the land should reckon its value at 100 times however many years he estimates remain between the time of his purchase and the end of the world. That no one in fact reckons value in this way indicates the existence of time preference.

A refusal to acknowledge the phenomenon of time preference leaves an observer completely unable to account for basic economic phenomena. For instance, business firms can often increase their production by adopting more time-consuming production processes. If time preference did not exist, a business firm would always choose this option, preferring whatever production process yielded the greatest output regardless of how much time it took to complete. That business firms do not always choose to do so is yet another example of time preference at work. It is time preference, explains Mises, that accounts for why "less time-consuming methods of production are resorted to in spite of the fact that more time-consuming methods would render a higher output per unit of input."[81]

The problems with the interest prohibition come through most clearly when we appreciate the implications of time preference. The phenomenon of time preference, observable in countless aspects of human life, is really a matter of simple common sense: men prefer a given quantity of a good in the present to the same quantity of the good in the future, and only an increased amount of the good in the future can persuade them to forego a given amount of consumption in the present. People do not treat a given quantity of a good in the present and an equal quantity of the good years hence as the same good. Leaving aside the issue of inflation, people do not consider $100 today and $100 ten years from now to be the same good. From the point of view of an economic actor, *these are two different goods.* Refusing to allow the charging and payment of interest, therefore, amounts to forcing people to treat a present good and a future good *as the same good*—a flagrant violation of the universal phenomenon of time preference that we see all around us in the course of human affairs and that we view as perfectly harmless, indeed quite normal and sensible.

As we have seen, the phenomenon of time preference means that a good in the present will be valued more than the same quantity of that good in the future. Now some amount of time must pass between the moment a good (usually money) is lent and the moment it is repaid.[82] The borrower enjoys the benefits of money *in the present*, and repays the lender *in the future*. Since the idea of time preference tells us that a future good is valued less than the same good in the present, if the borrower repays only the nominal sum he originally borrowed, say $500, he is actually committing an injustice against the lender by forcing him to treat the $500 lent at the beginning of the loan period and $500 at the time of repayment—*two different goods*, according to the phenomenon of time preference—as *the same good*. This basic point helps us to appreciate that there is nothing sinister about the taking of interest; to the contrary, it would appear to be unjust *not* to pay interest, since the absence of an interest payment forces one side of the contract to treat the same quantity of the same good in the present and in the future as being equal in value—a requirement we would consider irrational and foolish in any other context.

Austrians have typically described the interest rate as the "social rate of time preference." In a truly free market, explains Rothbard, the interest rate is determined "purely by the 'time preferences' of all the individuals that make up the market economy." As we have seen, the phenomenon of time preference means that a sum of money in the present will command a premium over the same amount of money in the future. "This premium is the interest rate, and its height will vary according to the degree to which people prefer the present to the future, i.e., the degree of their time preferences."[83] The interest rate, therefore, as a premium on present goods as opposed to future ones, appears to be conceptually no different from any other price, and there seems to be no good reason why the rate of interest should not be determined in the same way that the scholastics had approved the determination of any other price: through the voluntary interaction of buyers and sellers on the market. Interestingly, the *Catholic Encyclopedia* essentially concedes this point: "In practice . . . as even the answer of the Sacred Penitentiary shows (18 April 1889), *the best course is to conform to the usages established amongst men, precisely as one does with regard to other prices*, and, as happens in the case of such prices, particular circumstances influence the rate of interest, either by increasing or lowering it."[84]

The idea of time preference peeks through fleetingly in the writings of the scholastics. Giles Lessines, one of St. Thomas Aquinas' most brilliant students, wrote in 1285 that "future goods are not valued so highly as the same goods available at an immediate moment of time, nor do they allow their owners to achieve the same utility. For this reason, it must be considered that they have a more reduced value in accordance with justice."[85] San Bernardino of Siena, one of the greatest economic thinkers of the Middle Ages, referred to the idea of time preference but appears not to have recognized its significance.[86] The scholastic theologian Martin de Azpilcueta Navarrus (1493–1586) had come very close to this insight in his own analysis of usury. Azpilcueta, a man noted for his personal holiness and his impressive command of canon law, built upon San Bernardino of Siena's insight into the phenomenon of time preference. He taught that "a claim on something is worth less than the thing itself, and . . . it is plain that that which is not usable for a year is less valuable than something of the same quality which is usable at once."[87] Azpilcueta is correct, of course. But as soon as the implications of this point are grasped, the interest prohibition collapses at once.

In the twentieth century, Catholic author Hilaire Belloc still attempted to justify the prohibition on interest. According to Belloc, usury is the taking of interest on what he calls an "unproductive loan." That is, it is not the taking of interest per se that calls down moral condemnation, but the purpose for which the loan is intended. "The *intention* of usury is present," he writes, "*when the money is lent at interest on what the lender knows will be an unproductive purpose*, and the actual *practice* of usury is present *when the loan, having as a fact been used unproductively, interest is none the less demanded.*"[88]

Belloc provides the following example. Suppose Mr. Jones should approach Mr. Smith, the owner of a ship, and propose that with the use of Mr. Smith's ship he could carry on such profitable international trade as to leave him with a handsome reward one year hence. Mr. Smith agrees to lend Mr. Jones the ship for this purpose, but requires that he (Smith) receive some portion of the profits that accrue to Mr. Jones. After all, it was only with the help of Mr. Smith's ship that Mr. Jones was able to secure his profit in the first place, so it is only fair that Mr. Smith enjoy a portion of the fruits.

Belloc insists that there is no moral difficulty whatever with charging interest on this kind of loan. Neither is the morality of the situation affected if Mr. Smith is the owner not of a ship but of a sum of money sufficient to purchase a ship, and Mr. Jones borrows the money in order to purchase and outfit a ship for international trade. Mr. Smith would still be entitled to some share of Mr. Jones' gain on this productive loan. What makes it a "productive" loan, therefore, is that it leads to the overall creation of wealth: society is richer at the end of the transaction than it was before.

An "unproductive" loan, on the other hand, is one in which additional wealth is not created by means of the funds lent. Suppose, says Belloc, that a man approaches a lender and explains that he needs six loaves of bread to sustain himself and his family through the next few days. They will simply be consumed, and will in no way contribute to the creation of additional wealth (as had Mr. Jones' work with Mr. Smith's ship). The lender replies that he will indeed lend him the six loaves, but on the condition that when the loan comes due he repay seven loaves—one additional loaf. This, says Belloc, is usury. The loaves are for the man's immediate consumption and are not used for any productive purpose:

> No more wealth is created by the act. The world is not the richer, nor are you the richer, nor is society in general the richer. No more wealth at all has appeared through the transaction. Therefore the extra loaf that you [the lender] are claiming is claimed out of nothing. It has to come out of the wealth of the community— in this particular case out of the wealth of the man who borrowed the loaves— instead of coming out of an increment or excess or new wealth.[89]

This explanation leaves a number of unanswered questions. Why is the morality of an individual's action dependent upon whether it has, upon its conclusion, created more wealth for "society in general"? This is a profoundly invasive criterion. All consumption by individuals leaves society with less wealth than before. Is it all to be condemned? If not, why should usury be a special case? Many people prefer to consume their incomes rather than assume the risk of investing them in potentially productive investments. Is this decision deserving of moral criticism, since as a result of such abstention "the world is not the richer, nor are you the richer, nor is society in general the richer"? It is strangely ironic that Belloc, the great champion of those who condemn Austrian economists for their alleged commitment to "efficiency," should himself be guilty of the very efficiency-driven analysis from which his followers have considered themselves exempt.

In claiming that the borrower is not "the richer" for the loan he takes out, Belloc falls victim to the ancient fallacy of attempting to evaluate from the point of view of a third party the satisfaction derived from a market exchange. If a borrower determines that six loaves of bread today are worth more to him than seven loaves two weeks from now, who will be so foolish as to tell him he is "wrong"? The man may not be maximizing the wealth of "society in general," but he certainly is maximizing his own *psychic income*, which takes into account not simply physical stocks of goods at his disposal but also his relative contentedness and state of mind—in short, his necessarily subjective evaluation of his well-being. If he believes he will have a surplus of psychic income as a result of having six loaves this week and not starving, in the knowledge that he will have to pay back seven loaves two weeks from now, that is all we can say about the situation. It should be obvious that if the man did not believe that taking out the loan would make him *in some way* richer, he would not have taken out the loan in the first place.

Consider another point: how would home mortgages escape Belloc's condemnation? Someone who borrows money in order to purchase a home is not engaged in "productive" activity. He is engaged in consumption. So by Belloc's reckoning, mortgage loans must amount to immoral usury, and would also have to be discontinued—unless, of course, lenders with a quarter million dollars to spare could be persuaded to lend their money for thirty years and receive nothing in return to compensate them for their trouble. That is probably unlikely.

Without a "usurious" loan, a man might perhaps live in some kind of shed, or content himself with renting living space for the rest of his life rather than owning his own home. He would thereby be deprived of the opportunity to own a major asset. Ironically, in such cases (of which there would certainly be very many) Belloc's own policy would itself be responsible for people's lack of significant property.

Therefore, because a home borrower is not, from Belloc's perspective, engaged in "productive" activity, because his loan to purchase his home will not leave "society in general" any the richer, and because according to Belloc's analysis it will not even leave the new homeowner himself any the richer, the loan is not to be allowed. But why not ask the homeowner himself? Does he not consider himself subjectively better off with the opportunity to live in a comfortable home than he would have been without this opportunity? Might he in fact consider it quite a rational decision to pay more for the enjoyment of the house right now, rather than be forced to save his money for decades to be able to purchase the house, even if he would thereby save himself the "usurious" interest payments? And since, all that time, he would probably have to live in rental housing and pay a monthly rent, it could not even be said that at least he would save himself the interest payments he would have had on the house—that money now has to be spent for rental payments on an apartment he doubtless considers far inferior to the house that he might otherwise have been living in, had it not been for Belloc's refusal to allow him to purchase it by means of a loan on mutually agreeable terms with a willing lender.

In the introduction to a recent reissue of Belloc's *Essay on the Restoration of Property*, the very idea of the home mortgage is in fact mocked: "Those who claim to be homeowners forget that in most cases the real homeowners are the banks, and that they themselves are on a rent-to-own program which normally lasts 30 years and sees a 'modest' compound interest rate translate into a payment in real terms of *several times* the value of the home."[90] Again, a critic is going to presume to tell the buyer what his purchase is objectively "worth." Naturally, the borrower pays more for his home in the long run by borrowing than he would have paid had he been able to amass the money for the $200,000 asking price from the beginning. But who is this critic to tell the borrower that he is *wrong* to value this house *right now* at a significant premium over this house *years and years in the future*, by the time he had been able to save the money to purchase it in cash? This is a typical error: the failure to realize that man values goods in the present more highly than the same quantities of the same goods in the future. It can hardly come as a surprise that he would be willing to pay even a fairly substantial premium for the good of enjoying his home in the present rather than in the distant future. A house today and the same house years from now are, from the point of view of acting man, not the same good.

Also forgotten in all this analysis is the fate of the man who needed the six loaves of bread for immediate use. If he is not permitted to borrow at interest—which simply means taking into account the universal phenomenon of time preference, evident throughout human behavior—what exactly is he to do? Does he deserve to starve simply because in paying interest on his loan he would be depriving "society" of a loaf of bread?

Yet when all is said and done, although Belloc no doubt considers his discussion an extension of medieval discussions on the subject, his "productive" and "unproductive" loans are nowhere to be found in traditional Catholic teaching as moral categories by which to evaluate the charging of interest. In fact, such a distinction is explicitly rejected as a basis for the charging of interest in Pope Benedict XIV's *Vix Pervenit* of 1745.[91] This is the conclusion of John T. Noonan's book *The Scholastic Analysis of Usury*, which is universally regarded as the classic study of the subject. Belloc's "chief distinction, between consumption and production loans, is totally unfounded," and Belloc is

> lacking in historical perspective when he denounces profit on credit extended to states and when he decries international moneylenders; historically the scholastics always approved the annuities which were the earliest form of state deficit finance, and historically, the exchange bankers, international financiers on a grand scale, were encouraged by the Church and approved by the developed scholastic theory. Again, authors professedly appealing to history have remade history to support their preconceived positions.[92]

The development of the teaching on usury has been so dramatic over the centuries that it inevitably prompts the question: has the Magisterium taught error anywhere along the line? The *Catholic Encyclopedia* says no, claiming that changing economic circumstances rather than changing teaching account for the new attitude toward the charging of interest. Thus in the article on interest, the *Encyclopedia* explains the situation as follows:

> What is the reason for this change in the attitude of the Church towards the exaction of interest? . . . [T]his difference is due to economical circumstances. The price of goods is regulated by common valuation, and the latter by the utility that their possession ordinarily brings in a given center. Now, today, otherwise than formerly, one can commonly employ one's money fruitfully, at least by putting it into a syndicate. Hence, today, the mere possession of money means a certain value. Whoever hands over this possession can claim in return this value. Thus it is that one acts in demanding an interest.[93]

This explanation, while reasonable enough, is still somewhat unsatisfying, since it takes no account of the development over time of the teaching on usury and interest, as their economic foundations were better and better understood. A more plausible explanation is provided by Patrick O'Neil, writing in *Faith and Reason*:

> The error concerning the charging of interest is an example of correct moral principles (against economic exploitation and so forth) mistakenly applied on account of the inadequacies of early economic theory. When better economic theory became available (along with the lessons of practical experience), the Church could change its position because the fundamental form of her judgment was: "If W is the economic function involved in the charging of interest, then the charging of interest is immoral, because economic activities must adhere to rule X (or rules X, Y, & Z)." Changes under these circumstances do not threaten

the claims of the magisterium of the Church in any way. The discovery that the charging of interest does not (necessarily) involve exploitation, but represents instead legitimate payment for the time-value of money and for the risk factors endured by the lender, denies the antecedent of the hypothetical.[94]

For this reason, combined with explicit Vatican statements over the past two centuries, no Catholic need trouble his conscience over the ordinary transactions involving the charging and earning of interest in which he engages over the course of his economic affairs.

In sum, the best monetary regime, from the point of view both of utility and of Catholic morality, is a 100 percent reserve commodity money. This system alone is free from all forms of fraud, requires no violent confiscation, prevents the business cycle, and avoids the immoral distribution effects and erosion of accumulated wealth that inevitably accompany a system of fiat money. What this means, in short, is that that monetary system is best which observes the most basic moral rules: do not steal and do not commit fraud. This was the message of the great Catholic thinkers of the late medieval and early modern period, and it is a message that deserves to be heeded by their modern-day counterparts.

NOTES

1. Needless to say, it is nothing about gold in itself that attracts supporters of a gold standard; it is, rather, the idea of a commodity money itself that holds the attraction. This obvious point would hardly need making were it not for the suggestions of a few critics that supporters of a gold standard possess some kind of "fetish" for gold as such. Thus when I speak of the absolute necessity of a gold standard, or about gold as the only honest money, in a sense I do not mean to be taken strictly literally. I am not ruling out the possibility that some other commodity might in different circumstances be used instead of gold; neither am I saying that only gold per se could be honest money. I am speaking of the virtues of a commodity standard in general, which in the history of the modern Western world happens to have been all but synonymous with gold.

2. I am borrowing this definition from Hans-Hermann Hoppe, "How Is Fiat Money Possible?—or, The Devolution of Money and Credit," *Review of Austrian Economics* 7, 2 (1994): 49.

3. Thus see Murray N. Rothbard, *The Mystery of Banking* (New York: Richardson & Snyder, 1983); idem, *What Has Government Done to Our Money?* 4th ed. (Auburn, Ala.: Ludwig von Mises Institute, 1990); idem, *The Case against the Fed* (Auburn, Ala.: Ludwig von Mises Institute, 1994); Hans-Hermann Hoppe, "Banking, Nation States, and International Politics: A Sociological Reconstruction of the Present Economic Order," in *The Economics and Ethics of Private Property* (Boston: Kluwer Academic Publishers, 1993), 61–92.

4. For important differences between the two, see Rothbard, *The Case against the Fed*, 55–58.

5. This description of the evolution of banking is a theoretical exposition of the appearance of various modern banking phenomena, rather than a strictly historical account.

6. Hoppe, *The Economics and Ethics of Private Property*, 72.

7. While the gold standard was still in effect, member banks were also required to store their gold reserves at the Federal Reserve, and redeem their own demand deposits in Federal Reserve notes. These notes, in turn, were theoretically convertible into gold, but thanks to the prestige of the government backing the notes and the various advantages they were given (e.g., legal tender status), people tended to demand gold less and less. (And in any case, the Federal Reserve itself engaged in fractional reserve banking, and did not possess enough gold to honor all of its liabilities.)

8. Rothbard, *What Has Government Done to Our Money?* 76.

9. Rothbard, *Mystery of Banking*, 135.

10. The entire process is explained in much greater detail in Rothbard, *Mystery of Banking*, 127–49, as well as in idem, *What Has Government Done to Our Money?* 43–53, 72–79, and idem, *The Case against the Fed*, 29–69.

11. The difficulty Mises sought to address was as follows. The value of money on individuals' value scales is determined by its purchasing power yesterday, but that purchasing power in turn is determined by the value of money. Mises explained the way out of this circularity. Although the value of money today depends on its value yesterday, and its value yesterday depended on its value the day before, the regression backward in time is not infinite. It ceases on the last day of the barter economy, the last day when the value of the commodity that came to be used as money was valued solely for its purpose in use, and not for any exchange value. (Of course, the terms "yesterday" and "last day" should not be understood in the crude sense of 24-hour periods; they are meant in each case to refer to the praxeologically relevant unit of time involved.) The regression theorem is explained in Ludwig von Mises, *The Theory of Money and Credit*, trans. H. E. Batson (Indianapolis, Ind.: Liberty Classics, 1981 [1912]), 136–44; see also Rothbard, *Man, Economy, and State*, 231–37.

12. The fifteenth-century scholastic Gabriel Biel argued the same point. Murray N. Rothbard, *An Austrian Perspective on the History of Economic Thought*, vol. 1, *Economic Thought before Adam Smith* (Brookfield, Vt.: Edward Elgar, 1995), 73–74, 89–90.

13. See Rothbard, *What Has Government Done to Our Money?* Rothbard's entire book, a true classic, deserves to be read far and wide. Here I refer simply to his critical point (p. 74) that the introduction of paper as a money substitute redeemable in gold, while theoretically unimpeachable, in practice prepares the ground for the abandonment of the commodity standard by acclimating people to the use of paper and making them less and less accustomed to direct interaction with the precious metal.

14. Ludwig von Mises, "Inflation and You," in *Economic Freedom and Interventionism*, ed. Bettina Bien Greaves (Irvington-on-Hudson, N.Y.: Foundation for Economic Education, 1990), ch. 18.

15. Rothbard, *What Has Government Done to Our Money?* 58–59.

16. Hans F. Sennholz, *Age of Inflation* (Belmont, Mass.: Western Islands, 1979), 148.

17. Steven Horwitz, "Inflation," in *The Elgar Companion to Austrian Economics*, ed. Peter J. Boettke (Aldershot, UK: Edward Elgar, 1994), 404.

18. Mises, "Inflation and You." Emphasis added.

19. See note 1 for this chapter.

20. Juan de Mariana, S.J., "A Treatise on the Alteration of Money," trans. Patrick J. Brannan, S.J., *Journal of Markets & Morality* 5 (Fall 2002): 537, 538.

21. Mariana, "A Treatise on the Alteration of Money," 540.

22. Mariana, "A Treatise on the Alteration of Money," 544.

23. Rothbard, *Economic Thought before Adam Smith*, 90.

24. Bernard W. Dempsey, *Interest and Usury* (London: Dennis Dobson, 1948), 210. Fr. Dempsey's book is especially valuable because of its author's economic knowledge: his textual references as well as his notes indicate a firsthand acquaintance with Hayek, Mises, Schumpeter, Fisher, Wicksell, and Keynes. Another scholar of late scholastic economic thought summarizes the matter by noting that loans that fractional-reserve banks issue out of thin air mean "the generation of purchasing power which does not require any prior saving or sacrifice and gives rise to important damage to a large number of third parties, who see how the purchasing power of their monetary units decreases as a consequence of the inflationary credit expansion of the banks." From the point of view of the scholastics, "this creation of purchasing power from nowhere, which does not imply any prior loss of other people's purchasing power, is contrary to essential legal principles, as constructed by Molina and Lugo themselves and, in this respect, should be condemned." Jesus Huerta de Soto, "New Light on the Prehistory of the Theory of Banking and the School of Salamanca," *Review of Austrian Economics* 9, 2 (1996): 80.

25. See Rothbard, *Mystery of Banking*, 89.

26. Rothbard, *Mystery of Banking*, 94.

27. Sennholz, *Age of Inflation*, 19.

28. Quoted in Sennholz, *Age of Inflation*, 19.

29. Frédéric Bastiat, "What Is Money?" in *Essays on Political Economy*, trans. David A. Wells (New York: G. P. Putnam's Sons, 1877), reprinted in *Quarterly Journal of Austrian Economics* 5 (Fall 2002): 87–105, quotation on 94.

30. Murray N. Rothbard, "Economic Depressions: Their Cause and Cure," in *The Austrian Theory of the Trade Cycle and Other Essays*, comp. Richard M. Ebeling (Auburn, Ala.: Ludwig von Mises Institute, 1996 [1978]), 71–73.

31. John A. Ryan, *Social Doctrine in Action: A Personal History* (New York: Harper & Bros., 1941), 248–49.

32. Rothbard, "Economic Depressions: Their Cause and Cure," 73–74. Emphasis in original.

33. Roger W. Garrison, "Business Cycles: Austrian Approach," in *An Encyclopedia of Macroeconomics*, eds. Howard Vane and Brian Snowden (Aldershot, UK: Edward Elgar, 2002).

34. Garrison, "Business Cycles: Austrian Approach."

35. For a graphical depiction of the mechanics of the Austrian theory, see Roger W. Garrison, *Time and Money: The Macroeconomics of Capital Structure* (London:

Routledge, 2000). For a rebuttal to the argument that businessmen would learn from experience and not be so eager to invest amid a Fed-induced boom, see Gene Callahan, *Economics for Real People* (Auburn, Ala.: Ludwig von Mises Institute, 2002), 217–29; see also Frank Shostak, "Expectations and Austrian Cycle Theory," Mises.org, January 6, 2003, at www.mises.org/fullarticle.asp?control=1131&id=69 (accessed January 7, 2003).

36. The Austrian theory does not necessarily imply that it is only the recent investments, undertaken since the beginning of the credit expansion, that are in danger of liquidation. Already established firms now face higher input prices, reflecting the scarcities introduced by the abnormally high amount of activity occurring in the higher-order stages of production as a result of central bank policy.

37. Don Bellante and Roger W. Garrison, "Phillips Curves and Hayekian Triangles: Two Perspectives on Monetary Dynamics," *History of Political Economy* 20 (Summer 1988): 207–34.

38. This fact is explainable by the phenomenon of compound interest. The longer the period of a loan, the greater the proportion of interest to principal involved in the loan's repayment. Changes in the interest rate one way or the other can therefore have dramatic effects on the profitability (or otherwise) of a long-term investment, considerably more so than for shorter-term loans.

39. I am purposely not entering into the dispute that exists among some Austrian economists regarding the proper monetary regime. All Austrians oppose a central bank with a monopoly of the note issue. Some Austrians, such as George Selgin and Larry White, favor in its place a system of so-called "free banking," whereby fractional-reserve banking would not be prohibited by law. Proponents of this view deny that any significant inflation would occur under such a system, since the ever-present threat of bank runs and the constant calls for redemption by competing banks would serve as salutary restraints. Other Austrians, such as Murray Rothbard, Hans Hoppe, Joseph Salerno, and Guido Hülsmann, favor a system in which banks would be legally required to hold 100 percent of their demand deposits on reserve, and would be prohibited from engaging in fractional-reserve banking. I myself hold the latter position. But whether the inflation that would be produced under a system of free banking would be sufficient to set the business cycle in motion is an issue I do not intend to explore here.

40. Rothbard, "Economic Depressions: Their Cause and Cure," 87.

41. Kevin E. Schmiesing, "Catholic Critics of the New Deal: 'Alternative' Traditions in Catholic Social Thought," *Catholic Social Science Review* 7 (2002): 154.

42. See Gary North, "Gertrude Coogan and the Myth of Social Credit," in *An Introduction to Christian Economics* (Nutley, N.J.: Craig Press, 1976), 124–62.

43. For an overview of Fr. Coughlin's monetary views, see Alan Brinkley, *Voices of Protest: Huey Long, Father Coughlin, and the Great Depression* (New York: Random House, 1982), 110ff.

44. A real critique of the Federal Reserve, which criticizes what the Federal Reserve does, rather than simply the fact that supposedly "private" forces are doing these things, can be found in Rothbard, *The Case against the Fed*.

45. Charles E. Coughlin, *Money! Questions and Answers* (Royal Oak, Mich.: National Union for Social Justice, 1936), 141; Rev. Denis Fahey, *Money Manipulation and Social Order* (Dublin: Browne & Nolan, 1944), 18–19.

46. Hilaire Belloc, *Economics for Helen* (London: J. W. Arrowsmith, 1924), 179–80.

47. Belloc, *Economics for Helen*, 184ff.

48. North, "Gertrude Coogan," 157.

49. Gary North, *Salvation through Inflation: The Economics of Social Credit* (Tyler, Tex.: Institute for Christian Economics, 1993), 63. Emphasis in original.

50. Coughlin, *Money! Questions and Answers*, 139.

51. North, *Salvation through Inflation*, 63–64.

52. Mises' theory of the business cycle involves money creation that occurs via loans to business. The Coughlin/Fahey brand of inflation, which would consist simply of printing up paper currency, would not have the same consequences. They would, however, disrupt business activity by means of Cantillon effects, since the new money would create expansion in certain segments of the economy whose prosperity would depend on continued, or perhaps even accelerated, money expansions in order to maintain these misdirections. See F. A. Hayek, *Unemployment and Monetary Policy: Government as Generator of the "Business Cycle"* (Washington, D.C.: Cato Institute, 1979). Thanks to Professor John P. Cochran for this reference.

53. North, "Gertrude Coogan," 142.

54. Fahey, *Money Manipulation and Social Order*, 14ff.

55. See Coughlin, *Money! Questions and Answers*, 136, but both key texts by these men feature this claim time and again.

56. Rothbard, *Economic Thought before Adam Smith*, 43.

57. Rothbard, *Economic Thought before Adam Smith*, 44.

58. A. Vermeersch, "Usury," *Catholic Encyclopedia*.

59. Rothbard, *Economic Thought before Adam Smith*, 105.

60. John T. Noonan, Jr., *The Scholastic Analysis of Usury* (Cambridge, Mass.: Harvard University Press, 1957), 390, 393.

61. Vermeersch, "Usury."

62. Rothbard, *Economic Thought before Adam Smith*, 43.

63. Thomas Aquinas, *Summa Theologiae*, II-II, q. 78, art. 1.

64. Noonan, *Scholastic Analysis of Usury*, 53–54.

65. Noonan, *Scholastic Analysis of Usury*, 133–34.

66. Noonan, *Scholastic Analysis of Usury*, 143.

67. Noonan, *Scholastic Analysis of Usury*, 143.

68. Noonan, *Scholastic Analysis of Usury*, 144.

69. Aristotle had famously argued that money was "sterile" or "barren," and that it was therefore unnatural to expect to earn money on money, in effect. This argument would be repeated throughout the medieval period. An eighteenth-century commentator suggested the obvious rejoinder: "A consideration that did not happen to present itself to that great philosopher, but which had it happened to present itself, might not have been altogether unworthy of his notice, is, that though a *daric* would not beget another daric, any more than it would a ram, or an ewe, yet for a daric which a man

borrowed, he might get a ram and a couple of ewes, and that the ewes, were the ram left with them a certain time, would probably not be barren. That then, at the end of the year, he would find himself master of his three sheep, together with two, if not three, lambs; and that, if he sold his sheep again to pay back his daric, and gave one of his lambs for the use of it in the mean time, he would be two lambs, or at least one lamb, richer than if he had made no such bargain." Jeremy Bentham, *Defence of Usury*, 1787, X. 4–5.

70. Noonan, *Scholastic Analysis of Usury*, 144–45.

71. Noonan, *Scholastic Analysis of Usury*, 118; Rothbard, *Economic Thought before Adam Smith*, 46.

72. Rothbard, *Economic Thought before Adam Smith*, 61.

73. Rothbard, *Economic Thought before Adam Smith*, 108.

74. Rothbard, *Economic Thought before Adam Smith*, 127.

75. Rothbard, *Economic Thought before Adam Smith*, 109.

76. Noonan, *Scholastic Analysis of Usury*, 262–64, 351; Rothbard, *Economic Thought before Adam Smith*, 124–25.

77. Rothbard, *Economic Thought before Adam Smith*, 125. "With Leonard Lessius, then," Rothbard writes, "the last of the barriers to interest or usury were smashed, and only the formal prohibition remained."

78. Vermeersch, "Usury."

79. Noonan, *Scholastic Analysis of Usury*, 377.

80. A. Vermeersch, "Interest," *Catholic Encyclopedia*. Emphasis added.

81. Ludwig von Mises, *Human Action: A Treatise on Economics*, Scholar's edition (Auburn, Ala.: Ludwig von Mises Institute, 1998 [1949]), 523.

82. Whether the amount of the loan is repaid in the form of monthly payments or in one lump sum at the conclusion of the loan period is, of course, immaterial to the present analysis.

83. Rothbard, "Economic Depressions: Their Cause and Cure," 81–82.

84. Vermeersch, "Interest." In his own study, Fr. Bernard W. Dempsey concurs, pointing out that "a rate of interest which expresses the common market valuation of the average opportunity current in the community to make a gain by the use of funds saved and loaned, would be satisfactory to the Schoolmen." Dempsey, *Interest and Usury*, 196.

85. De Soto, "New Light," 80, n. 50.

86. Rothbard, *Economic Thought before Adam Smith*, 85.

87. Rothbard, *Economic Thought before Adam Smith*, 107.

88. Belloc, *Economics for Helen*, 221. Emphasis in original.

89. Belloc, *Economics for Helen*, 220.

90. Editors of IHS Press, "Introduction," in Hilaire Belloc, *An Essay on the Restoration of Property* (Norfolk, Va.: IHS Press, 2002 [1936]), 13.

91. "One cannot condone the sin of usury by arguing that the gain is not great or excessive, but rather moderate or small; neither can it be condoned by arguing that the borrower is rich; *nor even by arguing that the money borrowed is not left idle, but is spent usefully, either to increase one's fortune, to purchase new estates, or to engage in business transactions.*" Benedict XIV, *Vix Pervenit* 3, November 1, 1745.

Emphasis added. Professor Noonan comments that "Lessius and Lugo could still have accommodated most interest-bearing credit transactions within the confines of the encyclical; and St. Alphonsus does so accommodate them." Noonan, *Scholastic Analysis of Usury*, 357.

92. Noonan, *Scholastic Analysis of Usury*, 403.

93. Vermeersch, "Interest."

94. Patrick M. O'Neil, "A Response to John T. Noonan, Jr., Concerning the Development of Catholic Moral Doctrine," *Faith & Reason* (Spring/Summer 1996).

Chapter Four

The Economics and
Morality of Foreign Aid

In April 2003, written testimony before Congress on behalf of the U.S. Bishops' Conference and Catholic Relief Services called for billions of dollars in additional U.S. foreign aid. At a time when the failures of foreign aid have become increasingly obvious even to those who may have favored them in the past, the American bishops continue nevertheless to advocate more of the same. It was a terrible shame, according to Catholic Relief Services spokesman Fr. William Headley, that over the years the United States had devoted a smaller and smaller percentage of its wealth to foreign aid. The demands of morality, he insisted, required that this trend be reversed.[1]

Unfortunately, this line of argument fails to reckon with the well-documented problems associated with foreign-aid programs—problems so serious that they have led many former supporters of these programs to turn against them. Foreign aid has served to prop up brutal and corrupt regimes and shelter them from the economic consequences of their interventionist policies. Foreign aid has subsidized policies that have destroyed developing countries' export sectors. It has politicized life in these countries, as hostile groups struggle with each other to seize control of the increasingly lucrative coffers of the state apparatus. And after more than five decades of such assistance, developing countries have little or nothing to show for it.

Peter Bauer was one of those lucky few intellectuals who lived to see his own vindication. Bauer taught economics at Cambridge University and later at the London School of Economics, where he spent the bulk of his career. Often dismissed for his refusal to go along with the conventional wisdom regarding less-developed countries (LDCs) and the proper strategy for their rise to economic development and prosperity, Bauer insisted that the policy recommendations of the foreign aid establishment were fundamentally wrongheaded and counterproductive.

Since the 1980s, more and more development officials and scholars have
begun to concede that Bauer's market-oriented approach to economic development makes more sense than the massive state planning that had
proven so disastrous throughout the Third World. For years, the field of development economics had remained, in Bauer's words, "immune to incon-
venient evidence."[2] By the last two decades of his life, that had begun to
change.

The conventional wisdom during the first few decades following World
War II held that without significant infusions of Western aid, the world's
LDCs would remain forever mired in poverty. Economic development
could not be achieved without outside assistance in the form of government-to-government grants. These countries were said to be trapped in a
"vicious circle of poverty"—their low income made impossible the substantial savings necessary to fund the investment and capital accumulation
that would ultimately raise incomes. This idea played a significant role in
the development of foreign-aid programs, which were intended to provide
the capital that was allegedly the indispensable ingredient of economic
progress in the LDCs.[3]

One of Bauer's brilliant insights, which has since all but become the conventional wisdom, was that development was not a function of capital accumulation. Rather, capital was created in the process of economic development.[4] As Bauer put it, "To have money is the result of economic
achievement, not its precondition . . . . Indeed, if the notion of the vicious circle of poverty were valid, mankind would still be living in the Old Stone
Age."[5] This is what the Development Group for Alternative Policies was getting at when it concluded in a 1988 report: "Money—or the lack thereof—is
not a significant constraint on development."[6]

It is cultural attitudes and institutional arrangements, according to Bauer,
that have played a far more decisive role in determining the economic fates
of the various nations. A people who believe in fatalism or collectivism,
rather than in personal responsibility, will be less likely to undertake the risks
associated with capitalist entrepreneurship. As for institutions, Hernando de
Soto demonstrated their importance in his investigation of the poor economic
performance of his native Peru. He concluded that insecure and poorly de-
fined property rights were at the root of much of what ailed his country. He
also showed that the suffocating effects of regulation, a factor almost entirely
neglected in this literature, had played a significant role in Peru's woes. He
found, for instance, that it took "the equivalent of 289 work days, 81 meters
of forms, and eight overt bribes to legally establish a small clothing factory."[7]
(Such sheer destructiveness suggests why Pope Paul VI may perhaps have
been too hasty in concluding in *Octogesima Adveniens* that government "al-

ways intervenes with care for justice and with devotion to the common good, for which it holds final responsibility."[8])

By the end of the Cold War, over \$2 trillion in inflation-adjusted dollars had been given to the Third World. Tom Bethell rightly notes that this immense fortune may simply have served to retard economic development, since it inevitably functioned as an emollient that masked the destructive consequences of these governments' interventionist policies. It is revealing that South Korea, Taiwan, and Chile, faced with a cutoff in U.S. aid and therefore having little choice, ultimately embraced the free market.[9] Naturally, they prospered.

By the 1980s, the conventional view was in clear retreat. A 1983 study by the World Bank found that rates of economic growth in developing countries fell as market distortions increased, and eleven years later the World Bank drew the same conclusion in a special report on conditions in Africa. E. Dwight Phaup and Bradley Lewis noted what more and more scholars were beginning to concede: "Resource endowment, lucky circumstances, former colonial status, and other similar factors make little difference in the speed with which countries grow economically. But the results of domestic policy choices pervade every economic area."[10]

Even major aid agencies have at last begun to acknowledge the errors of development planning. The remarks of Alan Waters, former chief economist for the U.S. Agency for International Development (AID), are now commonplace:

> Foreign aid is inherently bad. It retards the process of . . . economic growth and the accumulation of wealth (the only means of escape from poverty and degradation); it weakens the coordinating effect of the market process; it pulls entrepreneurship and intellectual capital into non-productive and administrative activities; it creates a moral ethical tone which denies the hard task of wealth creation. Foreign aid makes it possible for . . . societies to transfer wealth from the poor to the rich.[11]

Alan Woods, who was appointed to head AID in 1987, echoed these sentiments. In a 1989 report, AID acknowledged that "only a handful of countries that started receiving U.S. assistance in the 1950s and 1960s has ever graduated from dependent status."[12] The following year, a draft paper of the Center for Institutional Reform and the Informal Sector at the University of Maryland conceded that AID had consistently neglected the role of "institutions and legal infrastructures." Economist Mancur Olson stated the matter directly, pointing out in 1993 that all economically successful countries possessed relatively secure property and contract rights, while all the unsuccessful ones did not.[13]

Even a task force during the Clinton administration was forced to concede that "despite decades of foreign assistance, most of Africa and parts of Latin America, Asia and the Middle East are economically worse off today than they were 20 years ago."[14] Likewise, the *New York Times* admitted during the 1990s that "three decades of foreign development assistance in the Third World has failed to lift the poorest of the poor in Africa and Asia much beyond where they have always been." It had simply "fattened political elites."[15] In a 1997 report, the World Bank described results that sounded much like what Bauer had predicted all along: "Governments embarked on fanciful schemes. Private investors, lacking confidence in public policies or in the steadfastness of leaders, held back. Powerful rulers acted arbitrarily. Corruption became endemic. Development faltered, and poverty endured." (The economic arbitrariness encouraged by foreign aid was to be expected: since governments do not have to pass the profit-and-loss test that private investors do, they can get away with allocating money toward economically dubious projects that yield high-profile jobs, and therefore support for the regime, in the short run.[16]) "State-led intervention," the report went on, "emphasized market failures and accorded the state a central role in correcting them. But the institutional assumptions implicit in this world view were, as we all realize today, too simplistic."[17] *As we all realize today*, but as Bauer knew decades ago.

This is why it is so disappointing to learn that in his 1967 encyclical *Populorum Progressio*, Pope Paul VI had urged the Catholic world to support the very foreign aid transfers and state-led development programs that contributed to this debacle, confident that they would provide economic well-being and security to the nations that took part in them. The Pope argued that private efforts were insufficient, and that the public sector must assume considerable responsibility for development. He declared: "It is for the public authorities to establish and lay down the desired goals, the plans to be followed, and the methods to be used in fulfilling them; and it is also their task to stimulate the efforts of those involved in this common activity."[18] People in more prosperous countries, he said, had an obligation to contribute to these ventures: "Each man must examine his conscience, which sounds a new call in our present times. Is he prepared to support, at his own expense, projects and undertakings designed to help the needy? Is he prepared to pay higher taxes so that public authorities may expand their efforts in the work of development?"[19]

It might be argued in his defense that the Pope could not have known the outcome of the policies he favored, or that they would be exactly contrary to what he had wanted. But people like Professor Bauer had been writing for years by the time *Populorum* appeared, so cautionary material was available.

Secondly, the very fact that we are dealing here with *policies*, which are all too fallible, rather than with Catholic doctrine per se, means that we are in a realm in which Catholics ought to be free to debate and discuss various morally licit alternatives. This is not to say that Catholics must be united only at the level of official doctrine and are entitled to take any position at all at the policy-making level, for no Catholic may support a policy that is intrinsically evil. The point is simply that when several morally licit policy alternatives are available, choosing between them becomes a matter of informed judgment and the proper exercise of reason. Recall Pope Leo XIII's important statement: "If I were to pronounce on any single matter of a prevailing economic problem, I should be interfering with the freedom of men to work out their own affairs. Certain cases must be solved in the domain of facts, case by case as they occur. . . . [M]en must realize in deeds those things, the principles of which have been placed beyond dispute. . . . [T]hese things one must leave to the solution of time and experience."[20] Through the endorsement he gave to mainstream development programs, writing an entire encyclical on the subject, Paul VI moved beyond the limits suggested by Leo XIII, and with very unfortunate consequences.

Populorum Progressio takes for granted that the developing world needs outside assistance from the developed world. But according to Bauer, there is not "a single instance in history when external donations were required for the economic development of a country." This only stands to reason, he explains. Economic achievement depends on "people's attributes, attitudes, motivations, mores and political arrangements. . . . If the conditions for development other than capital are present, the capital required will either be generated locally or be available commercially from abroad to governments or to businesses. If the required conditions are not present, then aid will be ineffective and wasted."[21]

One of the difficulties of the old argument that LDCs could not enjoy economic progress without foreign aid is that it cannot explain how any country ever developed. Where was the external aid for the first developing countries? If anything, LDCs today are in a far more enviable position from the point of view of development than were Western societies, since they can benefit from external capital markets and enormous technological knowledge that were unavailable during the West's rise to economic prosperity.[22]

Part of the reason that the LDCs lack capital is that some of them restrict or prevent foreign investment in their countries, or have an abysmal record of disregard for private property. Socialist political leaders, who foolishly pose as the defenders of their peoples by nationalizing foreign properties, can only get away with such behavior for so long before outside investors learn their lesson and refuse to pour any more resources into so risky a venture. If they

are to attract outside investment, the leaders of such countries need to stop behaving like spoiled children and acknowledge the inviolability of property
rights.

Tragically overlooked in the Pope's moral analysis is the contribution of
foreign aid to the politicization of life in the LDCs. This was another
of Bauer's crucial insights. Since foreign aid inevitably amounts to a
government-to-government transfer, ethnic and other tensions are likely to
rise as competition for control of the state apparatus grows correspondingly
more intense. The results can be violent—Bauer cites such substantial Western aid recipients as Burundi, Kampuchea, Ethiopia, Indonesia, Iraq, Nigeria,
Pakistan, Tanzania, Uganda, Vietnam, and Zaire. Indeed the tensions thus introduced into political life can become positively frightful, including "large-
scale expulsion and even massacre, tolerated, encouraged or perpetrated by
the rulers." "By helping to politicize life," Bauer contends, "aid has contributed to such policies and results."[23] Even when violence does not result,
the consequences of the politicization of life are nevertheless all too real, as
more and more people devote their energies to efforts to gain political favor
(whether through bribery or other means) and less and less time to productive
effort in satisfaction of consumer needs. Surely there is room for such considerations in our moral evaluation of foreign aid.

Bauer himself, evaluating *Populorum Progressio*, pointed out the crucial
differences between coerced government-to-government wealth transfers and
the activity of voluntary organizations:

> The Pope regards official transfers as a discharge of moral duty and as action
> substantially similar to voluntary charity. Yet there is an evident difference in
> moral content between voluntary sacrifice to help one's fellow men and public
> spending out of taxes. Taxpayers have no choice, and many may not know that
> they contribute for this particular purpose. The political and economic effects of
> the two forms of transfer also differ profoundly. The activities of voluntary
> agencies, especially nonpoliticized charities, do not politicize life as does offi-
> cial foreign aid, and thus they avoid the baleful results of the politicization of
> life promoted by official transfers. Moreover, voluntary charity is generally ad-
> justed far more effectively to the conditions and needs of local people. In par-
> ticular, voluntary agencies are much more interested in alleviating the lot of the
> poorest than are most rulers in the Third World.[24]

Even a policy as apparently noncontroversial to the average person as food
aid is fraught with destructive potential, and for similar reasons. As many in
the West have finally learned, recipient governments very often use the food
not to feed the hungry in their countries, but rather to prop up support for their
regimes by making food available to groups whose political support is

deemed important. ("The poor," Bauer once noted, "particularly the rural poor who are the great majority, are politically ineffective and thus of little interest to the rulers."[25]) As one critique put it:

No wonder the effectiveness of food aid around the world is under suspicion in the United States. Some critics have concluded that this low-cost food is merely a device for keeping elites in power by propping up foreign-government budgets and feeding influential middle classes. Food aid has discouraged food production, these analysts say, and has failed to address the basic challenge of helping the poor earn enough to buy the food already available.

In Bangladesh, for example, the food never reaches the hungry since it is used by the regime to win support:

It comes as a surprise to a layman, but not at all to the experts that food aid arriving in Bangladesh and many other places isn't used to feed the poor. Governments typically sell the food on local markets and use the proceeds however they choose. Here, the government chooses to sell the food in cut-rate ration shops to members of the middle class.[26]

To buy food in a cut-rate ration shop, one needs a ration card (necessary because the low prices create artificial shortages). The poor have no way of acquiring them.[27]

It is often the policies of many recipient governments themselves that are to blame for the poverty of their people. For instance, they "expel the most productive groups from their countries, or restrict the inflow and the deployment of private capital or the expansion of certain types of enterprise, both domestic and foreign."[28] This self-inflicted poverty, in turn, is used to justify aid payments from the West. "Redistribution from rich to poor countries as an objective of policy brings it about that lower incomes resulting from the policies of Third World governments serve as grounds for taxing Western citizens for the direct benefit of those who brought about these lower incomes."[29] When the issue is framed in this way, how can foreign aid payments be considered a moral imperative?

Paul VI also pointed to the disadvantages from which the underdeveloped countries allegedly suffered under what economists call "deteriorating terms of trade":

Highly industrialized nations export their own manufacturing products, for the most part. Less developed nations, on the other hand, have nothing to sell but raw materials and agricultural crops. As a result of technical progress, the price of manufactured products is rising rapidly and they find a ready market. But the basic crops and raw materials produced by the less developed countries are

subject to sudden and wide-ranging shifts in market price; they do not share in
the growing market value of industrial products.[30]

Here again we see the pitfalls of rendering moral judgments on the basis of
faulty economics, since the terms of trade argument defended by Paul VI
turns out to be fallacious. Following World War II, Raúl Prebisch and Hans
Singer had popularized the thesis that Paul VI adopted in *Populorum Progressio*: there is a tendency over time for the prices of commodities to fall and
of manufactured goods to rise, and since Third World countries tend to be
producers of commodities and developed countries tend to produce manufactured goods, the terms of trade between the two would inevitably undergo
secular deterioration.

Yet far from being proven, this thesis had been thrown into question from
the very beginning. Economist Gottfried Haberler observed as early as 1957
that "the alleged historical facts lack proof, their explanation is faulty, the ex-
trapolation [into the future] is reckless and the policy conclusions are irresponsible." Over thirty years later, Haberler revisited his earlier statements
and concluded that they had been "fully confirmed by later research."[31] For
example, Robert E. Lipsey's *Price and Quantity Trends in the Foreign Trade
of the United States* concluded:

> Two widely held beliefs regarding net barter terms of trade found no confirma-
> tion in the data for the United States. One is that there has been a substantial
> long-term improvement in the terms of trade of developed countries including
> the United States; the other, that there has been a significant long-term deterio-
> ration in the terms of trade of primary as compared to manufacturing products.
> Although there have been very large swings in U.S. terms of trade since 1879,
> no long-run trend has emerged. The average level of U.S. terms of trade since
> World War II has been about the same as before World War I.[32]

As Melvyn Krauss concludes, "Any argument based on the assumption of a
secular decline in the terms of trade of Third World countries with the industrialized North must be false, since no such decline has been observed."[33]

In some cases, the destructive policies that foreign aid makes possible are
the very ones advocated by *Populorum Progressio* as positive goods and sure
paths to prosperity. Having deplored the allegedly deteriorating terms of trade
between the Third World and the industrialized nations, Paul VI looked away
from trade as a path to Third World prosperity and economic well-being. He
described it as "evident" that "the principle of free trade, by itself, is no longer
adequate for regulating international agreements. It certainly can work when
both parties are about equal economically; in such cases it stimulates progress
and rewards effort. . . . But the case is quite different when the nations in-

volved are far from equal. Market prices that are freely agreed upon can turn out to be most unfair."[34] The Pope came out in favor of trade policies "favoring certain infant industries."[35]

TRADE AND THE LDCs

But consider the cases of Taiwan and South Korea, where import-substitution policies—that is, the use of tariffs and other government action to support domestic industry—were instituted to protect high-cost domestic industries from foreign competition. It was only when, in anticipation of the end of American aid in 1965, the Taiwanese government began to move away from these policies that Taiwan's "economic miracle" began to develop. The same is true for South Korea, which also began to encourage an inflow of foreign capital and technology.[36] Not only does foreign trade encourage efficient specialization, but it also holds out significant dynamic effects. Professor Evan Osborne refers to "the economies of scale that result when firms in a small, poor economy begin exporting to much larger, more prosperous global markets, as well as the ability of trade to promote learning of modern industrial techniques and other important knowledge."[37]

The eminently defensible conclusion is that it was precisely the economic recommendations of *Populorum Progressio* that had held these countries in relative poverty and stagnation. Again, therefore, we should bear in mind that the specific application of Catholic social principles, which is a debatable matter of rational judgment based on circumstances and contingent factors rather than a matter of strict Catholic doctrine, can never bind the Catholic conscience—especially, as in the present case, when a trained economist knows very well what their outcome will be. Since there is nothing morally wrong with the free exchange of goods between peoples, and since the Pope claims that *his own purpose* is to increase the material well-being of these peoples, Catholics must be permitted to hold another view if the Pontiff's recommendations are bound to have the opposite effect.

Indeed, it is theoretically unavoidable that the import-substitution policies favored in *Populorum Progressio* must do considerable damage to a country's export sector—and there is no obvious moral criterion according to which the benefits that accrue to domestic industry by such policies must outweigh the damage done to the export sector. Since domestic markets are inevitably limited in the LDCs, any hope of economic progress there depends on a healthy export sector. At least three reasons can be cited in support of the claim that import substitution must harm exports. First, the protected good may be an important input in the production process of export-oriented industries. The

higher prices that protectionism makes possible, therefore, put export industries at an artificial disadvantage vis-à-vis their competitors in countries that
do not engage in such policies. Tariffs on steel may "protect" some steel-
workers' jobs, for example, but at the expense of destroying jobs in all industries in which steel—artificially overpriced as a result of the tariff—is an
input. Those industries are now less competitive in international trade. Such
policies are all the more insidious because their negative consequences go essentially unnoticed, while their "benefits" are visible for all to see: everyone
sees the jobs in the steel industry that the tariff has protected, but hardly anyone is even aware that the job losses in industries throughout the economy
that use steel are attributable to the tariff.

Second, even if the good in question is a final consumption good and not a
potential input in the production process of an export-oriented industry, the
fact remains that in its artificially privileged position its production is able to
bid scarce resources away from export industries, and therefore make inputs
that much more expensive for the export sector. And finally, there is the very
real possibility of retaliation by other countries against the trade restrictions
imposed by the LDC. Such retaliation, naturally, means that the export sector's foreign markets are severely circumscribed or cut off altogether. No
wonder exports grew so dramatically in Taiwan and South Korea (between
1962 and 1970, from 13.2 percent of GNP to 31.1 percent and from 5.2 percent to 15 percent, respectively) when import substitution was ended.[38]

Policy analyst Doug Bandow describes the policy of import substitution as
"one of the most harmful strategies" offered to developing countries. "Today," he writes, "most development economists admit that this policy stifles
growth. The world's most rapidly growing economies, the East Asian states,
have eschewed import substitution and have instead concentrated on producing inexpensive exports."[39] Indeed, it is impossible to name a wealthy country that severely restricts either foreign trade or foreign capital.[40]

Since World War II, Raúl Prebisch had been one of the greatest champions
of import substitution in Latin America. Yet his predictions proved fantastically misguided. As we have seen, the claim of deteriorating terms of trade
turned out to be false, and the suggestion that Third World countries were incapable of developing new export industries could not have been more wrong
(labor-intensive manufacturing proved to be more than within their reach).[41]
Prebisch would later assess the consequences of following his own advice:
"[T]he proliferation of industries of every kind in a closed market has deprived the Latin American countries of the advantages of specialization and
economies of scale, and owing to the protection afforded by excessive tariff
duties and restrictions, a healthy form of internal competition has failed to develop, to the detriment of efficient production."[42]

But in the course of declaring protectionist trade policy to be all but a moral imperative for developing countries, Paul VI dismissed free trade as clearly detrimental to their interests. He asked, rhetorically, "Isn't it plain to everyone that such attempts to establish greater justice in international trade would be of great benefit to the developing nations, and that they would produce lasting results?"[43]

In fact, it is not. The logical conclusion of such reasoning would be that the less international trade the Third World has, the better, and that the ideal situation would be reached when the Third World had insulated itself entirely from external economic relations, at least with the West.[44] Of course, the very opposite is true: those places with the most Western contacts are far more prosperous than those with few or no such contacts.[45] As Bauer explains, inexpensive imports "extend the choice and economic opportunities of people in poor countries. These imports are usually accompanied by the expansion of other activities. If this were not so, the population would be unable to pay for the imports."[46] He bluntly addressed critics of trade:

> The allegations that external trade, and especially imports from the West, are damaging to the populations of the Third World reveal a barely disguised condescension towards the ordinary people there, and even contempt for them. The people, of course, want the imports. If they did not the imported goods could not be sold. Similarly, the people are prepared to produce for export to pay for these imported goods. To say that these processes are damaging is to argue that people's preferences are of no account in organizing their own lives.[47]

Although Paul VI had high hopes for what tariff barriers could accomplish, the reality has diverged rather radically from his predictions. "The economic landscape in some developing countries," writes Haberler, "is littered and disfigured by white elephants, modern factories unsuited to their productive resources, which either stand idle or operate inefficiently at exorbitant costs, *with protection from imports or direct subsidies at the expense of the taxpayer and the traditional export sector*—mainly agriculture."[48] That this is not a path to prosperity is about the least one can say about it. Paul Craig Roberts, former assistant secretary of the treasury, describes the actual consequences of these policies:

> Protectionism reigned as countries closed markets and raised tariff barriers to try to stimulate subsidized domestic industries under the guise of "import substitution." Capital controls were instituted, multiple foreign exchange rates were used to privilege favored importers, and the law was used to favor special interest groups at the expense of the general public. Latin American countries followed foreign advisers' recipes for high tax rates, currency devaluations, and a

plethora of regulations with the assurance that putting more resources into the hands of government would stimulate development. None of these policies promoted economic progress. Instead, they resulted in high inflation, high interest rates, political instability, poverty, and the flight of capital and people from the region.[49]

The case of Hong Kong, which ignored this terrible advice, is especially instructive. With no local power sources (such as coal or oil), shortages of land and water, and few raw materials, Hong Kong nevertheless became the envy of the world thanks to the explosion in economic growth and living standards made possible by its largely free economy. At the very time Paul VI was urging struggling families in the Western world to pay higher prices for goods from developing countries as a matter of moral obligation, Hong Kong was busily ignoring the implied suggestion that developing countries could get nowhere without special favors and condescension, and eventually created such a successful export sector that Britain and the United States actually began asking that small outpost of economic freedom to implement voluntary export restrictions.[50]

During a worldwide recession in the early 1980s, Hong Kong's unemployment rate peaked at 5.2 percent, when Britain's was more than twice as high.[51] The example of Hong Kong, then, is the kind of information that needs to be taken into account if the American bishops wish to issue a statement regarding what the government should do about unemployment. Hong Kong suggests to us the type of economic environment in which unemployment is minimized.

INTERNATIONAL AGENCIES

While development aid from Western governments has proven counterproductive at best, the records of the World Bank and the International Monetary Fund (IMF) have not been much better.[52] What these institutions have succeeded in doing is getting less-developed nations addicted to debt—some 70 countries have been on the receiving end of IMF loans for over 20 years. Although we hear a great deal about the allegedly stringent conditions that the World Bank and IMF impose on recipient nations, the reality was summed up in a recent Bank paper: "There is no systematic effect of aid on policy."[53] Russia, for example, was notorious for receiving aid for years while disregarding IMF requirements.

These institutions have rightly been criticized for the indiscriminate nature of their lending. As economist David Osterfeld explains, "Since the [World] Bank is a lending institution, but a lending institution that because of its quasi-governmental status is largely insulated from market forces, job promotions have come to be obtained more by meeting or exceeding lending targets than by worrying about the soundness of loans." One World Bank official admitted, "We're like a Soviet factory. The . . . pressures to lend are enormous and a lot of people spend sleepless nights wondering how they can unload projects. Our ability to influence in a way that makes sense is completely undermined."[54]

IMF loans and bailouts have had the effect of encouraging corruption and unwise economic policy by shielding the regimes perpetrating them from the consequences of their actions. In the absence of IMF loans, these countries would be forced to reform, to abandon the political favoritism, subsidies, state domination of the economy, and the rest of the political apparatus that keeps their people in poverty. Secure in the knowledge that the IMF is generally loath to cancel aid packages outright, such regimes can essentially continue their profligate ways while bilking taxpayers around the world and diverting investment funds away from profitable uses elsewhere.

The record of these institutions has been one of extraordinary profligacy, poor investments, and growing indebtedness among recipient nations.[55] Needed reforms are simply not made and Third World poverty is perpetuated because these outside loans shield recipient regimes from the consequences of their bloated bureaucracies and their depredations against private property. One example among many is Tanzania, which continued to be one of the largest recipients of World Bank money even after a report by the Bank itself had pointed out that the reason for the depressed condition of Tanzanian agricultural production was the oppressive tax burden imposed by the government.[56]

Even where the World Bank has funded projects that have turned out to be successful, the recipient country has still suffered. Such projects would likely have been financed by private capital, and thus the net effect of World Bank funding of state-owned enterprises has been to dissuade private capital from entering the country—once the state has achieved domination of some economic sector, private firms find the idea of investing there far less attractive. Not surprisingly, a correlation has even been observed between Third World borrowing on the one hand and decreases in foreign direct investment on the other.[57]

FOREIGN AID AND THE MAGISTERIUM

There is a larger issue at stake in all of this. *Populorum Progressio* recommended a course of action for less-developed nations whose results have not been good, and which fewer and fewer people continue to advocate now. Bauer warned that the Pope's writing on the subject "promotes policies directly at variance with the declared sentiments and objectives of the papal documents."[58] Were people who were aware of Bauer's analysis morally obligated to cooperate in development ventures whose consequences they knew perfectly well had to end in destruction and chaos, or at the very least do more harm than good? Recall Paul VI's examination of conscience for the lay person: "Is he prepared to pay higher taxes so that public authorities may expand their efforts in the work of development?" Now that it is now more or less established that—as Peter Bauer was already trying to explain when Paul VI was writing—the interference of "public authorities" in the work of development is precisely what has hurt so many developing countries, particularly in Africa, what is the status of the papal demand that people support state-led development? These are some of the problems that arise when general principles about generosity to our neighbor are translated into specific policy proposals in a papal encyclical. Not only are specific policy proposals all too fallible, but when enjoying the prestige of an encyclical, they can unnecessarily trouble the consciences of good Catholics—whose disagreements are based not on any perverse desire to oppose the Holy See, but on specialized secular knowledge that they happen to possess.

The Pope is surely free to instruct the Catholic population of our responsibilities toward our fellow men, but as Pope Leo suggested, he has no right as Pope to baptize one economic approach as the one most likely to be effective.[59] The grace of state attached to his office gives him no special insights into what the best strategy for economic development might be. By any standard, the issue of (for example) whether free trade or a system of protective tariffs is better for a developing country—clearly a matter of legitimate disagreement among Catholics—is not one on which the Pope may appear to make a morally binding judgment.

The 2003 proposal put forward by the U.S. Conference of Catholic Bishops for still more foreign aid reflects a continuation of the policies of Paul VI long after the international consensus behind them has collapsed in the face of overwhelming failure. On the grounds of morality and of economic science it is long past time to change course, and never again to associate the Church's good name with such disastrous—if "well-intentioned"—policies as "foreign aid."

NOTES

1. "U.S. Bishops Urge More Foreign Aid to Help Ensure Peace," *Zenit*, April 4, 2003.

2. Peter Bauer, "Subsistence, Trade, and Exchange: Understanding Developing Economies," in *The Revolution in Development Economics*, ed. James A. Dorn, Steve H. Hanke, and Alan A. Waters (Washington, D.C.: Cato Institute, 1998), 279.

3. Bauer, "Subsistence, Trade, and Exchange: Understanding Developing Economies," 279; idem, *From Subsistence to Exchange and Other Essays* (Princeton, N.J.: Princeton University Press, 2000), 45.

4. Alan Rufus Waters, "Economic Growth and the Property Rights Regime," in Dorn et al., eds., *The Revolution in Development Economics*, 109.

5. James A. Dorn, "Economic Development and Freedom: The Legacy of Peter Bauer," *Cato Journal* 22 (Fall 2002): 361.

6. Doug Bandow, "The First World's Misbegotten Economic Legacy to the Third World," in Dorn, et al., eds., *The Revolution in Development Economics*, 223.

7. Waters, "Economic Growth and the Property Rights Regime," 123.

8. Paul VI, *Octogesima Adveniens* 46.

9. Tom Bethell, *The Noblest Triumph: Property and Prosperity through the Ages* (New York: St. Martin's, 1998), 190–91. On foreign aid as an emollient, see, for example, Waters, "Economic Growth and the Property Rights Regime," 118.

10. Bandow, "The First World's Misbegotten Economic Legacy," 208.

11. Alan Waters, "In Africa's Anguish, Foreign Aid Is a Culprit," *Heritage Foundation Backgrounder*, August 7, 1985.

12. Bandow, "The First World's Misbegotten Economic Legacy," 223; Bethell, *The Noblest Triumph*, 201.

13. Bethell, *The Noblest Triumph*, 201.

14. Bandow, "The First World's Misbegotten Economic Legacy," 223.

15. Thomas J. DiLorenzo, "Ron Brown's Corporate Welfare Scam," *The Free Market*, June 1996.

16. Evan Osborne, "Rethinking Foreign Aid," *Cato Journal* 22 (Fall 2002): 309.

17. Dorn, "Economic Development and Freedom: The Legacy of Peter Bauer," 360, 362.

18. Paul VI, *Populorum Progressio* 33. Although the Pope added that the public authorities "must also see to it that private initiative and intermediary organizations are involved in this work," he nevertheless insisted that "[o]rganized programs are necessary for 'directing, stimulating, coordinating, supplying and integrating' the work of individuals and intermediary organizations" (internal footnote removed).

19. Paul VI, *Populorum Progressio* 47.

20. Quoted in Katherine Burton, *Leo the Thirteenth: The First Modern Pope* (New York: David McKay Co., 1962), 171.

21. P. T. Bauer, *Equality, the Third World and Economic Delusion* (Cambridge, Mass.: Harvard University Press, 1981), 100. Bauer includes the Marshall Plan in his statement that external donations have never been necessary for development. On the myth of the Marshall Plan, see Tyler Cowen, "The Marshall Plan: Myths and Realities," in *U.S. Aid to the Developing World*, ed. Doug Bandow (Washington, D.C.: Heritage Foundation, 1985), 61–74.

22. Bauer, *Equality, the Third World and Economic Delusion*, 99.

23. Bauer, *Equality, the Third World and Economic Delusion*, 104; George B. N. Ayittey, "The Failure of Development Planning in Africa," in *The Collapse of Development Planning*, ed. Peter J. Boettke (New York: New York University Press, 1993), 173.

24. Bauer, *From Subsistence to Exchange and Other Essays*, 105. Bauer's analysis of *Populorum Progressio* and *Octogesima Adveniens* is withering, and should be read by anyone interested in the subject. (It appears as "Ecclesiastical Economics" in *From Subsistence to Exchange and Other Essays*.) "The Pope's arguments and allegations," he writes (p. 107), "reflect unthinking surrender to intellectual fashion and political nostrums. This is obvious in the major themes, particularly the insistence on large-scale official aid. . . . The spirit of these documents is contrary to the most durable and best elements in Catholic tradition. They are indeed even unChristian. Their Utopian, chiliastic ideology, combined with an overriding preoccupation with economic differences, is an amalgam of the ideas of millenarian sects, of the extravagant claims of the early American advocates of foreign aid, and of the Messianic component of Marxism-Leninism."

25. Bauer, *Equality, the Third World and Economic Delusion*, 111.

26. Cited in Melvyn Krauss, *Development Without Aid: Growth, Poverty and Government* (New York: McGraw-Hill, 1983), 158–59.

27. Krauss, *Development Without Aid*, 159.

28. P. T. Bauer, *Dissent on Development* (rev. ed., Cambridge, Mass.: Harvard University Press, 1976), 101.

29. Bauer, *Equality, the Third World and Economic Delusion*, 118.

30. Paul VI, *Populorum Progressio* 57.

31. Gottfried Haberler, *International Trade and Economic Development* (San Francisco: International Center for Economic Growth, 1988), 67.

32. Haberler, *International Trade and Economic Development*, 68.

33. Krauss, *Development Without Aid*, 156.

34. Paul VI, *Populorum Progressio* 58.

35. Paul VI, *Populorum Progressio* 61.

36. Krauss, *Development Without Aid*, 160.

37. Osborne, "Rethinking Foreign Aid," 299.

38. Krauss, *Development Without Aid*, 52–56.

39. Bandow, "The First World's Misbegotten Economic Legacy," 217.

40. Cf. D. Eric Schansberg, *Poor Policy: How Government Harms the Poor* (Boulder, Colo.: Westview Press, 1996), 215–16.

41. Brink Lindsey, *Against the Dead Hand: The Uncertain Struggle for Global Capitalism* (New York: John Wiley & Sons, 2002), 103.

42. Quoted in Lindsey, *Against the Dead Hand*, 104.

43. Paul VI, *Populorum Progressio* 61.

44. Bauer, *Equality, the Third World and Economic Delusion*, 78; see also Peter Bauer, "The Disregard of Reality," in Dorn, et al., eds., *The Revolution in Development Economics*, 28.

45. Bauer, *From Subsistence to Exchange and Other Essays*, 5.

46. Bauer, *Equality, the Third World and Economic Delusion*, 79.

47. Bauer, *Equality, the Third World and Economic Delusion*, 80.

48. Haberler, *International Trade and Economic Development*, 77. Emphasis added.

49. Paul Craig Roberts, "Shut Down the Architects of a Failed Policy," in Dorn, et al., eds., *The Revolution in Development Economics*, 231.

50. Robert A. Peterson, "Lessons in Liberty: Hong Kong, 'Crown Jewel' of Capitalism," in *The Industrial Revolution and Free Trade*, ed. Burton W. Folsom, Jr. (Irvington-on-Hudson, N.Y.: Foundation for Economic Education, 1996), 109.

51. Peterson, "Lessons in Liberty," 109

52. On the World Bank and IMF, see *Perpetuating Poverty: The World Bank, the IMF, and the Developing World*, eds. Doug Bandow and Ian Vásquez (Washington, D.C.: Cato Institute, 1994).

53. Ian Vásquez, "Poor Country Debt Relief, Rich Country Shenanigans," Cato Institute, July 30, 2001 at www.cato.org/dailys/07-30-01.html (accessed October 29, 2002).

54. David Osterfeld, "The World Bank and the IMF: Misbegotten Sisters," in Boettke, ed., *The Collapse of Development Planning*, 190–91.

55. If anything, the *successes* of the Bank have been exaggerated. Osterfeld, "The World Bank and the IMF," 194–95.

56. Osterfeld, "The World Bank and the IMF," 197–98.

57. Osterfeld, "The World Bank and the IMF," 200.

58. Bauer, *From Subsistence to Exchange and Other Essays*, 108. "There is profound truth," Bauer goes on, "in Pascal's maxim that working hard to think clearly is the beginning of moral conduct. This applies with altogether special force to the head of a worldwide Church issuing major pronouncements."

59. As Bauer correctly notes, "The Pope's diagnosis and proposals are remarkably commonplace. There is nothing distinctively Christian or Catholic about them. They were already in vogue when the pronouncements were issued." Bauer, *From Subsistence to Exchange and Other Essays*, 99.

Chapter Five

The Welfare State, the Family, and Civil Society

On a fairly regular basis, committees of the U.S. Conference of Catholic Bishops and, at one point, the Conference itself, have been heard advocating a substantial expansion of the vast network of social and economic programs collectively known as the welfare state. The desirability of these programs, however, is by no means self-evident. In fact, the failure of the Great Society welfare programs of the 1960s had become so patent by the 1990s that even a Democratic president could promise to "end welfare as we know it."

Recent Church documents have sent mixed signals on the issue. Certain encyclicals of Pope John Paul II appear to call for a fairly substantial and expensive array of government welfare programs, while *Centesimus Annus* (1991) warns that such bureaucratization of the welfare function both violate the principle of subsidiarity and threaten to undermine the spirit of civic involvement:

Malfunctions and defects in the Social Assistance State [the welfare state] are the result of an inadequate understanding of the tasks proper to the State. Here again *the principle of subsidiarity* must be respected: a community of a higher order should not interfere in the internal life of a community of a lower order, depriving the latter of its functions, but rather should support it in case of need and help to coordinate its activity with the activities of the rest of society, always with a view to the common good.

By intervening directly and depriving society of its responsibility, the Social Assistance State leads to a loss of human energies and an inordinate increase of public agencies, which are dominated more by bureaucratic ways of thinking than by concern for serving their clients, and which are accompanied by an enormous increase in spending. In fact, it would appear that needs are best understood and satisfied by people who are closest to them and who act as neighbors to those in need. It should be added that certain kinds of demands often call for a response which is not simply material but which is capable of perceiving the deeper human need. One thinks of the condition of refugees, immigrants, the elderly, the sick, and all those in circumstances which call for assistance, such as drug abusers: all these people can be helped effectively only by those who offer them genuine fraternal support, in addition to the necessary care.[1]

The Pope's concern is a legitimate one, of course. David Beito studied the fraternal organizations of the late nineteenth and early twentieth centuries and found that they had once provided the services we now associate with the welfare state, and had done so with the kind of individual attention and concern that must forever elude any bureaucracy.[2] A reviewer for the *American Journal of Sociology* agreed with Beito that the welfare state had definitely crowded out mutual aid.[3]

THE WELFARE STATE AND THE FAMILY

Along these lines, Wilhelm Röpke once told a revealing anecdote: "A short time ago, a member of the House of Commons movingly described her father's plight in order to prove how inadequate the welfare state still is. But this is no proof of the urgency of public help; it is merely an alarming sign of the disappearance of natural feelings in the welfare state. In fact, the lady in question received the only proper answer when another member of Parliament told her that she should be ashamed if her father was not adequately looked after by his own daughter."[4]

The welfare state also amounts to a direct assault on the extended family. Present-day conservatives place great emphasis on the nuclear family, but it is the extended family, consisting of grandparents, aunts, uncles, and cousins, that is far more capable of providing a whole variety of useful and desirable functions and of lending health and vitality to the whole. An extended family whose members live within a reasonable distance from one another is able to provide child care, provide for members temporarily out of work, take care of the sick, and engage in a variety of other tasks that are today routinely transferred to the state. It can also do things that no state could ever do: transmit the family's history, cultural inheritance, and traditional beliefs.

If the state (at any level) takes on these tasks, though, it effectively subsidizes the breakup and dispersal of these extended family units. If the state is prepared to provide the services that until now had to be provided primarily by members of the family (or by neighbors that people had known for years), then it is much easier for one of its nuclear families to take that job in Spokane. Should times get tough, the state will always subsidize their child care, unemployment insurance, health care, and so on. The extended family is, in large part, almost the only community left in America, and it is scarcely to be believed that some Catholics, in the name of "social justice," would want to subsidize its breakup. But that is precisely what the welfare state does, trite blandishments to the contrary notwithstanding.

The intergenerational consequences of the welfare state, particularly Social Security, have been especially unfortunate. Traditionally, older people had relied for their well-being on their own savings as well as on the assistance of their grown children. Social Security has undercut the importance of saving and, more importantly, severed this critical bond between parents and children. One can hardly improve upon one writer's recent description of the consequences:

A life of isolation from children and grandchildren, an "independence" that many of them would cheerfully trade for closeness to the people whom they nurtured throughout their lives. Instead they subsist on e-mails, semi-annual visits, some Hallmark cards, a Web-ordered floral bouquet on Grandparents' Day — even as their descendants grow up with little or no exposure to their elders' wisdom and cultural memory. My own nephews and nieces know little of their grandfather's history, have absorbed almost nothing of his worldview, heard few of his tales, his recollections of the Great Depression and his service in occupied Germany — much less of our family's origins in the Adriatic islands long ruled by Venice. I do not think that my clan is exceptional in its rootlessness; in fact, we are all too typical. The chain of memory that has traditionally linked the generations has been stretched almost to snapping, with the hearty encouragement of a government policy that reduces elders to a second adolescence — an over-funded independence, shorn of responsibilities or community.[5]

For reasons such as these, Hans-Hermann Hoppe has emphasized the importance for conservatives to adopt a radically antistatist stand:

In conjunction with the even older compulsory system of public education, these institutions and practices [of the welfare state] amount to a massive attack on the institution of the family and personal responsibility. By relieving individuals of the obligation to provide for their own income, health, safety, old age, and children's education, the range and temporal horizon of private provision is reduced, and the value of marriage, family, children, and kinship relations is lowered. Irresponsibility, shortsightedness, negligence, illness and even destructionism (bads) are promoted, and responsibility, farsightedness, diligence, health and conservatism (goods) are punished. The compulsory old age insurance system in particular, by which retirees (the old) are subsidized from taxes imposed on current income earners (the young), has systematically weakened the natural intergenerational bond between parents, grandparents, and children. The old need no longer rely on the assistance of their children if they have made no provision for their own old age; and the young (with typically less accumulated wealth) must support the old (with typically more accumulated wealth) rather than the other way around, as is typical within families. Consequently, not only do people want to have fewer children—and indeed, birthrates have fallen in half since the onset of modern social security (welfare) policies—but also the respect which the young traditionally accorded to their elders is diminished, and all indicators of family disintegration and malfunctioning, such as rates of divorce, illegitimacy, child abuse, parent abuse, spouse abuse, single parenting, singledom, alternative lifestyles, and abortion, have increased.[6]

Sweden is frequently cited as a model welfare state, prosperous yet boasting an overwhelming array of social-welfare programs. We shall return in a moment to the question of just how prosperous Sweden really is; let us limit ourselves for now to the social consequences of Swedish policy. The roots of the Swedish welfare state can be found in several relatively early legislative acts. First, coming in the 1840s, was a mandatory school attendance law, justified as a measure to increase the welfare of the people. The deeper dynamic at work, explains a scholar of the Swedish system, was "the socialization of children's time, through the assumptions that state functionaries—the Swedish kingdom's bureaucrats—knew better than parents how children's time should be spent, and that parents could not be expected or trusted to protect their children from exploitation." The same kind of thinking was evident in the 1912 law that banned child labor in factories and to some extent on farms as well. Finally, a system of old-age insurance, introduced at about the same time, had the effect of reducing the traditional dependence of older people on their children. Now the state would take care of them.[7]

Today, such measures seem so noncontroversial to many people that their inevitable effects are simply not considered. But the net result of these policies was that children were now less of an economic asset to their parents but equally as much of an economic liability as they had been previously. "The natural economy of the household," writes Allan Carlson, "and the value that children had brought their parents—be it as workers in the family enterprise or as an 'insurance policy' for old age—was stripped away."[8] Hence "society" enjoyed the financial benefits of children, but only their parents had to bear the economic burdens.

The result, says Carlson, was a population crisis in Sweden, as the logic of the welfare state worked its way throughout society. Under these conditions, it can scarcely come as a surprise that dramatically fewer children were born. Sweden, in fact, by the early decades of the twentieth century, faced a demographic crisis, with the lowest birthrate in Europe by 1935.

Gunnar and Alva Myrdal, two of the most influential social scientists of the twentieth century, acknowledged that the Swedish demographic catastrophe was indeed the result of welfare-state policies that socialized the economic benefits of children but imposed on parents the entire costs of raising them. Young couples were thereby given strong incentive not to have children, and fewer and fewer did. The Myrdals concluded from this that Sweden had two choices: either repeal the welfare-state policies that had created the demographic problem in the first place (a solution they described as "not even worthy of being discussed"), or press on to the total welfare state, in which the government (via the taxpayers, of course) would provide children with clothing, housing, health insurance, day care, summer camps, free breakfasts and lunches, and a great many other things. As avowed socialists, the Myrdals considered the choice an easy one.

The author of a book-length study of the Swedish welfare state describes the fairly predictable consequences:

> With the family stripped, by state fiat, of all productive functions, of all insurance and welfare functions, and of most consumption functions, it should cause little surprise that ever fewer Swedes chose to live in families. The marriage rate fell to a record low among modern nations, while the proportion of adults living alone soared. In central Stockholm, for example, fully two-thirds of the population lived in single-person households by the mid-1980s. With the costs and benefits of children fully socialized, and with the natural economic gains from marriage intentionally eliminated by law, the bearing of children was also severed from marriage: by 1990, well over half of Swedish births were outside of marriage.[9]

There, in all its devastating effect, is the welfare state, taken to its logical conclusion.

The example of Sweden helps to put into perspective some relatively recent recommendations for the future direction of the welfare state in America. For instance, in a 1991 book, economist Sylvia Ann Hewlett pointed out that in the modern world, "not only are children 'worthless' to their parents, they involve major expenditures of money. . . . In return for such expenditures, 'a child is expected to provide love, smiles, and emotional satisfaction,' but no money or labor."

> Which brings us to a critical American dilemma. We expect parents to expend extraordinary amounts of money and energy on raising their children, when it is society at large that reaps the material rewards. The costs are private; the benefits are increasingly public. . . . In the modern age, relying on irrational parental attachment to underwrite the child-rearing enterprise is a risky, foolhardy, and cruel business. It is time we learned to share the costs and burdens of raising our children. It is time we take some collective responsibility for the next generation.

And with this logic, and the legislative agenda Hewlett accordingly promotes, it is the Myrdals all over again.

POVERTY

The welfare state is typically justified with reference to poverty in America. But by any conceivable standard, the "poor" in America enjoy a standard of living that people in previous ages (and indeed elsewhere in the world today) could scarcely have imagined. Some 41 percent of our "poor" own their own homes, with another 75 percent owning automobiles and VCRs and two-thirds having air conditioning and microwave ovens. Virtually all own telephones, refrigerators, and television sets, all of which were once considered luxuries. The *average poor person in America* has more living space and is more likely to own a car and a dishwasher than the *average European*. Recalling that we live in a society in which among the poor obesity is a greater problem than malnourishment further helps to put the alleged poverty problem in the U.S. into perspective.[10]

It is almost charming to find people on the left who still seriously propose increased spending and a federal commitment to job training as the solution to "poverty" without so much as hinting at the $5.4 trillion dollars spent on various federal, state, and local welfare programs since 1965 or the scores of federal job training programs that currently exist for welfare recipients.[11]

And no wonder they would rather make placards demanding job training than actually discuss the programs that already exist: federal job training has been one of the most notoriously wasteful government boondoggles of the past thirty-five years. Consider the Job Corps, a well-known vocational training program for the unemployed that began in 1965. Early on, studies found that those who completed the program had no better success in the job market than so-called "no shows" (people who had been accepted into the Job Corps but who had never shown up), despite the fact that the program cost about the same as providing a Harvard education for every participant. Worse still, throughout the program's first decade two-thirds of participants never even finished.[12] Let me repeat that: two-thirds of these people *did not even bother to complete a free job-training program.* Is it a hate crime to suggest that perhaps we have happened upon one of the reasons they have had such difficulty finding work?

We might also recall the Boston Compact, a much smaller-scale program in the early 1990s by which private employers guaranteed a job to anyone who graduated from high school. The dropout rate actually *rose* after the Compact was announced.[13] Such examples could be multiplied ad infinitum.

In many cases, perfectly respectable jobs that require only the most basic skills are easily available, but applicants lack even these. Unless agitators for "economic human rights" are prepared to argue that the poor are complete imbeciles who cannot even be expected to learn basic math, these unsuccessful job seekers can hardly be held blameless for their situation. According to Myron Magnet, the "higher skills" that a steel mill near Chicago recently needed to fill jobs for which it could not find qualified applicants "amounted to little more than being able to divide 100 by four and, going one step further, to understand the concept of 75%." Moreover, it generally takes "only basic math for a worker to handle the statistical process control that is one of the key recent technological advances in manufacturing." He continues:

> One didn't think of secretarial skills as being particularly elevated until recently, when corporations in big cities found that increasing numbers of applicants lacked them. Now anxious companies pay their employees bounties for bringing in qualified applicants for secretarial jobs. Anyone who wants her children . . . to escape poverty needs only to make sure they learn basic literacy, computer typing, and polite, businesslike demeanor in high school.[14]

Surely these minimal requirements cannot be too much to ask.[15] But to demand anything of the poor calls forth the wrath of the hard left, whose "welfare rights" philosophy requires them to believe that for doing nothing at all they are *entitled* to food, clothing, a home, an education, comprehensive health care, and who knows what else. Still, sensible people probably do not consider marriage and a high school education to be insuperable hurdles or a society that demands them akin to Nazi Germany.

Of course, the incentives that exist within welfare policy have in fact served to *dis*courage marriage. By providing government assistance to unwed mothers, these programs have subsidized the problem of out-of-wedlock births by making single motherhood more financially viable (even if still very difficult) for young mothers. The income of a man becomes commensurately less important. Such policies, while superficially generous and kind, by encouraging destructive behavior and setting people on the road to dependency and despair, have ruined countless lives.

More important are the social consequences of these programs, since they undermined the stigma that had historically been attached to single motherhood. Doubtless some find the idea of a "stigma" against single motherhood undesirable or even repellent, but society has to have some way to discourage lifestyle decisions that are easy to make but have terrible consequences, both for the mother and her children. Not only are such women much more likely to be poor, but studies have also consistently found children in single-parent households to be far more likely to have behavioral problems, suffer from mental illness, perform poorly in school, exhibit criminal behavior, and commit suicide. They are also much more likely to wind up on welfare themselves later in life.[16]

The state's decision to assume the role of the absent father, as well as its erosion of the stigma, have contributed significantly to the breakdown of the family and to social dysfunction. "Until fairly recently," writes welfare scholar James Payne, "girls who got 'in trouble' were whispered about—and expelled from school. Seeing this social disapproval, other girls made a great effort to avoid pregnancy. Today programs like free day care for student mothers make unwed teen pregnancy seem almost normal—not 'trouble' at all, but a viable option intentionally chosen by girls in certain subcultures."[17]

The results should have surprised no one: from 1960 to 1990, out-of-wedlock births increased from 5 percent to 28 percent overall, and from 23 percent to 65.2 percent among blacks. Incentives really do matter. Policy analyst Michael Tanner observes that "by removing the economic consequences of out-of-wedlock births, welfare has removed a major incentive to avoid them. A teenager looking around at her friends and neighbors is likely to see several who have given birth out of wedlock. When she sees that they have suffered few visible consequences (the very real consequences of such behavior are often not immediately apparent) she is less inclined to modify her own behavior to prevent pregnancy."[18]

There are always those who, despite the overwhelmingly destructive effects of the Great Society welfare state,[19] will nevertheless come up with nothing more creative than more of the same. Perhaps the solution, they argue, is a still greater welfare state, or still more government intervention. Such observers like to point to Sweden, supposedly an example of a prosperous country that nevertheless provides a systematic package of "benefits" from the cradle to the grave.

In fact, though, a major study released in May 2002 by the Swedish Institute of Trade (HUI) decisively punctured the myth of welfare-state "prosperity" in Sweden: by the end of the 1990s, Sweden's median income was $26,800, compared to $39,400 in the United States. More to the point, the HUI economists specifically pointed out: "Black people, who have the lowest income in the United States, now have a higher standard of living than an ordinary Swedish household."[20]

Further solidifying the moral and practical superiority of free markets and less government, and nicely complementing the HUI study in Sweden, is the work of Professor Robert Lawson. Professor Lawson recently demonstrated graphically that even if we accept the Rawlsian premise that the just society is the one in which the condition of the least well-off is maximized, we still have to favor the free market, since the condition of the poorest is consistently far higher in market societies than in heavily interventionist ones with heavy wealth redistribution.[21] Recent Catholic social thought has spoken of a "preferential option for the poor," whereby this or that policy or approach is to be evaluated in terms of its effects on the poorest. As Professor Lawson has abundantly demonstrated, the market *is* the preferential option for the poor.

The fact that a few people own yachts is not a cause of the condition of the poor. But it is not difficult to find things that do worsen the condition of the poor. For one thing, consistently burdening the private sector with allegedly worker-friendly regulations—including such seemingly harmless requirements as minimum-wage legislation, "employer contributions" to the employee's Social Security, mandated leave, and the like—naturally makes it more expensive and less desirable to hire people in the first place, and therefore creates more unemployment. This is one reason that some companies have simply left the United States altogether, all too happy to leave yelping economic "activists" behind. Taxation, particularly on capital, means lower productivity, less production and wealth, and a lower standard of living. For its part, the Federal Reserve system has consistently and drastically undermined the value of the currency we use, a fact that is likely to be felt more acutely by those with less money.

The suffocating effects of federal regulation also reduce our standard of living. The 1994 *Code of Federal Regulations*, which lists all federal regulations currently in effect, was composed of some 201 books, taking up an incredible 26 feet of shelf space. Its index alone numbered 754 pages.[22] This makes business more costly and all of us less wealthy; some businesses never get started at all because they cannot survive the regulatory regime that has been fastened upon us. When retired Senator George McGovern attempted to open his own hotel and encountered the regulatory morass that the American business climate had become, he publicly regretted ever having allowed the regulatory apparatus to become so suffocating. (His hotel never opened, needless to say.) Walter Williams wrote an entire book showing how government regulations have (at times deliberately) had disproportionately adverse effects on blacks.[23]

The Social Security system confiscates wealth in exchange for a pitiful return (and indeed very likely for no return at all given the way the program is going). In what way can one suggest even jokingly that such a program does anything but defraud the poor, taking money from them that they need in the present in exchange for some indeterminate but certainly minuscule return in the future? Furthermore, the money taken from them is not invested, as in a real retirement plan, but spent on current expenditures. This massive squandering of savings translates into lower productivity and a lower standard of living for everyone than if the program had not existed.

The perverse incentives of the welfare state have all too frequently enticed the poor, blacks included, away from finding remunerative work and toward a destructive mentality of dependency and entitlement. Given the realities of original sin and the disutility of labor, it is already difficult to persuade people to work and easy to persuade them to enjoy leisure. When economic incentives not to work are added to the mix, the results can be readily predicted. In 1995, the Cato Institute examined the welfare packages (which, recall, are tax free) in all 50 states and the District of Columbia. In 40 states, the study found, welfare paid more than an $8 per hour job; in 17 it paid more than a $10 per hour job; and in 6 states and the District of Columbia it paid more than a $12 per hour job. According to Michael Tanner, "In 9 states welfare pays more than the average first-year salary for a teacher. In 29 states welfare pays more than the average starting salary for a secretary. In 47 states welfare pays more than a janitor makes." In the six most generous states, welfare benefits even constitute more than the entry-level salary for a computer programmer. Such incentives only reinforced the suffocating welfare dependency and sense of entitlement that has wrought such havoc in poor communities.[24]

It is revealing that when the Bureau of the Census asked the unemployed poor in 1990 why they were not working, only 4.1 percent gave as the reason an inability to find work.[25] Likewise, when Harvard economist Richard Freeman surveyed unemployed inner-city black youths in 1980, 70 percent of them told him they could easily find a job. By the end of the enormously prosperous 1980s, the figure had risen to 75 percent. They simply refused to take the relatively low-paying jobs open to them, even though the interpersonal and other skills one learns at such jobs have traditionally been the first step toward prosperity for countless Americans.

The corruption that the bureaucratization of charity brings in its wake hardly needs documenting. In 1988, a midwestern researcher, having gained the confidence of twenty-five women receiving assistance through Aid to Families with Dependent Children (AFDC), found that *all of them* had unreported income. It came from boyfriends, family members, unreported full- or part-time jobs, and the like.[26] Corruption in the Special Supplemental Income (SSI) program is almost beyond belief, with entire clinics having been found specializing in providing phony diagnoses in order to win SSI support for their clients.[27] Meanwhile, a considerable tax burden overwhelms honest working families.

Naturally, the welfare bureaucracy itself prospers as its reach is extended and more and more people are brought into these programs. It measures success by how fast it increases the number of people on the rolls, an attitude no charitable institution relying on voluntary contributions could possibly afford to hold. A social security official in a Midwest field office candidly admitted:

> In the field—I was a supervisor out there for years and years—your staffing, your budget for supplies, and your awards money for the employees was based on work units. Now, work units were assigned based on the number of claims you took. So we would sit around and figure out how we could get more people on the SSI rolls, because it would benefit us. The more applications we took, the more work units, the bigger the staff: we could build up an empire.[28]

Just keeping track of all the federal government's programs is an undertaking in itself. Several years ago, Heritage Foundation researchers, looking exclusively at employment and job training programs, came up with nine of them, whose combined price tag was $5.3 billion. But a year later, a more thorough examination by the General Accounting Office found "about" 163 programs, costing $20 billion.[29] *There* is an accounting irregularity: even the government's own budget office was not certain that it had counted all the job training programs to which the taxpayers' money is allocated.

Ultimately, however, it is not these accounting irregularities, or the drags on productivity, or even the enormous sums of money poured into failed programs—important as all these factors are—that constitute the fundamental Catholic critique of the welfare state. The real problems are cultural, social, and moral. The welfare state has not only encouraged perverse and destructive behavior, but it has also led to an idolatrous devotion to the central state, with its implied promise of a simple and costless political solution to every social ill. Hilaire Belloc described such an outcome as the "servile state," in which a spiritless population is cared for, from the cradle to the grave, by a state apparatus to which it gives its highest allegiance. Over and against such false promises, we should turn once again to the families, churches, and local institutions that we have allowed to atrophy under the domination of the central government, and which constitute what Edmund Burke aptly called the "little platoons" of civilization.

NOTES

1. John Paul II, *Centesimus Annus* 48. Emphasis in original.

2. David T. Beito, *From Mutual Aid to the Welfare State: Fraternal Societies and Social Services, 1890–1967* (Chapel Hill: University of North Carolina Press, 2000).

3. Charlotta Stern, review of David T. Beito, *From Mutual Aid to the Welfare State*, *American Journal of Sociology* 106 (May 2001): 1834. On this point, see also Charles

Murray, *In Pursuit of Happiness and Good Government* (New York: Simon and Schuster, 1988).

4. J. P. Zmirak, "Honor Thy Fathers," *The American Conservative*, June 16, 2003.

5. Zmirak, "Honor Thy Fathers."

6. Hans-Hermann Hoppe, *Democracy, the God that Failed: The Economics and Politics of Monarchy, Democracy, and Natural Order* (New Brunswick, N.J.: Transaction, 2002), 195–96.

7. Allan Carlson, "What Has Government Done to Our Families?" *Essays in Political Economy*, Ludwig von Mises Institute, November 1991, 2–3.

8. Carlson, "What Has Government Done to Our Families?" 3.

9. Carlson, "What Has Government Done to Our Families?" 3. See also idem, *The Swedish Experiment in Family Politics: The Myrdals and the Interwar Population Crisis* (New Brunswick, N.J.: Transaction, 1990).

10. For a proper perspective on rich and poor in the United States, see W. Michael Cox and Richard Alm, *Myths of Rich & Poor: Why We're Better Off than We Think* (New York: Basic Books, 2000).

11. The $5.4 trillion figure covers only through 1995, and is cited in Michael Tanner, *The End of Welfare: Fighting Poverty in the Civil Society* (Washington, D.C.: Cato Institute, 1996), 69.

12. Allen J. Matusow, *The Unraveling of America: A History of Liberalism in the 1960s* (New York: Harper & Row, 1984), 237–39.

13. Jared Taylor, *Paved with Good Intentions: The Failure of Race Relations in Contemporary America* (New York: Carroll & Graf, 1992), 292.

14. Myron Magnet, *The Dream and the Nightmare: The Sixties' Legacy to the Underclass* (1993; repr., San Francisco: Encounter Books, 2000), 48–49.

15. A mere 3 percent of married couples who have a high school education are poor. Linda J. Waite and Maggie Gallagher, *The Case for Marriage* (New York: Doubleday, 2000), 122. *The Economist* reported in 1988 that an American had a less than 1 percent chance of being poor if he simply completed high school, got (and stayed) married, and held a job, even a minimum-wage job, for at least a year. "Politics Without Economics," *The Economist*, August 6, 1988, 8.

16. For a good summary of the literature on the effects of divorce and/or single parenting on children, see Waite and Gallagher, *The Case for Marriage*, ch. 9.

17. James L. Payne, *Overcoming Welfare* (New York: Basic Books, 1998), 34.

18. Tanner, *The End of Welfare*, 76.

19. The destruction wrought by the welfare state is famously described in Charles Murray, *Losing Ground: American Social Policy 1950–1980* (New York: Basic Books, 1984). Less well known but also excellent is Payne, *Overcoming Welfare*.

20. "Study Discovers Swedes Are Less Well-Off than the Poorest Americans," Reuters, May 5, 2002.

21. Robert A. Lawson, "We're All Rawlsians Now!" *Ideas on Liberty*, June 2002, 49–50.

22. Hoppe, *Democracy*, 62.

23. Walter E. Williams, *The State against Blacks* (New York: McGraw-Hill, 1982).

24. Tanner, *The End of Welfare*, 67–68.
25. Tanner, *The End of Welfare*, 21.
26. Payne, *Overcoming Welfare*, 79.
27. Payne, *Overcoming Welfare*, 80.
28. Payne, *Overcoming Welfare*, 73.
29. Payne, *Overcoming Welfare*, 59.

Chapter 6

Answering the Distributist Critique

Some Catholics who object to the market order belong to a school of thought known as distributism. According to the celebrated Catholic writers G. K. Chesterton and Hilaire Belloc, who popularized the idea in the early twentieth century, that social system is best in which "productive property" is widely dispersed rather than concentrated. They contend that the market order introduces an intolerable level of insecurity and anxiety into the economic life of the ordinary person. They typically favor a variety of measures intended to reverse this situation, including prohibitive taxation of chain stores, department stores, and large distributors, in order to level the playing field for the smaller operation. Plenty of orthodox Catholics agree with both the diagnosis and the remedy, convinced that they are striking a blow for traditional Catholicism and against liberalism and the Enlightenment by supporting distributism and opposing the free market.

There is no reason to doubt for a moment the good will and pure intentions of those who support distributism. For that matter, if someone wishes to live in relative self-sufficiency and to retreat, to a degree, from the division of labor, that is his decision. What this chapter intends to suggest is that the purported advantages of distributism as well as the alleged iniquities of the market have both been greatly exaggerated.

Let us consider Belloc's fundamental claim for distributism. As he sees it, distributism brings freedom:

A family possessed of the means of production—the simplest form of which is the possession of land and of the implements and capital for working the land—cannot be controlled by others. Of course, various producers specialize, and through exchange one with the other they become more or less interdependent, but still, each one can live "on his own": each one can stand out, if

161

necessary, from pressure exercised against him by another. He can say: "If you will not take my surplus as against your surplus I shall be the poorer; but at least I can live."[1]

For Belloc, then, the great advantage of distributism is that it gives the household a significant measure of independence. A new introduction to his *Essay on the Restoration of Property* describes his view of "economic freedom" as something that "comes from the possession of sufficient productive property, such that a man need not depend upon his employer for a wage, but has rather to depend upon himself and *his* land, craft, tools, and trade for his sustenance."[2] Belloc acknowledges in passing that of course anyone selling to others is in some way dependent on those others, thereby conceding that risk and uncertainty are unavoidable aspects of life rather than unique to a system of economic freedom. If the price and quality of his goods do not remain sufficiently competitive, he is surely bound to lose business. However, Belloc points out, the family can nevertheless live on its own, even if buyers refuse to purchase its surplus goods. They can live on what they themselves produce. At heart, then, Belloc's promise of security amounts to the distributist family's ability in the last resort to retreat altogether from the division of labor and live in a condition of self-sufficiency.

Yet the advantages of the division of labor are so clear that relatively few people have found Belloc's proposal attractive enough to attempt to observe it in practice. Practically anyone in the United States today who possesses the requisite knowledge and modest capital can acquire farmland and chase after the kind of self-sufficiency advocated by Belloc. Producing their own necessities and in possession of the means of production, so to speak, such a family would be utterly independent of employers or anyone else. They would probably also enjoy a standard of living so depressed and intolerable as to throw the rationality of the entire enterprise into question. This certain outcome probably accounts for why the overwhelming majority of people choose to take their chances within the division of labor, balancing the risks from which this earthly life is never entirely secure against the unparalleled wealth and comfort they can enjoy by not retreating into semi-autarky.

Even granting the distributist premise that smaller businesses have been swallowed up by larger firms, that it is always preferable for a man to operate his own business rather than to work for another is by no means obvious. It may well be that a man is better able to care for his family precisely if he does not own his own business or work the backbreaking schedule of running his own farm, partially because he is not ruined if the enterprise for which he works should have to close, and partially because he doubtless enjoys more leisure time that he can spend with his family than if he had the cares and responsibilities of his own business. Surely, therefore, we are dealing here with a matter for individual circumstances rather than crude generalization.

The way distributists portray the situation, the wage earners of today are where they are as a result of forces beyond their control: an ineluctable process of wealth concentration brought about by capitalism has deprived them of the possibility of owning "productive property" and avoiding the dependency that the wage relation implies. But the fact is, many people clearly prefer to be wage earners rather than own their own businesses. Belloc and his followers are free to insult such people by calling them "wage slaves"— the distributists' favorite slur—but wage earners have made an entirely rational choice. And it *is* a choice. As Sadowsky observes,

> The fact is that in the nineteenth century, when workers had far less disposable income than their counterparts today, a remarkable number of them became capitalists. It is all too often the *unwillingness* to restrict consumption, a grasshopper attitude, that prevents workers like me from becoming capitalists. In our day we see especially among immigrants from Asia what is, for us, an amazing willingness to defer present consumption. We find these people living initially in conditions that we should judge to be absolutely impossible. Yet before we know it, they are operating successful businesses.[3]

"INSECURITY" AND THE FREE ECONOMY

Pope Pius XI spoke in *Quadragesimo Anno* of "the insecure lot in life in whose uncertainties non-owning workers are cast"; a distributist commentator on *Quadragesimo* referred to the "hand-to-mouth uncertainty" of workers in a capitalist economy.[4] Now to the extent that someone who owns the means of production is able to work for himself and for that reason is not required to work for another, then we have here simply the argument of Thomas Jefferson, who admired the independent farmer for this very reason. But by no means does it follow that by not working for another, one thereby avoids "hand-to-mouth uncertainty." Those who work for wages in fact enjoy a kind of security that is simply not acknowledged at all by distributists—namely, that the worker receives his pay whether or not the goods toward whose production he contributes ever sell. It may be many months or years before they make it to market at all. During all that time, instead of suffering the anxieties and uncertainties of the independent craftsman or shop owner, the worker consistently earns his wage. He need not wait until—if ever—his product is actually sold in order to reap his benefit. While Karl Marx claimed that any differential between capitalist profit and wages paid to labor constituted "surplus value" whereby capital exploited labor, the Austrian economist Eugen von Böhm-Bawerk attributed such differentials to the time factor involved: rather than having to wait, say, the full year that must ordinarily elapse before the product on which he has worked is sold, the laborer can be paid immediately. Since present goods are preferred ceteris paribus to future goods, the capitalist is entitled to his profit since he compensates his workers in the present for the production of goods that will be sold only in the future. The worker, on the other hand, prefers a lesser amount in the present to the greater amount he could have received in the future had he been willing to wait that long. He is clearly benefited by the wage relation.[5]

To be sure, the worker does labor under the very real uncertainty that he may lose his job. But this is inevitable due to technological improvements, changing tastes, new methods of production, and the like. The advent of the automobile meant that carriage manufacturers would have to shift into some other line of production. The introduction of fax machines and electronic mail must have cut into the business of couriers and package delivery. The net result of these changes is greater abundance and a higher standard of living, as fewer resources are now necessary to accomplish our ends, thereby freeing up resources for the production of goods that prior to these technological advances we could not have enjoyed.

What would the distributists have us do about these benign phenomena? Shall we establish a board of economic commissars to dictate which improvements will be permitted and which not? No one has a "right" to a particular job. Put another way, no one has a right to demand that society continue to compensate him for performing a task they no longer require, whether he is a wage earner or a shop owner. An economy based on the division of labor does not tolerate such a self-centered, antisocial attitude. Instead, it encourages us to satisfy the needs of our fellows.

Moreover, it is profoundly misleading to suggest that the "uncertainty" or "insecurity" of the modern worker is a uniquely reprehensible aspect of modern society, rather than an inevitable aspect of life that has been with us since the beginning of time. Were peasants in preindustrial France—who were among the freest, most independent peasantry in Europe—free of "hand-to-mouth uncertainty"? (Try telling that to a fourteenth-century mother who has just lost her fourth child before his first birthday, lives one bad harvest away from starvation, and resides in nearly intolerable squalor.) As late as the eighteenth century, travelers consistently spoke of the appalling conditions of the French peasantry and the shockingly dilapidated state of rural housing. The same held true for many who sought employment in a trade. A Norman parish priest described the situation in 1774:

> Day laborers, workmen, journeymen and all those whose occupation does not provide for much more than food and clothing are the ones who make beggars.

As young men they work, and when by their work they have got themselves decent clothing and something to pay their wedding costs, they marry, raise a first child, have much trouble in raising two, and if a third comes along their work is no longer enough for food, and the expense. At such a time they do not hesitate to take up the beggar's staff and take to the road.[6]

Taking up the beggar's staff and taking to the road: that is what was left to them. To say that the free market led to the destruction of some previously existing, harmonious community life is simply to defy historical testimony. How could "community" exist when people were starving and forced to take to the road for sustenance? In what way is the alleged "independence" of farmers and craftsmen in evidence here? These appalling conditions applied at times to as much as one third of the French population—some eight million people.[7]

What sets apart the condition of laborers in market economies is precisely that they do *not* live in a condition of "hand-to-mouth" uncertainty. To be sure, terrible misfortunes can befall people, but this is true whether they are ordinary laborers or independent shopkeepers (the distributist ideal), whether medieval, early modern, or present day. The difference is that in a prosperous society like that of the United States, such tragedies essentially never mean utter destitution or starvation. The fantastic wealth made possible by the division of labor, by which we all enjoy the benefits of each person's specialization in that line of work that suits him best, makes such tragedies far less likely. It is not in free societies but in centrally planned economies where the most recent famines have occurred. As of this printing, North Korea still cannot feed itself, while South Korea continues to enjoy prosperity. The situation in North Korea helps to remind us of the kinds of conditions that were a single bad harvest away in previous centuries. That, and not the prosperity of the South and of market economies in general, is real hand-to-mouth uncertainty.

In light of this point, it is difficult to see how Belloc can be excused from this comment: "[I]t is a necessary inference that there will be under capitalism a conscious, direct, and planned *exploitation* of the majority (the free citizens who do not own) by the minority who are owners. . . . If you left men completely free under a capitalist system, there would be so heavy a mortality from starvation as would dry up the sources of labor in a very short time."[8] This is something like the opposite of what has actually happened in practice, and what could have been expected to happen based on economic theory. If businessmen really are as greedy as Belloc believes they are, wouldn't their greed lead them to produce food for profit? Wouldn't they have a ready market for so necessary a commodity?

Nevertheless, Belloc argues that "the twin evils of Insecurity and Insufficiency" are inevitably associated with capitalism. "The main body of citizens, the Proletariat, are not sufficiently clothed, housed and fed, and even their insufficient supply is unstable. They live in a perpetual anxiety."[9] As we shall see, this was not even true at the height of the Industrial Revolution, let alone in the early twentieth century when Belloc was writing. Perhaps the benefits of industrialization were not as apparent in Belloc's day as they are now. But the overall material level of the vast bulk of the population was certainly higher than it had ever been before.

Faced with this point, distributists frequently make the rhetorically effective argument that there is more to life than material possessions, and that economic relations should be such that man is enabled to enjoy and cultivate higher tastes and virtues. This is a straw man, of course, since hardly anyone arguing in favor of the market suggests that material possessions are ends in themselves or bring the highest kind of fulfillment. Furthermore, it is precisely the wealth that market mechanisms create and the leisure that the market makes possible that make the enjoyment of higher things practicable in the first place. A man living at the level of bare subsistence is not likely to be able to cultivate an interest in opera, or Renaissance painting, or nineteenth-century literature.

Partisans of the market are often portrayed as morally stunted for their emphasis on economic efficiency, an emphasis that supposedly fails to reckon with other values whose importance is said to be greater than that of mere efficiency. But the point is, the more efficient we are in producing the goods we need, the more leisure we can enjoy to pursue the very "higher things" that economists allegedly leave out of account. The more capital-intensive our economy the greater the productivity of labor, the greater the output, the greater our overall wealth, and the less time we need to work in order to earn the money necessary to purchase the goods we need. (I am speaking here of the normal workings of a genuinely free market economy, not the mixed economy we have today, where this happy outcome is relentlessly undermined by countless forms of government intervention.) Greater leisure and greater wealth are precisely what make it possible for people to spend more time doing the things in life that really matter. A man forced to work 80 or more hours per week because, as in the early Industrial Revolution, his labor is so unproductive that 80 hours of labor is necessary for his sheer survival, cannot even dream of such things. The real friends of the "higher things" in life, therefore, are the supporters of the market, whose favored system makes those things readily available to more people than anyone centuries ago would have thought possible.

The net result of all of the obstacles to prosperity inherent in distributism *must* be a far poorer society. At times, distributists even concede this point. One writer acknowledged that one of the reasons it would be especially difficult to "restore the small craftsman" was that "in many cases mass methods produce not somewhat cheaper but enormously cheaper than individual methods."[10] Is there not a kind of security in being able to acquire the necessities of life cheaply? It is doubtful that many families today would be comforted by the chimerical "security" of distributism when they find out that everything they now need would cost, say, two, three, or four times as much as before.

Now Belloc and his followers are free to argue that relative impoverishment is a small price to pay for economic "independence." But they have no right to accuse anyone of moral perversity for remaining unconvinced. Yes, there is "insecurity" in a free society, in that no one has a right to demand that his fellow men continue to pay him for performing a task they have indicated they no longer require. This is a feature of any economic system—unless we guarantee every business owner a share of the market regardless of his abilities, courtesy toward the customer, and responsiveness to the needs of society. At the same time, the "insecurity" of the free society is more than compensated for by the unique security enjoyed by members of such a society vis-à-vis members of a distributist society, in the form of fantastic, unheard-of levels of wealth and the benefits of the large-scale social cooperation of the division of labor. An eleventh-century serf may have enjoyed a great deal of job security, but few envy him his position.

Every one of the agricultural revolutions through which the Western world has passed since the ninth century has involved the introduction of new farming implements, methods, or fertilizers whose net result has been that fewer people are needed to produce the same amount of agricultural output. Naturally, these advances meant the displacement of some people, as the economy adjusted to new circumstances. Would Belloc have permitted any of these agricultural revolutions to occur? After all, they led to a great deal of what Belloc calls insecurity. But they also made possible the sheer survival of far more people, now that food could be more readily produced. The same is true of any innovation that increases the productivity of agricultural labor: it makes possible a considerable increase in population. Can this consideration be weighed against Belloc's desire for stability? We are not told.

Moreover, it is not clear what precisely is so "secure" about deliberately spurning the material benefits of the division of labor, which are not inconsiderable, in favor of the kind of self-sufficiency that Belloc describes. As Belloc and other distributists have said, the self-sufficient man, while certainly benefiting from specialization and exchange with others, can if necessary rely on himself alone for the things he needs. That is certainly true, but that would make Robinson Crusoe one of the most secure men who ever lived, since he was in no danger (until Friday came along, that is) of being lured into the temptations of the division of labor and thereby finding himself in a state of interdependence with his fellows.

The man who relinquishes so many of the benefits of the division of labor, moreover, invites a level of insecurity with which the so-called "wage slave" of capitalism need never be confronted. What does Belloc's isolated farmer do during a drought? By the time normal channels of trade are hastily reopened, it may be too late. What consolation will such a family be afforded by reassuring themselves at such a time that at least they are not "wage slaves"? Who in the present United States suffers from such fears?

Belloc claims to support private property, of course, since his aim is to diffuse "productive property" as broadly as possible throughout society, but his claim rings hollow, since his entire system rests on consistent, sustained aggression against private property, involving punitive taxation and restrictions on the use of property. It rests on coercion and threats of violence and imprisonment, and could not function without them. People who have contributed absolutely nothing to the creation or acquisition of a man's property somehow arrogate to themselves the right to dispose of it, or to dictate to him the terms on which he is permitted to use it. It is taken for granted that the consequences of original sin are such that the wealthy man cannot be permitted the full enjoyment of his property, but it is rarely if ever acknowledged that the same effects of original sin are at work in the man whose job it is to confiscate property on behalf of the state. At least some check exists against a wealthy manufacturer: he will be able to maintain his wealth only to the extent that he makes prudent investments and continues to satisfy the needs of his fellow man. This is what Mises meant when he said that ownership of the means of production "is not a privilege, but a social liability":

> Capitalists and landowners are compelled to employ their property for the best possible satisfaction of the consumers. If they are slow and inept in the performance of their duties, they are penalized by losses. If they do not learn the lesson and do not reform their conduct of affairs, they lose their wealth. No investment is safe forever. He who does not use his property in serving the consumers in the most efficient way is doomed to failure. There is no room left for people who would like to enjoy their fortunes in idleness and thoughtlessness. The proprietor must aim to invest his funds in such a way that principal and yield are at least not impaired.[11]

What more salutary check against arbitrariness could exist than that? The state, on the other hand, since it never has to pass any such market test, is insulated from the consequences of arbitrariness. In fact, the worse a government agency performs, the higher its budget tends to be the following year. This is one reason so many of us are loath to entrust our well being to such an institution.

There is also something of a contradiction involved in using the state to bring about independence. If state privilege alone is what keeps a man in business, then it is only in a very strained sense of the word that we may call him independent. He is utterly dependent on the continuing good will of the state authorities. "The outward appearance of economic independence may be retained," Mises once said, "but in fact the beneficiary of government support turns more and more into a ward of the administration. He is no longer a self-reliant citizen, but depends on the disposition of government officers and politicians. His discretion is restricted and finally entirely nullified by a bureaucratic apparatus."[12]

THE INDUSTRIAL REVOLUTION

Suppose, moreover, that distributism had been in effect as the Industrial Revolution was developing in Britain in the late eighteenth century. We would have heard ceaseless laments regarding the increasing concentration of economic power and the dramatic growth in the number of people working for wages. What we probably would not have heard about was the actual condition of those people who were seeking employment in the factories, or the rise in living standards for a rapidly growing population—a phenomenon never before seen.

What follows will come as a surprise to some, since the standard view of the Industrial Revolution among the general public and shared by prominent distributists (including Belloc himself) is that it led to the widespread impoverishment of people who had hitherto been enjoying lives of joy and abundance. For at least the past several decades, however, alternative interpretations of this critical period have grown so abundant that even Western civilization textbooks, always the last to adapt to new trends in scholarly thinking, have been forced to concede the existence of what is referred to as the "standard of living debate" surrounding the Industrial Revolution. In a major 1985 study, economist Nicholas F. R. Crafts estimated that real income per capita doubled in England between 1760 and 1860.[13] The economic historian R. M. Hartwell devoted much of his career to this debate, and by 1970 he could proclaim, "Is the controversy over? As regards the standard of living—the bundle of goods—it should be, and, indeed, appears to be. Even E. P. Thompson, the most convinced pessimist, now agrees that 'no serious scholar is willing to argue that everything got worse.'"[14]

[N]one of the suggested immiseration models fit the facts of history. On the contrary, the historical facts were: average per capita real income increased . . .

after 1815 prices fell more than money wages; per capita consumption of food
and other consumer goods increased. . . . To these facts should be added evidence about population. Population was rising rapidly after 1780, the result almost certainly of a rising birth rate and, more important, of a falling death rate,
the consequence not of improved medicine but of environmental and nutritional
improvements. As living standards rose with industrialization parents had more
children and more survived.[15]

Naturally, for reasons discussed in chapter 2, the conditions of the workers in
eighteenth- and nineteenth-century England were unspeakably poor compared to the conditions of workers today (whose improved living standards
are themselves the logical result of the capital accumulation that occurs in a
free market). The point is that prior to the Industrial Revolution, conditions
had been considerably worse. For the first time, it appeared that greater and
greater numbers of people would be able not only to survive but also to enjoy a rising standard of living.[16]

Already in the 1940s and 1950s, Hayek and Mises were among those who
advanced this newer view of the Industrial Revolution. One of the reasons
that so many falsehoods and fallacies had come to surround our understanding of the Industrial Revolution, according to Hayek, was that the historians
who had studied the matter had been blinded by their own ideological preconceptions. Many of them were Marxists, who believed as part of their creed
that industrialization simply *had* to have made the workers miserable. As
Hayek puts it: "[B]ecause the theoretical preconceptions which guided them
postulated that the rise of capitalism must have been detrimental to the working classes, it is not surprising that they found what they were looking for."
In short, they had not approached the evidence in the spirit of impartial rationality that befits a scholar, but rather with the ideological ax to grind that
characterizes the propagandist.[17]

Economist and philosopher Leopold Kohr was far from alone among intellectuals suspicious of capitalism when he suggested in his book *The Breakdown of Nations* (1957) that the tremendous rise in reform movements and
social criticism in the wake of the Industrial Revolution must have been an
indication of worsening conditions. "[A]n increase in reform movements,"
wrote Kohr, "is a sign of worsening, not of improving, conditions. If social
reformers were rare in former ages, it could only have been so because these
were better off than ours."[18]

But according to Hayek, this is not necessarily so; in fact, the exact opposite is more likely the case. The very fact that we hear complaints in the late
eighteenth and early nineteenth centuries about the appalling conditions in
which many people lived and worked is, ironically enough, actually a point
in the Industrial Revolution's favor. Prior to the Industrial Revolution, *every-*

one fully expected to live in abject poverty and, what is more, they fully expected a similar fate for their descendants. The astonishing wealth that the Industrial Revolution made possible now made people impatient with any remaining pockets of poverty. Before the Industrial Revolution, no one would have been especially outraged at the notion that the vast majority of people would spend their lives at an appallingly low material level—this was simply assumed to be an unavoidable fact of life. Charity could partially alleviate the worst suffering, and the Church constantly exhorted the wealthy to lend their assistance to the poor. Still, even with such palliative measures, the wealthy were far too few and the poor far too numerous for most of the population to have much hope of living at a level that we would today consider tolerable. Thus, as Hayek notes, we see in the eighteenth century "an increasing awareness of facts which before had passed unnoticed." He goes on:

> The very increase of wealth and well-being which had been achieved raised standards and aspirations. What for ages had seemed a natural and inevitable situation, or even as an improvement upon the past, came to be regarded as incongruous with the opportunities which the new age appeared to offer. Economic suffering both became more conspicuous and seemed less justified, because general wealth was increasing faster than ever before.[19]

Hayek points out that the "actual history of the connection between capitalism and the rise of the proletariat is almost the opposite of that which these theories of the expropriation of the masses suggest."[20] In Hayek's view, capitalism created the proletariat not in the Marxist sense that it took an already existing segment of the population and reduced it to poverty, but in the sense that the new opportunities for work that it created meant that many, many more people could now survive. "The proletariat which capitalism can be said to have 'created' was thus not a proportion which would have existed without it and which it had degraded to a lower level; it was an additional population which was enabled to grow up by the new opportunities for employment which capitalism provided."[21] Before the Industrial Revolution, anyone who had not been lucky enough to be able to make a profitable living in agriculture, and who had not been provided by his family with the tools necessary to enter an independent trade and operate one of the small shops that delight the distributist, found himself in dire straits indeed. What the Industrial Revolution made possible, then, was for these people, who had nothing else to offer to the market, *to be able to sell their labor to capitalists in exchange for a wage.* That is why they were able to survive at all. Capitalism, and not distributism, literally saved these people from utter destitution, and made possible the enormous growth in population, in life expectancy, health, and living standards more generally that England experienced at the time and which later spread to western Europe at large. The Industrial Revolution therefore made possible a population explosion that could not have been sustained under the stagnating conditions of the preindustrial age.

Any suggestion that the situation before the Industrial Revolution was prosperous and satisfactory flies in the face of reality. Mises relates the standard tale:

> The peasants were happy. So also were the industrial workers under the domestic system. They worked in their own cottages and enjoyed a certain economic independence since they owned a garden plot and their tools. But then "the Industrial Revolution fell like a war or a plague" on these people. The factory system reduced the free worker to virtual slavery; it lowered his standard of living to the level of bare subsistence; in cramming women and children into the mills it destroyed family life and sapped the very foundations of society, morality, and public health.[22]

In fact, conditions prior to the Industrial Revolution were catastrophically poor. The economy on the eve of the Revolution was hopelessly static, and possessed no outlet whatever for the increasingly sizable number of people for whom a living in agriculture or domestic manufacture was impossible. Professor Hartwell makes quick work of the mythology surrounding an allegedly idyllic preindustrial society:

> Thus much misunderstanding has arisen because of assumptions—mainly misconceptions—about England before the industrial revolution; assumptions, for example, that rural life was naturally better than town life, *that working for oneself was better and more secure than working for an employer*, that child and female labor was something new, that the domestic system (even though it often involved a house crammed with industrial equipment) was preferable to the factory system, that slums and food adulteration were peculiar products of industrialization, and so on; in other words, the perennial myth of the golden age, the belief that since conditions were bad, and since one did not approve of them, they could not have been worse, and, indeed, must once have been better! But, as Alfred Marshall pointed out, "Popular history under-rates the hardships of the people before the age of factories."[23]

The fact is, such views as Hartwell identifies among opponents of industrialism are nothing but myth. Rural life was no better than urban life, as eyewitness testimony amply reveals. Conditions were described by contemporaries as "a violation of all decency" and "altogether filthy and disgusting." As many as twelve people were in a single room. A modern scholar of the situation speaks of "depravity which the towns could scarcely have rivaled."[24] Insecurity was as prevalent in the eighteenth century as in the nineteenth. And the domestic system and agriculture both relied heavily on the labor of women and children.[25]

As Mises argues, the very fact that people took factory jobs in the first place indicates that these jobs, however distasteful to us, represented the best opportunity they had. (This is an illustration of Murray Rothbard's concept of "demonstrated preference," according to which an individual's preferences, when expressed in voluntary action, provide the only absolutely reliable indicator that he has substituted what he believes will be a more satisfactory state of affairs for a less satisfactory one.) "The factory owners," he writes, "did not have the power to compel anybody to take a factory job. They could only hire people who were ready to work for the wages offered to them. Low as these wage rates were, they were nonetheless much more than these paupers could earn in any other field open to them. It is a distortion of facts to say that the factories carried off the housewives from the nurseries and the kitchens and the children from their play. These women had nothing to cook with and to feed their children. These children were destitute and starving. Their only refuge was the factory. It saved them, in the strict sense of the term, from death by starvation."[26] Distributism, in such a context, would have spelled certain doom for the proletariat it claims to defend.

Another central point is that industrial capitalism is dedicated to mass production. "The processing trades of earlier ages," Mises explains, "had almost exclusively catered to the wants of the well-to-do. Their expansion was limited by the amount of luxuries the wealthier strata of the population could afford."[27] Factory production, on the other hand, was geared toward the mass production of inexpensive goods for the common man. This represents an extraordinary step forward in *everyone's* standard of living. And it is this principle on which the entire capitalist system is based:

> The outstanding fact about the Industrial Revolution is that it opened an age of mass production for the needs of the masses. The wage earners are no longer people toiling merely for other people's well-being. They themselves are the main consumers of the products the factories turn out. Big business depends on mass consumption. There is, in present-day America, not a single branch of big business that would not cater to the needs of the masses. The very principle of capitalist entrepreneurship is to provide for the common man. . . . There is in the market economy no other means of acquiring and preserving wealth than by supplying the masses in the best and cheapest way with all the goods they ask for.[28]

T. S. Ashton observed that the central problem of the first half of the nineteenth century involved "how to feed and clothe and employ generations of children outnumbering by far those of any earlier time." England, of course, was not alone in facing it. "Ireland was faced by the same problem. Failing to solve it, she lost in the forties about a fifth of her people by emigration or starvation and disease." Ashton's point is that such a terrible outcome would certainly have befallen England as well had there been no Industrial Revolution and the distributist ideal of small farmers and shops had remained as before:

> If England had remained a nation of cultivators and craftsmen, she could hardly have escaped the same fate, and, at best, the weight of a growing population must have pressed down the spring of her spirit. She was delivered, not by her rulers, but by those who, seeking no doubt their own narrow ends, had the wit and resource to devise new instruments of production and new methods of administering industry. There are today on the plains of India and China men and women, plague-ridden and hungry, living lives little better, to outward appearance, than those of the cattle that toil with them by day and share their places of sleep at night. Such Asiatic standards, and such unmechanized horrors, are the lot of those who increase their numbers without passing through an industrial revolution.[29]

Thanks to industrial society, few of us live in fear of dying of the countless diseases since tamed by medical science. We enjoy sanitary conditions, personal comforts, and opportunities for education that the greatest kings of Europe could scarcely have imagined. Half of our children do not die by age five. People are free to consider these things trivial or unimpressive if they wish, but the judgment of mankind appears to run in the other direction.

ECONOMIC CONCENTRATION

The distributist argument contends, as did Marx, that economic concentration occurs systematically and inevitably under a capitalist system, and that over time fewer and fewer firms come to monopolize more and more of the economy.[30] It also alleges that there is no logical limit to the concentration of wealth under capitalism. Such claims, however, are considerably exaggerated.

In *Man, Economy and State*, his classic treatise on economics, Rothbard suggested that Mises' insights into the socialist calculation problem could shed light upon constraints to *the size of the firm*.[31] Recall our discussion of higher-order and lower-order stages of production. A fifth-order capital good is a good that is five stages of production away from a consumer good; it is therefore of a higher order than, say, a third-order capital good, which is only three stages away from a consumer good. Now imagine a vertically integrated firm—that is, a firm that produces at more than one stage of production—that produces a fifth-order capital good, then uses that fifth-order capital good in the production of a fourth-order capital good, which it in turn uses in the production of a third-order capital good, which it then sells. As long as external markets exist in the production of the fifth- and fourth-order capital goods—that is to say, as long as this firm is not the *only* producer of these goods—the firm can engage in profit-and-loss calculation.

Rothbard provides the following example. Imagine an economy in which the going rate of interest is 5 percent. Suppose a firm spends $100 on factors of production at the fifth stage and $15 on factors at the fourth stage, and sells the resulting third-order good for $140. An attractive profit is evidently being made here, but the question arises as to which stage is yielding this profit (if in fact the profit is concentrated at a particular stage or stages).

With a functioning external market at the fourth stage, the firm can estimate an implicit price for the fourth-order good. Suppose that fourth-order good sells on the market for $103. This is the firm's implicit price for that good, since this is what it could have earned on the market if it had sold the fourth-order good. Add to that $103 the $15 spent on original factors at the fourth stage, and the total is $118.

At this point, the firm can calculate its profits at each stage of the production process. At the fifth stage, $100 in factors yielded a product implicitly priced at $103—for a profit of three percent. At the fourth stage, $118 in factors yielded a third-order good that sold for $140—a profit of 29 percent. Far from enjoying general profitability, then, it is now obvious that the vast bulk of the firm's profits come from the later–fourth–stage of the production process. In fact, when we recall that the going rate of interest is 5 percent, the firm actually suffered a 2 percent entrepreneurial loss on its production at the earlier stage, and a 24 percent profit at the later stage. This valuable information aids the firm in its allocation of resources in the future. It will almost certainly shift resources away from the fifth stage and toward the fourth stage, and may even abandon its production of the higher-order good altogether, simply purchasing it on the market instead.

But suppose that our vertically integrated firm is so dominant that it is the only producer of the fourth-order capital good. Without an external market generating an implicit price for that good, economic calculation for this firm, with regard to the fourth-order good, becomes impossible. It faces, on a much smaller scale of course, the same difficulty faced by the socialist planning board described in chapter 1. In the case of this vertically integrated firm, there is no rational way of allocating resources among the various stages of production, or pinpointing the source of its profitability (or otherwise).

Since such an arrangement inevitably produces all the misallocation and inefficiency we would expect from a firm unable to calculate profit and loss, market forces will tend to discourage it from occurring in the first place. As Rothbard explains,

> Since the free market always tends to establish the most efficient and profitable type of production (whether for type of good, method of production, allocation of factors, or size of firm), we must conclude that complete vertical integration for a capital-good product can never be established on the free market (above the primitive level). *For every capital good, there must be a definite market in which firms buy and sell that good.* It is obvious that this economic law *sets a definite maximum to the relative size of any particular firm on the free market.*[32]

Even if distributists were to concede the existence of Rothbard's limits to the size of the firm, they would be unmoved in their broader argument about the success in a capitalist system of larger stores at the expense of smaller ones. The process whereby larger stores are alleged to win market share at the expense of smaller stores is that of "predatory pricing." In this familiar scenario, the larger store sells below cost in order to drive out its competitors, and then recoups its losses by raising its prices once its rivals have folded. Not surprisingly, Belloc himself dutifully echoed this widely held notion: "The larger institution can undersell the smaller one at a loss, until the smaller one is imperiled or killed."[33]

There has developed over the years a considerable literature on predatory pricing as a monopolizing device, very little of which has been favorable to the theory. Economist George Stigler has gone so far as to declare, "Today it would be embarrassing to encounter this argument in professional discourse."[34] One problem with the "predatory pricing" scenario is that it is next to impossible to find an actual example. To be sure, there is no shortage of examples of large stores offering low prices, but the windfall that is supposed to occur when they allegedly raise prices again once they have the field to themselves seems to be the stuff of myth.

As Thomas DiLorenzo has shown, this has been true ever since the passage of the Sherman Antitrust Act in 1890, which was allegedly intended to prevent "anticompetitive practices" and protect consumers from "predatory" firms and strategies. In an important article in the *International Review of Law and Economics*, DiLorenzo showed that the industries most frequently accused at that time of holding a "monopolistic" position were not in fact behaving in conformity with standard neoclassical models of monopoly.[35] A monopolistic firm, goes the standard definition, is economically benefited by restricting output and raising prices. But these industries were doing neither. During the 1880s, when gross domestic product rose 24 percent in real terms, output in the allegedly monopolized industries for which data was available rose 175 percent in real terms.[36]

At the same time, prices in these industries were generally falling — considerably faster than the 7 percent decline in the price level observable in the economy as a whole. Thus, for example, the average price of steel rails fell from $68 to $32 between 1880 and 1890 (a 58 percent decline), zinc from $5.51 to $4.40 per pound (20 percent), and refined sugar from 9¢ to 7¢ per pound (22 percent).[37] Lester Telser confirmed DiLorenzo's findings in a book of his own. Successful firms achieved their position by serving the consumer, not by exploiting him. "The oil trust did not charge high prices because it had 90 percent of the market," Telser wrote. "It got 90 percent of the refined oil market by charging low prices."[38]

One of the classic studies of predatory pricing is John W. McGee's 1958 journal article on Standard Oil, in which he decisively refuted the standard charges that John D. Rockefeller had engaged in the practice. Rockefeller acquired his position, McGee showed, by means of mergers and acquisitions, voluntarily entered into by his opponents. Anticipating the objection that these opponents were browbeaten into accepting poor offers from Rockefeller, McGee points out that "Standard's usual practice during this time was to employ the managers and owners of the firms they absorbed, and often to make them shareholders as well." Had they been treated poorly, of course, they would not have been particularly desirable employees: "Victimized ex-rivals might be expected to make poor employees and dissident or unwilling shareholders."[39] There are also a number of cases of people who made excellent livings establishing refinery concerns and selling them to Rockefeller.[40] The result of Rockefeller's work was a dramatic decrease in prices to consumers. "Before 1870, only the rich could afford whale oil and candles," one historian observes. "The rest had to go to bed early to save money. By the 1870s, with the drop in the price of kerosene, middle and working class people all over the nation could afford the one cent an hour that it cost to light their homes at night."[41] Prices continued to decline during the next two decades of Standard's dominance.[42]

Although dissolved by antitrust prosecution in 1911, Standard Oil, as even a New Left historian concedes, had from 1899 on "entered a progressive decline in its control over the oil industry, a decline accelerated, but certainly not initiated, by the dissolution." Contrary to what distributist preconceptions would lead us to expect, competition grew dramatically in the following two decades. Consider:

In 1899 there were sixty-seven petroleum refiners in the United States, only one of whom was of any consequence. Over the next decade the number increased steadily to 147 refiners. Until 1900 the only significant competitor to Standard was the Pure Oil Company, formed in 1895 by Pennsylvania producers with $10 million capital. It concentrated on the heavy lubricants field and grew despite Standard attacks, and after 1900 spread into other important phases of refining. By 1906 it was challenging Standard's control over pipe lines by constructing its own. And in 1901 Associated Oil of California was formed with $40 million capital stock, in 1902 the Texas Company was formed with $30 million capital, and in 1907 Gulf Oil was established with $60 million capital. In 1911 the total investment of the Texas Company, Gulf Oil, Tide Water-Associated Oil, Union Oil of California, and Pure Oil was $221 million. From 1911 to 1926 the investment of the Texas Company grew 572 percent, Gulf Oil 1,022 percent, Tide Water-Associated 205 percent, Union Oil 159 percent and Pure Oil 1,534 percent. In 1926 all of the Standard companies combined represented only 60 percent of the industry's investment.[43]

Standard's decline, historian Gabriel Kolko explains, was "primarily of its own doing—the responsibility of its conservative management and lack of initiative."[44] Thus even Standard Oil must remain innovative and dynamic or lose market share.

George Reisman's lengthy discussion of the predatory-pricing doctrine in his magisterial treatise on the market economy treats the theoretical reasons as to why predatory pricing is both extraordinarily difficult as well as positively irrational. Belloc claims that the "larger unit of capital can afford to lose on its wares for a longer time than the smaller unit. If both the larger and the smaller unit are producing a particular product at a pound, both in competition sell it at fifteen shillings, each will be losing five shillings on every sale."[45] This analysis, while superficially plausible, is certainly mistaken. For one thing, a large firm attempting predatory pricing *must endure losses commensurate with its size*. That is to say, a firm holding 90 percent of the market competing with a firm holding 10 percent of the market makes losses *on its 90 percent market share*, while his smaller competitor makes losses only on its 10 percent share. As Reisman writes, "It is difficult to see the advantage constituted by nine times the wealth and nine times the business if money is lost at a rate that is nine times as great." This is, indeed, hardly a sane long-term strategy.[46] A scholar writing in the *Journal of Political Economy* concurs:

> Price wars are far more expensive than is often realized. For one thing, it takes quite a long time to drive a rival from the field. The smaller firms may simply close down and wait and then reopen when the larger firm, in the expectation of recovering its losses, raises its prices. Even if the large firm succeeds in driving one set of owners into bankruptcy, the capacity does not thereby disappear from the area. The small company may now reopen under new management with

plant bought at knock-down prices and capable, as a consequence, of marketing a product at very low cost. Only when the small plant is worn out or becomes obsolete, a matter of years, is it out of the picture, and only then is the large firm in a position to raise its prices to recoup its losses. After that the prolonged period over which prices must be kept high in order that the large business can entirely recover its losses may simply invite new entrants or new expansion and start the whole period of unprofitably low prices over again.[47]

There is also a chain-store variant of the predatory pricing argument. Opponents of chain stores seem to believe that by virtue both of their size and of the resources at their disposal, these stores will nearly always win out in direct competition with smaller stores. They possess enormous resources, and they can draw on the profits they earn in other markets to sustain them while they suffer losses in a particular new market in their efforts to drive out their competitors there.

As superficially plausible as this scenario may appear, the reasoning employed here is, on further examination, once again incorrect. First, all the difficulties associated with any kind of predatory pricing scheme apply here as well. But let us consider the specifics of the case of the chain store. Take the hypothetical case of MegaMart, a nationwide chain of grocery stores.[48] Suppose MegaMart has a thousand stores around the country, and $1 billion of total capital invested, for an average of $1 million per store. Distributists appear to believe that MegaMart can bring to bear its entire fortune in order to drive competitors out of a new market into which it seeks to expand. In fact, however, it would be an example of ludicrously poor business strategy and economic judgment for MegaMart to do so.

Suppose, for the sake of argument, that in the face of all the theoretical and empirical evidence to the contrary, we nevertheless conceded the possibility that MegaMart could in fact drive all its competitors from the field in a given market and keep them out forever simply through the implicit threat of crushing any new competitor who should emerge on the scene. MegaMart would indeed enjoy abnormally high profits in that market should it be successful, and the prospect of those premium profits could well entice the company into making the effort. But as Professor Reisman observes, "Such a premium profit is surely quite limited—perhaps an additional $100,000 per year, perhaps even an additional $500,000 per year, but certainly nothing remotely approaching the profit that would be required to justify the commitment of [the firm's] total financial resources."[49]

Let us suppose that the premium profit that could be reaped by MegaMart after removing all its competitors fell in the middle of those two figures: $300,000 per year. Let us assume also that the average rate of profit in the economy is 10 percent. That means that MegaMart can afford to lose $3 million in order to seize this market for itself. Three million dollars is the capitalized value of $300,000 per year. If MegaMart devoted any more than $3 million to the acquisition of this market, it would be a bad investment. They would earn a lower than average return on their capital—that is, they would earn less than 10 percent on this investment. Despite their billion dollars of capital, even MegaMart would find it absurd and self-destructive to devote anything above $3 million to the capture of this market, since they would earn a better return investing their money elsewhere in the economy. If they spent $9 million to capture this market, they would earn a profit of only 3.33 percent, instead of the going rate of 10 percent. It would make no economic sense.

A very important consequence follows from this. As Professor Reisman explains,

> everyone contemplating an investment in the grocery business who has an additional $5 million or even just $1 million to put up is on as good a footing as [MegaMart] in attempting to achieve such [premium] profits. For it simply does not pay to invest additional capital beyond these sums. In other words, the predatory-pricing game, if it actually could be played in these circumstances, would be open to a fairly substantial number of players—not just the extremely large, very rich firms, but everyone who had an additional capital available equal to the limited capitalized value of the "monopoly gains" that might be derived from an individual location.[50]

In some cases, of course, the larger firm can undersell the smaller on the basis of advantages it enjoys in terms of economies of scale and other benefits that can accrue to a firm on the basis of its size. This is not necessarily to be deplored; there clearly *are* advantages that accrue to everyone from business concentration. "In the precapitalistic ages," Mises writes, "the difference between rich and poor was the difference between traveling in a coach and four and traveling, sometimes without shoes, on foot. Today in the industrialized parts of the U.S. the difference between rich and poor is the difference between a late model Cadillac and a second-hand Chevrolet. It is difficult to see how this result could have been achieved without bigness in business."[51]

In this case, however, it is not the larger firm with which the distributist has a just dispute, but with the consumers who freely purchase the firm's goods. It is only the consumers' buying or abstention from buying that determines the composition of a given industry. Apart from consumers' freely demonstrated preferences, made explicit through their voluntary purchases in the market, there is no nonarbitrary way of determining the proper size of a store or the infrastructure of a particular industry, or indeed how many stores or firms there should be. It is ultimately the consumers, who wish to acquire the things they need at least sacrifice to themselves and their families, and not the large store per se, whom distributists should logically condemn.

And the consumers do not always prefer the large firm or the chain store: surely I am not alone in my willingness to drive 30 miles if necessary to avoid a Pizza Hut. I rarely have to, though, since independent pizzerias are practically everywhere. There are always plenty of opportunities for astute small-scale entrepreneurs to carve out niches for themselves. In early 2003, McDonald's reported its first-ever quarterly loss (for the last quarter of 2002). Consumers simply did not want its fatty food as much as they used to. The person who opened up a deli or a health food store in correct anticipation of consumer demand prospered, while McDonald's, the giant among giants, posted a loss. This is what Mises meant by consumer sovereignty.

Moreover, if it were true that capitalism tended naturally toward a greater and greater concentration of wealth in the hands of ever fewer firms, we should expect to see a tendency toward fewer and fewer sellers during the period of American history when capitalist activity was least restricted, and a tendency toward more and more competition during the period since, when capitalist activity has been most regulated. Unfortunately for the distributists' allegation, the very opposite is true. Gabriel Kolko's famous study of economic conditions in the late nineteenth and early twentieth centuries finds that the economy was extraordinarily competitive in the sense that quite a number of competitors could be found in virtually every industry, and it was often difficult for the top firms to maintain their dominant positions. This was essentially the case across the board, spanning industries as diverse as iron, steel, oil, automobiles, agricultural machinery, copper, meat packing, and telephone services. It was only after voluntary efforts—pools, secret agreements, mergers, etc.—had failed to stabilize this highly competitive environment that some firms began to look to the federal government and its regulatory apparatus as a way to reduce competition coercively. "Ironically, contrary to the consensus of historians," Kolko concludes, "it was not the existence of monopoly that caused the federal government to intervene in the economy, but the lack of it."[52]

The irony of the distributists' desire to use state coercion to bring about what they consider a more desirable dispersion of property is that it is precisely state coercion that has contributed to some of the advantages that larger firms enjoy. In an enormously influential journal article, Nobel Prize-winning economist George Stigler contended that "as a rule, regulation is acquired by the industry and is designed and operated primarily for its benefit." He defended the hypothesis that "every industry or occupation that has enough political power to utilize the state will seek to control entry. In addition, the regulatory policy will often be so fashioned as to retard the rate of growth of new firms."[53] Thus the regulatory apparatus tends to favor established firms at the expense of upstarts.

BRING BACK THE GUILDS?

It is in the context of established firms using the force of law to suppress competition that we should consider another proposal frequently heard among distributists: restoring the medieval craft guilds, which are sometimes cited as a morally superior alternative to the free market. These guilds operated as follows. Each occupation had its own guild, to which all employers and employees in that occupation belonged. The guild regulated minimum prices, wages, hours of operation, and product quality. In this way, one shop was prevented from underselling another. Cooperation rather than competition was the rule, and the result was occupational stability: there was a niche for everyone in a given line of work.[54]

The guild system possesses a superficial plausibility, which gives it what attractiveness it may have. But let us consider how a guild system *must* work in practice. The logic of the guild is such that certain people who wish to enter a particular trade are denied entry. If a particular guild should happen to have a relatively liberal policy of admitting new producers to its craft, it will certainly insist on a minimum price at which all producers will be allowed to sell the good in question, and/or will limit the amount of the good that any given master will be permitted to produce. Whatever the case, the outcome is the same: higher prices and less production than if free entry into the profession, a free price system, and unrestricted production had been allowed.

Aspects of the guild system have existed in our economy in the past and some continue through the present. Their consequences have been less than desirable, to say the least. Perhaps the most obvious example, which lasted only two years, is the National Recovery Administration, established by the New Deal's National Industrial Recovery Act in 1933. President Franklin Roosevelt believed that business competition had to be restricted in order to tame the alleged problem of "overproduction" and to spread among as many firms as possible what consumer demand existed.

There is no need here to attempt to explain FDR's economic reasoning, if such an explanation is even possible. Speaking of the president's acquaintance with economics, biographer John T. Flynn noted that "it is entirely possible that no one knew less about that subject than Roosevelt."[55] Ignorance was indeed bliss for FDR, who seems to have held that no so-called economic law was any match for his iron will. (Thus H. L. Mencken's "Constitution for the New Deal," which appeared in the June 1937 issue of the *American Mer-*

cury, gave the president the power to "repeal or amend, in his discretion, any so-called natural law, including Gresham's law, the law of diminishing returns, and the law of gravitation.")

What is important is that his egregious errors in economic reasoning would have terrible consequences. The president's faulty grasp of what had caused the Depression led him to introduce a system whose operation was quite similar to the old guild structure, with the explicit intention of reducing competition.

Under the NRA, each industry was invited to establish a production code, which would set minimum wages, minimum prices, and a variety of other regulations to be observed by the firms in that industry. (A system not entirely dissimilar had been established in Mussolini's Italy.) Note that the code established *minimum* prices. All sellers would have to sell their products for *at least* the prescribed minimum. This meant a dramatic reduction in the intensity of economic competition, since with an established minimum price in effect it was not really possible to undersell one's competitors.

New York Times editorial writer Henry Hazlitt had no illusions about the NRA:

> [T]he American consumer is to become the victim of a series of trades and industries which, in the name of "fair competition," will be in effect monopolies, consisting of units that agree not to make too serious an effort to undersell each other; restricting production, fixing prices—doing everything, in fact, that monopolies are formed to do. . . . Instead of a relatively flexible system with some power of adjustment to fluid world economic conditions we shall have an inadjustable structure constantly attempting—at the cost of stagnant business and employment—to resist these conditions.[56]

This description actually sounds rather like what the admirers of the guilds consider the *ideal* economic arrangement. It gave the force of law to producers' collusion with regard to minimum prices and wages, hours of operation, amount of output, and still other factors. This way, there would be less competition among producers. This is nothing other than the guild system in modern form.

But it was a complete disaster, both logically and in practice. First, although such a system would indeed raise prices, such an outcome obviously defeated the program's other aim of increasing wages, since a rise in prices must reduce the real value of wages (that is, what those wages can buy). Second, in practice the program produced such an outcry among sensible people that the U.S. Senate finally managed to force FDR into appointing a commission to investigate the NRA. Its report, issued in 1934, described the agency as "harmful, monopolistic, oppressive, grotesque, invasive, fictitious, ghastly, anomalous, preposterous, irresponsible, savage, wolfish."[57] The act establishing it was declared unconstitutional the following year.

So much for the NRA. But a great deal of the guild mentality remains in the U.S. economy, and can be seen in the behavior of such organizations as the American Medical Association, the American Bar Association, and others. Very often, such bodies lobby the government to institute stiff requirements in order to acquire a license to practice, and to place obstacles in the path of anyone else who might want to provide medical, legal, or other services. Nobel Laureate Milton Friedman suggests what is often really at work in such agitation:

> The *justification* offered is always the same: to protect the consumer. However, the *reason* is demonstrated by observing who lobbies at the state legislature for the imposition or strengthening of licensure. The lobbyists are invariably representatives of the occupation in question rather than of the customers. True enough, plumbers presumably know better than anyone else what their customers need to be protected against. However, it is hard to regard altruistic concern for their customers as the primary motive behind their determined efforts to get legal power to decide who may be a plumber.[58]

Consider, first, the American Medical Association, which operates in a manner very similar to that of the medieval guilds.[59] AMA activity serves to reduce the number of people who can practice medicine, and thereby increases the cost of medical treatment beyond what it would be in a competitive market. According to Clark Havighurst, Duke University Professor of Law, "Professional licensure laws have long made the provision of most personal health services the exclusive province of physicians. Obviously, such regulation limits consumers' options by forcing them to use highly trained, expensive personnel when other types might serve quite well."[60]

Consider Friedman's description of the guild's operations:

> One effect of restricting entry into occupations through licensure is to create new disciplines: in medicine, osteopathy and chiropractic are examples. Each of these, in turn, has resorted to licensure to try to restrict its numbers. The AMA has engaged in extensive litigation charging chiropractors and osteopaths with the unlicensed practice of medicine, in an attempt to restrict them to as narrow an area as possible. Chiropractors and osteopaths in turn charge other practitioners with the unlicensed practice of chiropractic and osteopathy.[61]

Doubtless most members of the AMA believe that such requirements work to the consumer's benefit by protecting him from substandard medical care, but this only shows the extent to which interest groups subconsciously conflate their own interests with those of society as a whole. Mancur Olson cautions people to "note that the [medical] examinations are almost always imposed only on entrants. If the limits [on entry into the field] were mainly motivated by the interest of patients, older physicians would also be required to pass periodic qualifying examinations to demonstrate that they have kept their medical knowledge up to date."[62]

The fact is, studies find that nonphysician providers of medical care, such as midwives, nurses, and chiropractors, "can perform many health and medical services traditionally performed by physicians—with comparable health outcomes, lower costs, and high patient satisfaction."[63]

Government regulations on the chiropractic profession, lay midwifery, and on the freedom of nurse practitioners to offer services within their competence, all of which make perfect sense from the point of view of the medical guild that lobbied for them, make no sense at all from the point of view of consumer wishes (as repeatedly expressed in polling data) or from economic considerations. In many cases, such people can provide health services far more cheaply than can licensed physicians (or, in the case of chiropractors, can provide services that licensed physicians do not provide at all), but consumers are prevented from making their own decisions regarding their medical care. Given the logic of the guild structure, no one has the right to be surprised to find that the AMA has put so much effort into undermining its professional opposition.[64]

Private certification boards, providing certification to physicians who met certain standards, would of course be welcome and extremely likely in a society without state-imposed licensing requirements. Lacking a coercive element, such boards would be limited to providing information to consumers of health care services and would be unable to use their position to transform the entire profession into a guild or cartel able to crush all competition. As George Reisman suggests:

> [T]he members of the various state medical licensing boards around the country could constitute themselves into private certification agencies and give or withhold their seal of approval to individual medical practitioners on any basis they wished. They would simply lack the power to make the absence of their particular seal of approval the basis of fining or imprisoning anyone who chose to practice medicine without it. The consumers of medical care, who presently retain the right to judge the qualifications of the state governors and legislators who are responsible for the appointment of the members of the medical licensing boards, would decide for themselves the value of certification by this or that organization. . . . Indeed, if ordinary men and women are to be allowed to vote in elections in which their votes ultimately determine the most complex matters of foreign and domestic policy, and thus where their decisions affect not only their own lives and those of their immediate families but also the lives of everyone else in

the country, then surely they are entitled to the responsibility of determining matters pertaining exclusively to their own well-being.[65]

Reisman further observes that if government regulations allowed only automobiles less than five years old on the roads, there would certainly be an overall increase in the quality of automobiles on the roads. But a great many perfectly serviceable automobiles would thereby become unavailable for use at all. The main victims of such alleged largesse would be, as usual, the poor.[66]

The legal profession in the United States is also akin to a guild—or, what is the same thing, a cartel. Everyone knows that legal services are expensive, but few realize that the barriers to entry erected by what is in effect a lawyers' guild bear much of the responsibility. Thanks to the lobbying of bar associations, the only people who may enter the legal profession are those who possess a license from the state, which is available only to those able to afford the extraordinarily costly path of law school and the bar exam. The outcome is the desired one: fewer lawyers, and therefore higher fees.[67]

As with the medical profession, where costs could be dramatically reduced by allowing medical personnel below the rank of physician to perform routine work, paralegals are more than capable of performing a variety of legal tasks, but the guild reserves them for lawyers only. That means people wind up paying more—a lot more—for basic legal services. In 1987, the chairman of the Legal Services Corporation, W. Clark Durant, made an extraordinary address to the American Bar Association in which he suggested that his agency be abolished and that all barriers to competition in the market be removed. One day later, the president of the ABA was calling for Durant's resignation.[68]

One paralegal in Portland, Oregon, decided that enough was enough. Robin Smith, who worked for several years in a large law office, had grown tired of lawyers charging exorbitant fees that their clients could barely afford, all for work that she herself had done. She opened her own business, People's Paralegal, Inc., where she and her colleagues offered basic legal services, such as the drafting of common legal documents, at lower prices.

Not surprisingly, however, the guild went into action. People's Paralegal found itself on the receiving end of a lawsuit by—who else?—the Oregon State Bar, accusing the firm of violating Oregon's prohibition on the "unauthorized practice of law." (Thanks to bar association lobbying, every state but Arizona has such a law.) People's Paralegal was shut down, and even ordered to pay the legal fees incurred by the Oregon State Bar when litigating them out of business.[69] This is the ineluctable outcome of the guild mentality. A privileged few reap abnormally high salaries while the vast majority are made poorer by higher fees—and if anyone should attempt to give consumers an alternative to this kind of exploitation, the guild springs into action to quash the challenge. An entire society organized along these lines is scarcely conceivable, but that is what the guild system amounts to, romantic illusions notwithstanding.

Lesser examples abound. During the 1990s, 15-year-old Monique Landers of Kansas opened her own African hair-braiding business. Upon returning from a visit to New York, where she was honored as one of five outstanding high school entrepreneurs, she was informed that the state licensing board of Kansas was shutting her down. Not because of customer complaints, but because of the guild mentality of already existing establishments, which typically use mandatory licensure by the state as a way of limiting competition. She was told that she could stay in business if she spent a year at a licensed cosmetology school, but few of them taught the particular skill she already possessed, and none of them would admit her prior to her seventeenth birthday. "The Board won't let me earn my own money, and won't let kids like me learn to take care of ourselves," she said. "I think owning your own business is a way of being free."[70]

Landers' case is absolutely typical. In *The State against Blacks*, Walter Williams provides a lengthy catalog of occupational licensure laws and other barriers whose effect is to place overwhelming obstacles in front of those who wish to enter an industry.[71] The New York taxicab industry is the classic example. To operate a taxi in New York City, a potential driver needs a medallion from the city. In a free market, such a medallion would cost precisely nothing. But in the market as rigged in favor of the taxi guild, these medallions cost in the hundreds of thousands of dollars. It is impossible to measure how many jobs are destroyed by this kind of behavior, or how much higher taxi fares are for hapless city residents. But again, this restrictionist policy is precisely the kind of antisocial behavior that the infrastructure and indeed the very logic of the guild encourage.

Agriculture provides perhaps the most disgraceful example of what the guild mentality amounts to in reality. (Although proponents of the guild systems do not generally have farmers' guilds in mind, my point is to show where the logic of the guild system, in whatever section of the economy, must inevitably lead.) The federal government's assistance to farmers has often amounted to encouraging them to destroy (or not plant in the first place) huge stocks of crops, in order to increase their selling prices. This, in effect, is what a guild would do, though the guild would more likely keep supplies down and prices up by allowing fewer people entry into the guild in the first place, and/or requiring existing guild members to adhere to a production quota.

The costs and consequences of such an antisocial policy are staggering, and are all the more insidious because, as usual, the beneficiaries of these policies are clear and visible, while the victims are dispersed and largely unaware that an organized cabal is taking advantage of them. Here again we see the importance of Hazlitt's lesson: the need to be aware of the long-term consequences for all groups, rather than the short-term gains of one group, that a given policy must produce. How many Americans realize that the price they have to pay for sugar—and, for that matter, all foods containing sugar as an ingredient—is much higher than necessary as a result of a government program? Indeed, for most of the twentieth century the price of sugar to Americans was 500 percent higher than the world price, thanks to government price supports.[72] This is certainly a boon to sugar producers, who receive an average of $235,000 a year from the policy. But it costs consumers well over $3 billion per year, and it puts all American industries that use sugar at a competitive disadvantage vis-à-vis foreign producers who are not forced to pay such an inflated price for sugar.[73] This latter point is always overlooked by opponents of free trade, who in their zeal to protect jobs in Industry X from foreign competition neglect altogether the destructive effects that their preferential policy for Industry X has for Industries A, B, and C that use X as an input in the production of their own products. Job losses in those industries, though, will hardly ever be attributed to the tariff or other privilege shown to Industry X. Meanwhile, the government can point with pride to the jobs it has "saved." What is seen and what is not seen indeed.

Since 1937, as much as 40 percent of all oranges grown annually in the U.S. have, by law, been destroyed, fed to livestock, or exported in order to raise domestic prices. Quotas on peanuts—which, again, have exactly the effect on peanut production that a guild restricting entry into the field would have—effectively double the price of peanuts and peanut butter. Dairy subsidies are more outrageous still, with every dairy cow in America subsidized to the tune of $700 per year—"an amount greater than the income of half the world's population," Professor Eric Schansberg points out.[74] All this inefficiency and destruction of wealth impoverishes society as a whole, and hurts the neediest the most. We will never know the full cost of these policies, since many of their costs include jobs never created and businesses never started. Let us be serious: is this really how we would like *our entire economy* to be run?

All of these examples of genuine exploitation amount to one of many reasons that free-market economists hold the beliefs that they do. The greater the scope of state activity, the greater the potential for each pressure group to use the state apparatus for its own enrichment, at the expense of the rest of society. As the Public Choice school of economics teaches, since the benefits that accrue to such pressure groups from their political agitation are sizable and concentrated while their costs are dispersed and hidden, the tendency over time is for more and more of this kind of activity to go on at the expense of the ordinary person. Even if someone does make the connection between the higher prices he has to pay for peanuts and the government's restrictionist peanut policy, the amount of his individual loss is low enough that he has next to no incentive to devote himself to lobbying for its repeal. The relatively few beneficiaries, on the other hand, since they benefit so handsomely, have every reason to devote energy and resources to the maintenance of the policy. Bastiat called all this looting "legal plunder," and who can blame him?

Since guilds operate to restrict competition and price cutting, and since guilds are run by people not exempt from the consequences of original sin, we must expect that the monopoly power of the guilds will have consequences analogous to those of the government favoritism I have just described. Through a variety of methods, the federal government has granted special privileges to certain industries. In one way or another, these privileges dramatically limit competition—just what the guild system is supposed to do. No one has a right to expect that their effects would be any different if implemented by guilds.

No wonder the scholastic doctors, in those rare instances when they mentioned the guilds at all, chided them for their monopolistic behavior. "I do not find evidence in their treatises that they favored the guild system," writes de Roover, "which is so often pictured as an ideal organization for Christian society or is recommended as a panacea against the evils of modern industrialism."[75]

DISTRIBUTISM AND SUBSIDIARITY

Confronted with the problems and dangers associated with government control, some distributists will protest that they, too, oppose statism, and that their vision of Catholic social teaching takes into account the great principle of subsidiarity. As Pius XI put it in his frequently cited definition, "Just as it is gravely wrong to take from individuals what they can accomplish by their own initiative and industry and give it to the community, so also it is an injustice and at the same time a grave evil and disturbance of right order to assign to a greater and higher association what lesser and subordinate organizations can do. For every social activity ought of its very nature to furnish help to the members of the body social, and never destroy and absorb them."[76] Following Pius XI, they insist that they have no intention of strengthening a federal government that is, they agree, already far too powerful.

But despite distributists' protestations to the contrary, a massive dose of statism would be necessary both to inaugurate and to maintain the distributist utopia. As Joseph Zoric argues, a distributist social order "would be a giant leap backwards in many respects—and who would be willing to pay the cost? Precisely nobody, which is why the whole vision falls apart when one considers its fatal yet hidden flaw: only one institution in society has the absolute power to make it happen: the government."[77] In his *Essay on the Restoration of Property*, Belloc made clear that the power of government would have to be harnessed on behalf of distributism, in the form of punitive taxation against large concerns and other such coercive measures.

Zoric asks the distributists some tough questions:

> Who does the limiting in the distributist economy? If I have a bakery and my business includes the baking of bread, doughnuts, and wedding cakes, would I be allowed to expand my bakery to include cherry tarts and apple turnovers? Or would this expansion be looked upon by the distributionist police as an unfair advantage over the bakery across town whose owners don't have my vision of the growing market in tarts and turnovers? Would Michael Dell be limited to selling computers to his college dormmates at the University of Texas rather than to the entire nation (and the world)? It is nothing more or less than a thorough and ongoing socialist state that could limit my bakery's search for more markets or Michael Dell's quest to create the biggest computer company in the world. You may call it whatever name you want but the socialist state would most certainly be the result.[78]

Moreover, the limitations seem arbitrary. Should we have mom-and-pop potato chip makers? Mom-and-pop automobile manufacturers? Mom-and-pop airlines? And if not, why not? Who shall decide? Who would trust a government agency to make such decisions?

But this is just what distributists propose. A distributist tract from the mid-twentieth century raised concerns about the department store, which deals in a number of different categories of goods. Such a store "must be handicapped by taxation which should begin after a few categories and become prohibitive before it deals with many." This particular distributist recommended a licensing system "to prevent illegal expansion"—precisely what Professor Zoric proposed in jest. The license "would be granted as a matter of right to every applicant at a nominal cost, but this cost would rise very steeply as the number of licenses applied for by one man increased."[79]

The very logic of the distributist position makes any attachment to subsidiarity, however sincerely held, almost certainly unstable and short lived. Suppose Community A should wish to put distributism into practice, and gives special tax breaks to small and medium-sized businesses, while imposing punitive taxation on larger businesses. We shall leave aside the arbitrary nature of such designations, a problem made still worse by the fact that property holdings that constitute a "large" business in one industry may amount to a small business in another, given the greater capitalization that its product requires. We shall assume that all such disputes would be solved by government officials in a completely impartial manner and that no bribery or political manipulation would take place.

Suppose further that people eventually begin to make certain purchases one community over, in Community B, where larger firms are able to offer budget-conscious members of Community A substantial savings on some products. Let us also suppose that these purchases reach a level that begins to jeopardize the solvency of certain firms in Community A. If this process is allowed to continue, Community A's experiment in distributism will be seriously shaken. Businessmen in the affected firms could, of course, simply move into some other area of production, where they might be able to produce less wastefully, but this would run counter to the kind of conservatism distributists appear to seek.

Much more likely is that the people of Community A will begin to clamor for some kind of restrictive action to suppress the competitive pressures coming from Community B. Assuming that Community B does not voluntarily accede to Community A's demands, the only logical next step is to appeal to some authority above both communities. This authority will have to be the state, since in order for its intervention to have any salutary effect from Community A's point of view, it will have to possess some kind of coercive power. All the while, the people of Community A will claim to be loyal to the principle of subsidiarity. They will simply argue that their difficulties have proven that these issues cannot be dealt with by lower associations and that it has now become legitimate for some higher association—the central state—to intervene. In this way they will claim philosophical consistency just as they are implementing the very centralized economy that they originally claimed they wished to avoid.

For as time goes on, the people living in Communities A and B, whose economic policies have been homogenized by state authority at the demand of Communtiy A, will certainly repeat the process. People from Communities A and B, increasingly skeptical that the Catholic faith requires them to pay a 40 percent premium on all goods, and certain that local businessmen (who are not exempt from original sin) are taking advantage of their privileged status to extort unreasonable prices from their hapless neighbors, begin to patronize firms in Community C. (Distributists might claim at this point that distributist communities would work to prevent unreasonable prices from being charged, but this would only multiply their difficulties, as it would introduce yet another arbitrary grant of power to the community's government, and it is far from clear on what basis they could decide such questions.) And so action is now demanded against Community C for what will inevitably be described in such lurid terms as "cutthroat competition" and "'survival of the fittest' economics."

"SOCIAL JUSTICE" AND ITS CONSEQUENCES

Thus there is plenty of reason to believe, from a theoretical point of view, that distributism will tend toward a centralized and tightly controlled economy. In addition to this theoretical argument, the career of John A. Ryan provides a degree of empirical support for this contention. Ryan was not a distributist, so the example is not perfect, but he is consistently cited by distributists and others as a great exponent of the social teaching. When Roosevelt proposed his New Deal programs, which did so much damage to the economy as well as to the Constitution and which centralized power over the economy in the hands of the central government, *Ryan supported them all*, claiming that they were very much in line with what Pope Pius XI had advocated. He wrote in his autobiography, "Practically all the reform measures enacted during the Roosevelt Administration have met with my hearty approval."[80] No protest in favor of subsidiarity was to be heard. He went on: "Relief for the needy and helpless, minimum fair standards for work and wages, the right of employees to bargain collectively, larger incomes for labor and farmers, expenditure of public money for public works both to provide employment and to increase the purchasing power of the masses, reduction of the rate of interest both for the benefit of borrowers and in order to diminish the amount of national saving [!]—all these seemed to me to be highly desirable means and ends. . . ."[81]

Ryan's views on saving raise an additional concern. One distributist recently blamed "capitalism" for what he argued was the excessive indebtedness of Americans.[82] But what such commentators never address is that since the New Deal, *government policy* has been skewed in favor of consumption and against saving (in his quotation above, Msgr. Ryan even *boasts* of his support for less saving) thanks in large measure to the economic arguments of people distributists typically point to as their intellectual heroes and mentors.[83] Msgr. Ryan was far from alone among partisans of the social teaching in holding to a "purchasing power" theory of prosperity, contending that consumption drives the economy and saving drags it down. Of course, saving is the source of investment, which makes possible more wealth in the future; it is also the source of larger purchases in the future. Msgr. Ryan's Keynesian "purchasing power" theory has done untold damage to the American economy and to American households, whose economic decisions have been artificially skewed in favor of spending and consumption and away from saving. (The purchasing power fallacy dies hard: as I write, the president has just won congressional approval for a tax reduction package that he justifies as a spur to consumption—as if simply using things up could somehow make us wealthy.)

More to our present point, the measures to which Msgr. Ryan points with such pleasure and satisfaction prolonged the Great Depression and postponed the recovery. That Franklin D. Roosevelt lifted the United States out of the Great Depression has reached the status of something "everyone knows." The reams of social and economic legislation for which FDR was responsible are spelled out proudly in every American history textbook, one historian writes, "but the costs for the United States of his eight-year-long war against business recovery are mentioned in none."[84] Neither are they mentioned in Msgr. Ryan's analysis.

Unemployment remained in the double digits throughout the 1930s, and averaged a whopping 18 percent from 1933 to 1940. Its lowest point was 14.3 percent in 1937, but by the end of that very year the economy was nearly as bad as it had been when FDR entered office.[85] According to the econometric estimates of Richard Vedder and Lowell Gallaway, in the absence of Roosevelt's policies the Depression "would have been completely over (less than 5 percent unemployment) by 1936."[86] Among the most important factors that prevented such a happy outcome was the "high-wage" policy that FDR consciously pursued throughout his various programs. In particular, the National Industrial Recovery Act, which in effect organized businesses into industrywide cartels, forced member businesses to abide by the wage floors imposed by organized labor. Partisans of the social teaching got their "just wage." These minimum wages, however, were absurdly high in light of the depressed condition of American business. The general *minimum* was 90 percent of the *average* hourly wage of 1933.[87]

FDR and his administration thought they saw in high wages a way out of the Depression; high wages, they believed, would restore consumer "purchasing power." What they failed to realize is that wages are a cost of doing business, and that full employment can be achieved only by allowing wages on their own to clear the market and reach a sustainable level. The sadly predictable result of these policies was that a select few did indeed prosper during the Depression, enjoying the high wages that these programs made possible. Americans bought more than twice as many refrigerators in 1935, when unemployment was over 20 percent, as in 1929, when unemployment was 3.2 percent. But millions of Americans had no wages at all. Over the past several decades more and more economists have begun to concede the NRA's depressing effects on employment.[88]

The NRA was far from the only New Deal policy that kept people unemployed. The Wagner Act, which gave special legal benefits to organized labor, continued the high-wage policy. By 1938, an estimated 1.2 million people had become victims of unemployment as a result of the increased wage costs associated with Social Security.[89]

The New Deal programs kept the United States mired in the Depression. Msgr. Ryan, the greatest American exponent of Catholic social teaching, considered them morally imperative. If this was "social justice," American workers needed a lot less of it.

PROPERTY: AN ABSOLUTE RIGHT?

Thankfully, the more conservative distributists tend not to be supporters of the New Deal. They will insist, however, that it is not the New Deal's interference with the rights of private property per se to which they object, since they contend that the idea of an absolute right to private property is alien to Catholic tradition. St. Thomas Aquinas, for example, is frequently cited as having placed restrictions on people's use of their property. Yet when St. Thomas speaks of the circumstances in which it would be licit for a person in need to appropriate for his own use the property of another, it is plain that he is speaking only of the direst and most desperate conditions, which rarely if ever hold in a modern market society. He contends that "if the need be so manifest and urgent, that it is evident that the present need must be remedied by whatever means be at hand (for instance when a person is in some imminent danger, and there is no other possible remedy), then it is lawful for a man to succor his own need by means of another's property, by taking it either openly or secretly."[90] Thus we are speaking of cases in which the need is "manifest and urgent," possibly involving "some imminent danger, and *there is no other possible remedy*." Such a statement can hardly be cited in favor of the massive confiscations of wealth, done in the name of egalitarianism, on the part of modern welfare states.

Moreover, embedded within St. Thomas' discussion of the limits to property is the much broader question of the status of the right to property itself: is it a natural or divinely bestowed right, or a mere fixture of human positive law? St. Thomas opted for the latter position, and it is from this contention that we can trace the idea that private property, useful and important an institution though St. Thomas acknowledges it to be, may be restricted by lawful authority. He explicitly invokes this line of thinking elsewhere in the *Summa* question cited above.

Within Catholic tradition, however, there is also a venerable lineage of thinkers who treat property as a natural right, and whose thought could indeed lead to the conclusion that no one may justly engage in violent aggression against holders of legitimate property titles—i.e., people who have either homesteaded previously unused resources by means of the exertion of their own labor upon them, or who have acquired title to such property through voluntary cession by others.[91] Pope John XXII, in the course of refuting the radical anti-property views of the heretical Franciscan spirituals in his bull *Quia Vir Reprobus* (1329), made comments in this direction.[92] Still earlier, Henry of Ghent, one of the great masters at the University of Paris in the late thirteenth century, justified property rights on the basis of the individual's ownership of himself.[93] Brian Tierney's important book *The Idea of Natural Rights* (1997) has gone a long way toward dispensing with the simplistic view that finds such arguments developing spontaneously in the seventeenth century; they are, instead, part of a much older tradition.

Thus it is significant that Pope Leo XIII should speak of private ownership as a "natural right of man," and as something that must be held "sacred and inviolable."[94] It is not surprising, therefore, that the Pope was particularly careful in speaking of the obligations binding on the Christian conscience in the matter of the use of one's property.

"It is lawful," says St. Thomas Aquinas, "for a man to hold private property; and it is also necessary for the carrying on of human existence." But if the question be asked: How must one's possessions be used?—the Church replies without hesitation in the words of the same holy Doctor: "Man should not consider his material possessions as his own, but as common to all, so as to share them without hesitation when others are in need. Whence the Apostle with, 'Command the rich of this world . . . to offer with no stint, to apportion largely.'" True, no one is commanded to distribute to others that which is required for his own needs and those of his household; nor even to give away what is reasonably required to keep up becomingly his condition in life, "for no one ought to live other than becomingly." But, when what necessity demands has been supplied, and one's standing fairly taken thought for, it becomes a duty to give to the indigent out of what remains over. "Of that which remaineth, give alms." It is a duty, not of justice (save in extreme cases), but of Christian charity—*a duty not enforced by human law*. But the laws and judgments of men must yield place to the laws and judgments of Christ the true God, who in many ways urges on His followers the practice of almsgiving—"It is more blessed to give than to receive"; and who will count a kindness done or refused to the poor as done or refused to Himself—"As long as you did it to one of My least brethren you did it to Me." To sum up, then, what has been said: Whoever has received from the divine bounty a large share of temporal blessings, whether they be external and material, or gifts of the mind, has received them for the purpose of using them for the perfecting of his own nature, and, at the same time, that he may employ them, as the steward of God's providence, for the benefit of others.[95]

Such language, whether intentionally or not, builds upon the natural rights tradition evident among earlier Catholic thinkers. Thus in the sixteenth century, the Jesuit theologian Luís de Molina would write:

> When we say . . . that someone has a *ius* to something, we do not mean that anything is owed to him, but that he has a faculty to it, whose contravention would cause him injury.
>
> In this way we say that someone has a *ius* to use his own things, such as consuming his own food—that is, if he is impeded, injury and injustice will be done to him. In the same way that a pauper has the *ius* to beg alms, a merchant has the *ius* to sell his wares, etc.

It is significant that Molina should say that the pauper has the right to *beg* alms; he does not say that the pauper has the right to receive alms. Although his fellow men may be morally bound to help him, this moral imperative is altogether distinct from a legally binding obligation, enforceable by violence.[96]

To say that the demands of Christian charity are binding on the Catholic conscience, and that these demands must inform the pious man's disposition of his property, is something very different from claiming for the state a right to violent interference with a man's use of his property if he is considered not to be sufficiently generous toward his fellows. He will have to answer to God for his lack of charity toward his fellow man, to be sure. But to claim that the state is *obligated* to seize his possessions violently is a mere statement of opinion. Moreover, surely it is at least possible that the dangers inherent in granting the state such powers could be so great as to render wealth redistribution undesirable even to those who might otherwise support it.

This is a complex and contentious topic. For now, let me offer a few additional considerations. It would be foolish to pretend that we have not had decades, even centuries, of experience with the idea of a limited or conditional right of property, or that the results might not render necessary a prudent adjustment—a *development*, perhaps, to use Cardinal Newman's terminology—of this conditional view of property, or an increasing emphasis on the natural rights tradition within Catholic thought.

This is not to deny that people may use their property foolishly or selfishly; but St. Thomas himself is at pains to deny that all vices should be legally actionable. If St. Thomas could argue that, in some cases and given certain circumstances, even prostitution, a sin he strongly condemns on several grounds, must be tolerated, then surely it can be argued that private property can be tolerated.[97] And indeed there are good reasons—in addition to the instinctive moral argument that confiscating another's goods by force is wrong—for state interference with private property to be rejected. We have already seen the terrible consequences of the wealth redistribution inherent in the welfare state. Social security, which involves the confiscation of the property of current workers, has attenuated family relationships and contributed to a decline in the birth rate. After some had argued in the 1960s that the common good required that people be taxed in order to support massive anti-poverty programs, the result was that the once-declining poverty rate had come to an abrupt halt, and the perverse incentives involved in any form of wealth redistribution had contributed to the breakdown of the family and the collapse of civilized life in substantial portions of our cities.

In addition, we have already seen in chapter 2 just how counterproductive wealth redistribution can be. We have seen that confiscating the wealth of those individuals and firms who have shown themselves skilled at satisfying the needs of the people only lowers the overall standard of living, since it cuts into the funds available for the capital investment that alone increases our material well being. Such confiscation also tends to discourage entrepreneurs from creating new wealth in the first place, since the after-tax reward appears less and less worth the effort. Now it is possible that some people favor wealth redistribution out of sheer spite, or envy, or even from a misguided desire to bring about "equality." But those who favor such wealth redistribution because they believe it improves the lot of the less wealthy simply do not understand how the economy operates.

There are, therefore, certain consequentialist arguments that warn against state interference with private property. But at the very least, it would seem supremely inadvisable and profoundly imprudent to place great emphasis on state restrictions on private property at the present moment in particular. At a time of ongoing cultural revolution, when the adversaries of Catholicism and conservatism have made plain their intent to use the machinery of state to promote leftist social ideologies, it is hardly an opportune time to discuss how the rights of property might be compromised. Private property is the major bulwark against the leftist assault. Although those who consider themselves traditionalists would doubtless claim that they wish to interfere with the rights of property only to this or that extent, or only to bring about this or that allegedly desirable social outcome, there can be little excuse for such naivete in our day. No Catholic should want to build up an institution that he would be terrified to see in the hands of his ideological opponents.

Fred Foldvary has done considerable work demonstrating the viability of purely private communities, and how they make provision for those things that mainstream economists have historically labeled "public goods" whose nature allegedly requires that they be provided by the state.[98] There is in fact an enormous literature on this subject. It turns out that the reasons typically cited to justify taxation on behalf of the "common good" are entirely specious, since the goods and services in question can be provided by the private sector, without all the disadvantages of a public sector monopoly: calculation problems (the state has no nonarbitrary way of knowing, for any of the goods it supplies, just *how much* to produce), inefficiency, poor service, and contempt for the consumer.[99] As for such property-related issues as pollution, noise, and the like, Rothbard showed (as we saw in chapter 1) how such issues can be resolved within a common-law, property-rights framework. Such a framework possesses an overwhelming advantage over one that would decide such questions on the basis of the "common good," since such a vague concept could never provide the predictability, fixed rules, and peaceful social interaction that a property-rights regime makes possible.

During such times, far from looking around for excuses to curtail the right to private property, Catholics should want to have recourse to all the protections that private property can afford. If the rights of private property were respected across the board, without exception, we would have reason to expect a substantial improvement in the cultural and moral health of the American people. As Hans-Hermann Hoppe explains:

> [O]ne would be on the right path toward restoring the freedom of association and exclusion implied in the institution of private property if only towns and villages could and would do what they did as a matter of course until well into the nineteenth century in Europe and the United States. There would be signs regarding entrance requirements to the town, and, once in town, requirements for entering specific pieces of property . . . and those who did not meet these entrance requirements would be kicked out as trespassers. Almost instantly, cultural and moral normalcy would reassert itself.[100]

This is how Catholics faced with the collapse of civilized order should be thinking, rather than concocting rationales for state aggression against and expropriation of private property owners. Apart from the injustice involved, such misguided policy would only empower the state, the very institution that has done so much to undermine the kind of normal community life on which living out the Faith in practice has traditionally depended.

CATHOLICISM AND THE STATE

Against this critique of the state, some people who describe themselves as traditional Catholics will cite this or that passage from St. Thomas, or argue that the Catholic tradition requires a state that is far more active and energetic than the minimal state of classical liberalism. Indeed it is sometimes condescend-

ingly intimated that Catholics who insist on the strict limitation or even elimination of state power have been ensnared by a modern ruse, and if only they
had not been seduced by modern ideas they would be able to appreciate the
traditional Catholic position.

But if anyone has been seduced by modern ideas it is these critics themselves. The fact is, the "state" with which St. Thomas was familiar is qualitatively different from the modern state. This is another important contribution
of Pope John Paul II's *Centesimus Annus*: it finally recognized what should
have been clear for a long time—namely, that the modern state is something
altogether new and not to be treated analytically as merely an extension of the
political order that preceded it. *Centesimus* is, as one scholar rightly notes,
"the first major encyclical that treats the modern state for what it is, at least
as recent history has disclosed it: namely, a potentially dangerous concentration of coercive power that requires the most exacting juridical and structural
limitations lest it engulf the economic sphere on the one hand, or the cultural-
religious sphere on the other. The political state depicted in *Centesimus Annus* is no longer the classical or medieval *civitas*."[101]

The very idea of sovereignty, according to which there must exist a single,
sovereign voice, competent and forceful enough to make its will felt throughout society, would simply not have been recognized by the medievals whose
political order our critics think they are defending. In his classic study of Cardinal Wolsey, Alfred Pollard described the decentralization of power that char-
acterized medieval England—and, by extension, Western Europe at large:

> There were the liberties of the church, based on law superior to that of the King;
> there was the law of nature, graven in the hearts of men and not to be erased by
> royal writs; and there was the prescription of immemorial local and feudal cus-
> tom stereotyping a variety of jurisdictions and impeding the operation of a sin-
> gle will. There was no sovereignty capable of eradicating bondage by royal edict
> or act of parliament, regulating borough franchises, reducing to uniformity the
> various uses of the church, or enacting a principle of succession to the throne.
> The laws which ruled men's lives were the customs of their trade, locality, or es-
> tate and not the positive law of a legislator; and the whole sum of English par-
> liamentary legislation for the whole Middle Ages is less in bulk than that of the
> single reign of Henry VIII.[102]

Likewise, sociologist Robert Nisbet described medieval society as "one of
the most loosely organized societies in history."[103] Political leaders who desired centralization found themselves up against the historic liberties of
towns, guilds, universities, the Church, and similar corporate bodies, all of
whom guarded their (often hard-fought) liberties with great vigilance, and all
of whom would have been baffled at the modern idea that a single sovereign

voice, whether of a king or of "the people," could on its own authority have redefined or overturned those rights. The process of monarchical centralization, therefore, writes Bertrand de Jouvenel, "presupposed the complete subversion of the existing social order."[104]

In such a society, where competing legal jurisdictions abounded and no single sovereign voice could be found, the king did not make the law but was himself bound by it. Law was something to be *discovered*, not made, as with the absolute monarchs and parliaments of the modern age.[105] This is what colonial lawyer James Otis meant when he said in 1763—when this older view was on its last legs—that only *jus dicere* (to say or declare what the law was) rather than *jus dare* (to give the law, as something invented) fell to Parliament; *jus dare* ultimately rested only with God.[106]

Today, however, we have reached the point at which an institution called the state essentially defines its own powers. This is a far cry from the medieval model, in which the king possessed certain customary rights but could not define his own powers at will, or overturn the customary rights of the people or of the various subsidiary bodies of society. "Almost everywhere in Latin Christendom," writes A. R. Myers, "the principle was, at one time or another, accepted by the rulers that, apart from the normal revenues of the prince, no taxes could be imposed without the consent of parliament."[107] This point reflects the broader principle that the king could not arbitrarily step beyond the bounds of his customary rights.

How different is the situation today. As de Jouvenel observes,

> A landlord no longer feels surprised at being compelled to keep a tenant; an employer is no less used to having to raise the wages of his employees in virtue of the decrees of Power. Nowadays it is understood that our subjective rights are precarious and at the good pleasure of authority. But this was an idea which was still new and surprising to the men of the seventeenth century. What they witnessed were the first decisive steps of a revolutionary conception of Power; they saw before their eyes the successful assertion of the right of sovereignty as one which breaks other rights and will soon be regarded as the one foundation of all rights.[108]

It is entirely plausible to argue, therefore, that the authentically conservative position is not to embrace but rather to reject the modern idea of sovereignty altogether. Sovereignty is a thoroughly modern notion, and thus if anyone has made concessions to "modernity" it is those who ardently embrace a political philosophy that is not only at variance with, but which also helped to undermine and subvert, that of medieval Europe. It is they, rather than those of us skeptical of the state, who have the explaining to do.

As medieval historian Norman Cantor has observed of the Middle Ages:

In the model of civil society, most good and important things take place below the universal level of the state: the family, the arts, learning, and science; business enterprise and technological progress. These are the work of individuals and groups, and the involvement of the state is remote and disengaged. It is the rule of law that screens out the state's insatiable aggressiveness and corruption and gives freedom to civil society below the level of the state. It so happens that the medieval world was one in which men and women worked out their destinies with little or no involvement of the state most of the time.[109]

It is with these points in mind that we should evaluate the proposals of traditional Catholics to increase the authority of the state. Thus one Catholic critic of the market complains that "the capitalist seeks to neutralize the resolve of the State to ensure that all of a nation's wealth is equitably distributed so as to provide for the needs of all, that is, the common good."[110] But the idea of a single sovereign voice having control over all of "a nation's wealth"—an imprecise and question-begging phrase—would have been considered an intolerable innovation during the Middle Ages, the very period this critic thinks he is defending.

Returning to more strictly economic arguments, this critic's statement calls to mind Reisman's point from chapter 2 that "what made possible the rise in real wages and the average standard of living over the last two hundred years is precisely the fact that for the first time in history the redistributors were beaten back long enough and far enough to make large-scale capital accumulation and innovation possible."[111] Second, to speak of the "equitable distribution" of "a nation's wealth" only invites confusion. The market economy consists of voluntary property exchanges. There is no mechanism of "distribution" whatsoever. If the individual exchanges that make up the market economy are just (and it would be very difficult to argue that they are not), then it is nonsensical to judge the material outcomes of these exchanges as somehow "unjust." More to the point, if there is no distribution in a market economy, there can be no such thing as a "just distribution" or an "unjust distribution."[112]

"A nation's wealth" is not just sitting there in a pile, when one day a minority of the population surreptitiously grabs large chunks of it and vanishes into the night. Wealth is *created* in a dynamic economy, and therefore the enrichment of one party does not come at the expense of anyone else. Moreover, if someone invents, markets, or promotes an important cost-cutting innovation in, say, the production of the automobiles driven by millions of people, it can hardly be surprising or appear sinister that his salary should be many, many times greater than that of someone who sweeps the floor in a single office building in Hoboken. Whatever the *moral* claims on his generosity, to argue that the property of this hypothetical inventor should be *legally* considered part of "the nation's wealth," at the disposal of the state, to redistribute to those who had nothing to do with the creation of this new wealth–this really requires a much more elaborate philosophical defense than many Catholic critics of capitalism have provided. Such a view certainly has no roots in the political order of the Middle Ages, when the idea that the king should have control of all of the wealth in his realm would scarcely have been thought of, let alone accepted.

THE PROFIT MOTIVE

Given the kind of criticisms of the market that appear in distributist literature and argument, it may not be out of place to conclude with a word in defense of the so-called "profit motive." Now even a distributist would not deny — since he cannot — that it is morally licit for a man to want to improve his position, both for his own sake and for that of his family. Moreover, the restoration of Catholicism amid its present difficulties is certainly going to require the assistance of men of wealth to endow colleges and other salutary endeavors, and that wealth will have to be acquired somehow.

But without a "profit motive," there is no way to be sure that this morally legitimate desire to improve one's lot and provide for his family is pursued in a way that benefits society as a whole. A small industry has arisen over the years devoted to poking fun at Adam Smith's "invisible hand," the image by which the great eighteenth-century economist sought to describe the salutary process by which each man's desire to improve his condition benefits those around him as well; and some moralists have argued that the fact that the baker bakes his bread not out of universal benevolence but out of a desire for profit is so much the worse for him from a moral point of view.

But there are only two options here: either man can pursue his ends *without regard* for the needs and wishes of his fellow man, or he can act *with regard* to those needs. There is no third option. By seeking to "maximize profits," a motivation that is routinely treated as a terrible scourge on civilization, man ensures that his talents and resources are directed toward areas in which his fellow man has indicated the most urgent need. In other words, the price system, and the system of profit and loss that follows from it, forces him to plan his activity in conformity with the expressed needs of society and in the interest of a genuine stewardship of the things of the earth. This is how a rational and civilized society ensures that its resources are apportioned not according to some arbitrary blueprint but according to the needs of the people.

Profit signals, then, make for peaceful social cooperation and the most efficient use of scarce resources. Without them, as Mises showed in his classic essay on the impossibility of economic calculation under socialism, civilization literally reverts to barbarism. For his part, Röpke pointed to this marvelous coordination of the market, by which "anarchy in economics" produces "an orderly cosmos." "He who does not find this a wondrous phenomenon and thereby deserving of the most patient study," he concluded, "cannot be expected to take much of an interest in economics."[113] Indeed.

Moreover, no Catholic would deny that a life of pure self-indulgence is morally inferior to one in which one's wealth is put to lasting and productive use. But even to raise this point is to distract attention from the real issue. It should be obvious that to acknowledge a "profit motive" is not to say that people should think only about money, or that money is more important than God, or any other such nonsense. As Mises explains, "The immense majority strives after a greater and better supply of food, clothes, homes, and other material amenities. In calling a rise in the masses' standard of living progress and improvement, *economists do not espouse a mean materialism*. They simply establish the fact that people are motivated by the urge to improve the material conditions of their existence. They judge policies from the point of view of the aims men want to attain. *He who disdains the fall in infant mortality and the gradual disappearance of famines and plagues may cast the first stone upon the materialism of the economists*."[114] Any takers?

The point is, since we know that man has perfectly valid reasons for seeking the highest return on his investment, or earning the highest wage, then instead of wasting time on foolish and irrelevant lamentations regarding the greedy people in the world—a matter of moral philosophy rather than economics—we ought to employ human reason to learn how this perfectly moral desire for gain redounds to society's benefit by ensuring that people produce what society urgently needs rather than more of something that society already enjoys in abundance. Stated this way, the profit-and-loss system of an economy based on the division of labor, an indispensable institution of civilized society, suddenly appears not only profoundly moral but actually obligatory, which is perhaps why opponents of capitalism never do state it this way.

If the engine of the enormous improvement in living standards that everyone in the developed world has enjoyed these past two centuries is not to be ground to a halt, it is essential that we understand the mechanisms that have made it possible. Such an appreciation of these indispensable aspects of the free economy is altogether absent from most opponents of the market—who, in their eagerness to caricature the free economy as the site of ceaseless "exploitation" and greed, consistently neglect to acknowledge its achievements and virtues. Richard Tawney's characterization of Martin Luther's anger at and ignorance of economics may be apt here: "Confronted with the complexities of foreign trade and financial organizations, he is like a savage introduced to a dynamo or a steam engine. He is too frightened and angry even to feel curiosity. Attempts to explain the mechanism merely enrage him; he can only repeat that there is a devil in it, and that good Christians will not meddle with the mystery of iniquity."[115]

John Ryan, the American priest who perhaps more than any other attempted to reckon with the question of labor and wages, himself acknowledged that men are "more susceptible to religious influence [and] can know and serve God better when they are contented and comfortable than when they are impoverished and miserable."[116] If that is so, then we should expect Catholics to appreciate the market all the more, since it has made possible the greatest explosion of wealth the world has ever seen—including stunning increases in life expectancy, caloric intake, education, literacy, and countless other good things. Overwhelmingly it is the poor who have benefited from the extension of the market, and for whom the good things of civilization are available in much greater abundance than they were even for the greatest kings of centuries past. That includes better housing, better health and sanitation, and dramatic declines in famine, disease, and infant mortality. Donald Boudreaux offers a useful thought experiment: suppose an ancestor from the year 1700 could be shown a typical day in the life of software magnate Bill Gates. He would doubtless be impressed by some of what makes Bill Gates' life unique, but

a good guess is that the features of Gates's life that would make the deepest impression are that he and his family never worry about starving to death; that they bathe daily; that they have several changes of clean clothes; that they have clean and healthy teeth; that diseases such as smallpox, polio, diphtheria, tuberculosis, tetanus, and pertussis present no substantial risks; that Melinda Gates's chances of dying during childbirth are about one-sixtieth what they would have been in 1700; that each child born to the Gateses is [far] more likely than a preindustrial child to survive infancy; that the Gateses have a household refrigerator and freezer (not to mention microwave oven, dishwasher, and radios and televisions); that the Gateses's work week is only five days and that the family takes several weeks of vacation each year; that each of the Gates children will receive more than a decade of formal schooling; that the Gateses routinely travel through the air to distant lands in a matter of hours; that they effortlessly converse with people miles or oceans away; that they frequently enjoy the world's greatest actors' and actresses' stunning performances; that the Gateses can, whenever and wherever they please, listen to a Beethoven piano sonata, a Puccini opera, or a Frank Sinatra ballad.[117]

In other words, what would most impress our visitor are the aspects of Gates's life that the software giant *shares with ordinary Americans*.

It might be objected that such considerations as I have brought forth here are "materialistic," and that there is more to life than refrigerators and television sets. Such an objection is completely nonsensical. If it were true, then Catholic social teaching itself would stand condemned as "materialistic," since it too seeks an increase in material goods for workers and their families that they might live in reasonable comfort. The objection of materialism only reveals the incoherence of the antimarket position, which began as an argument that the market systematically exploited and impoverished the laborer. When the overwhelming weight of the evidence shows this opinion to be ludicrously at odds with reality, the accusation shifts ground. Now that the superiority of economic freedom has become all but impossible to deny, and the amazing abundance which we owe to such a social order no longer a matter of serious dispute, we are now told that even to think in such terms reveals a liberal attachment to the things of this world. This is what Joseph Schumpeter meant when he deplored those intellectuals for whom effective arguments on behalf of capitalism would lead them simply to move on to new criticisms of capitalism rather than to concede its value.[118]

As for decentralism, those who care to support locally based and smaller-scale agriculture have already been doing so for two decades now by means of community-supported agriculture, which is booming. On a purely voluntary basis, people who wish to support local agriculture pay a modest sum at the beginning of the year to provide the farmer with the capital he needs; they then receive locally grown produce for the rest of the year. The organizers of this movement, rather than wasting their time complaining about the need for state intervention, actually *did* something: they put together a voluntary program that has enjoyed considerable success across the country. Perhaps there is a lesson here.

Unlike any alternative, the market order does not require the use of coercion—the initiation of physical force—but amounts instead to a system of peaceful social cooperation. This fact alone lends a prima facie moral superiority to the market order. Moreover, it creates abundance that previous ages could scarcely have imagined, thereby freeing us to appreciate the good things of life. Any alternative must be based on coercion rather than voluntary consent, must tend relatively to impoverish the great mass of the population, and must contribute to a dangerous concentration of political power.

Belloc would have been the first to admit that no system is perfect, his own included. We must, therefore, make a prudent choice among imperfect alternatives. And in such a competition, the market wins hands down.

NOTES

1. Hilaire Belloc, *Economics for Helen* (London: J. W. Arrowsmith, 1924), 125.

2. Editors of IHS Press, "Introduction," in Hilaire Belloc, *An Essay on the Restoration of Property* (Norfolk, Va.: IHS Press, 2002 [1936]), 12.

3. James A. Sadowsky, "Capitalism, Ethics, and Classical Catholic Social Doctrine," *This World*, Fall 1983, 123.

4. Pius XI, *Quadragesimo Anno* 61. In "Liberal Economics vs. Catholic Truth" <http://www.seattlecatholic.com/article_20021103_Liberal_Economics_vs_Catholic _Truth.html>, John Sharpe renders Pius XI's phrase as "hand-to-mouth uncertainty," though I have been unable to find this particular translation used. Since Mr. Sharpe evidently agrees with this description of affairs, however, I continue to make reference to it within the text.

5. Eugen von Böhm-Bawerk, *Capital and Interest*, 3 vols., trans. George D. Huncke and Hans F. Sennholz (South Holland, Ill.: Libertarian Press, 1959), vol. 1, 269; see also Hans-Hermann Hoppe, *The Economics and Ethics of Private Property* (Boston: Kluwer Academic Publishers, 1993), 96–97.

6. Olwen H. Hufton, *The Poor of Eighteenth Century France, 1750–1789* (Oxford: Oxford University Press, 1974), 11.

7. William Doyle, *The Oxford History of the French Revolution* (Oxford: Oxford University Press, 1989), 14.

8. Hilaire Belloc, *The Servile State* (Indianapolis, Ind.: LibertyClassics, 1977 [1913]), 108, 114. Emphasis in original.

9. Belloc, *Essay*, 28.

10. Marion Mitchell Stancioff, "Distributism," *Integrity*, March 1949; reprinted in *The Angelus*, July 1998, 10–16, quotation on 14.

11. Ludwig von Mises, *Human Action: A Treatise on Economics*, Scholar's edition (Auburn, Ala.: Ludwig von Mises Institute, 1998 [1949]), 308. I owe this reference to Professor Jeffrey Herbener.

12. Ludwig von Mises, "Small and Big Business," in *Economic Freedom and Interventionism: An Anthology of Articles and Essays* (Irvington-on-Hudson, N.Y.: Foundation for Economic Education, 1990). Elsewhere in the same article, Mises observes that the best example of the contradiction involved in using state power to establish individual independence is provided by American farm policy. "Its objective was to preserve the 'family farm' and the free independent farmer, the type of man that made the United States and laid the foundations of its greatness. But the champions of farm aid were not aware of the insoluble contradiction between the ideal aimed at and the methods resorted to for its realization. A farmer supported by the government at the expense of the rest of the population, the immense majority of the people, is no longer independent. The government tells him what to produce and in what quantity, and thus virtually converts him into a public servant. The free farmer depended on the market; his income came from the consumers. The supported farmer depends on the discretion of a huge apparatus of government agencies. He is the lowest subordinate of a hierarchy of superiors. It is true that at the top of this hierarchy

stand the President and Congress in whose election he cooperates. Because they canvass his votes, the politicians promise him aid. But it is precisely this aid that necessarily obliterates his independence. One cannot subsidize a man to render him independent. The very fact of receiving aid deprives the recipient of his discretion to determine the conduct of his affairs."

13. Nicholas F. R. Crafts, *British Economic Growth during the Industrial Revolution* (Oxford: Clarendon, 1985).

14. R. M. Hartwell, "The Standard of Living Controversy: A Summary," in *The Industrial Revolution*, ed. R. M. Hartwell (New York: Barnes & Noble, 1970), 178.

15. Hartwell, "The Standard of Living Controversy," 177–78.

16. It should also be recalled that the years from 1793 to 1815 were a time of war for England, when she was involved in the wars of the French Revolution as well as the Napoleonic wars. This factor must necessarily have depressed the living standards of workers in comparison to what they would otherwise have been. T. S. Ashton, *The Industrial Revolution 1760–1830* (Oxford: Oxford University Press, 1947), 119ff.

17. F. A. Hayek, "History and Politics," in *Capitalism and the Historians*, ed. F. A. Hayek (Chicago: University of Chicago Press, 1954), 22.

18. Leopold Kohr, *The Breakdown of Nations* (New York: Rhinehart & Co., 1957), 155.

19. Hayek, "History and Politics," 18.

20. Hayek, "History and Politics," 15.

21. Hayek, "History and Politics," 16.

22. Mises, *Human Action*, 614.

23. R. M. Hartwell, *The Industrial Revolution and Economic Growth* (London: Methuen & Co., 1971), 340. Emphasis added.

24. F. M. L. Thompson, "English Landownership: The Ailesbury Trust, 1832–56," *Economic History Review* (August 1958): 128; cited in Hartwell, *The Industrial Revolution and Economic Growth*, 340.

25. Hartwell, *The Industrial Revolution and Economic Growth*, 341.

26. Mises, *Human Action*, 615.

27. Mises, *Human Action*, 616.

28. Mises, *Human Action*, 616.

29. Ashton, *The Industrial Revolution 1760–1830*, 129.

30. This is Belloc's contention, and is shared by other distributists as well. The Australian hierarchy made a similar statement in its 1949 document on economic issues. See "A Catholic Economics," *The Angelus*, June 1997, 34–35.

31. Murray N. Rothbard, *Man, Economy, and State: A Treatise on Economic Principles* (Auburn, Ala.: Ludwig von Mises Institute, 1993 [1962]), 544–50, but esp. 547–48; see also Peter G. Klein, "Economic Calculation and the Limits of Organization," *Review of Austrian Economics* 9, 2 (1996): 3–28.

32. Rothbard, *Man, Economy, and State*, 547–48. Emphasis in original.

33. Belloc, *Essay*, 43.

34. Quoted in Thomas J. DiLorenzo, "The Origins of Antitrust: An Interest-Group Perspective," *International Review of Law and Economics* 5 (June 1985): 82.

35. DiLorenzo compiled figures for salt, petroleum, zinc, steel, bituminous coal, steel rails, sugar, lead, liquor, twine, iron nuts and washers, jute, castor oil, cotton seed oil, leather, linseed oil, and matches.

36. DiLorenzo, "The Origins of Antitrust," 80.

37. DiLorenzo, "The Origins of Antitrust," 80.

38. Lester Telser, *A Theory of Efficient Cooperation and Competition* (Cambridge, UK: Cambridge University Press, 1987), 41.

39. John W. McGee, "Predatory Price Cutting: The Standard Oil (N.J.) Case," *Journal of Law and Economics* 1 (April 1958): 145.

40. McGee, "Predatory Price Cutting," 148 and *passim*; Gabriel Kolko, *The Triumph of Conservatism: A Reinterpretation of American History, 1900–1916* (New York: Free Press, 1963), 40.

41. Burton W. Folsom, Jr., *The Myth of the Robber Barons: A New Look at the Rise of Big Business in America* (Herndon, Va.: Young America's Foundation, 1991), 87.

42. Kolko, *Triumph of Conservatism*, 40.

43. Kolko, *Triumph of Conservatism*, 40–41.

44. Kolko, *Triumph of Conservatism*, 41.

45. Belloc, *Essay*, 48.

46. George Reisman, *Capitalism* (Ottawa, Ill.: Jameson Books, 1996), 399–408.

47. Wayne A. Leeman, "The Limitations of Local Price-Cutting as a Barrier to Entry," *Journal of Political Economy* 64 (August 1956): 330.

48. This example is modeled after one given in Reisman, *Capitalism*, 403–405.

49. Reisman, *Capitalism*, 404.

50. Reisman, *Capitalism*, 405.

51. Mises, "Small and Big Business."

52. Kolko, *The Triumph of Conservatism*, 5, 26–56 (quotation on 5); see also Hans-Hermann Hoppe, *A Theory of Socialism and Capitalism: Economics, Politics, and Ethics* (Boston: Kluwer, 1989), ch. 9.

53. The classic treatment is George Stigler, "The Theory of Economic Regulation," *Bell Journal of Economics and Management Science* 2 (Spring 1971): 3–21 (quotations on 3 and 5); see also Sam Peltzman, "Toward a More General Theory of Regulation," *Journal of Law and Economics* 19 (August 1976): 211–40.

54. As Will Durant observes, the guilds "were frankly institutions in restraint of trade. They usually persuaded their towns to keep out, by a high protective tariff or elsewise, goods competitive with their own; such alien goods, if allowed to enter the town, were sold at prices fixed by the affected guild . . . . By city ordinance or economic pressure the guild usually compelled craftsmen to work only for the guild or with its consent, and to sell its products only to or through the guild." Will Durant, *The Age of Faith* (New York: MJF Books, 1950), 634.

55. John T. Flynn, *The Roosevelt Myth*, 50th anniv. ed. (San Francisco: Fox & Wilkes, 1998 [1948]), 116.

56. Thomas J. DiLorenzo, "Franklin Delano Roosevelt's New Deal: From Fascism to Pork-Barrel Politics," in *Reassessing the Presidency*, ed. John V. Denson (Auburn, Ala.: Ludwig von Mises Institute, 2001), 433.

57. DiLorenzo, "Franklin Delano Roosevelt's New Deal," 438–39.

58. Milton and Rose Friedman, *Free to Choose: A Personal Statement* (New York: Avon, 1979), 229. Emphasis in original.

59. On the AMA, see Llewellyn H. Rockwell, Jr., "Medical Control, Medical Corruption," *Chronicles*, June 1994; on the rise of medical licensure, see Ronald Hamowy, "The Early Development of Medical Licensing Laws in the United States, 1875–1900," *Journal of Libertarian Studies* (1979): 73–119.

60. Quoted in Sue A. Blevins, "The Medical Monopoly: Protecting Consumers or Limiting Competition?" Cato Policy Analysis No. 246, December 15, 1995.

61. Friedman and Friedman, *Free to Choose*, 229–30.

62. Mancur Olson, *The Rise and Decline of Nations: Economic Growth, Stagflation, and Social Rigidities* (New Haven, Conn.: Yale University Press, 1982), 66.

63. Blevins, "The Medical Monopoly."

64. Blevins, "The Medical Monopoly."

65. George Reisman, *The Real Right to Medical Care versus Socialized Medicine* (Laguna Hills, Calif.: Jefferson School, 1994), 32; cf. on this overall argument Murray N. Rothbard, *Power and Market: Government and the Economy* (Kansas City, Mo.: Sheed Andrews and McMeel, 1970), 206–208 (but esp. 208); Ludwig von Mises, *Planning for Freedom* (South Holland, Ill.: Libertarian Press, 1952), 42–43.

66. Reisman, *The Real Right to Medical Care*, 31–32.

67. George C. Leef, "The Lawyer Cartel," *The Free Market*, November 1998.

68. Leef, "The Lawyer Cartel."

69. Leef, "The Lawyer Cartel."

70. D. Eric Schansberg, *Poor Policy: How Government Harms the Poor* (Boulder, Colo.: Westview Press, 1996), 67.

71. Walter Williams, *The State against Blacks* (New York: McGraw-Hill, 1982); see also Stigler, "Toward a General Theory of Regulation," 13–17.

72. James T. Bennett and Thomas J. DiLorenzo, *Official Lies: How Government Misleads Us* (Alexandria, Va.: Groom Books, 1992), 111.

73. Schansberg, *Poor Policy*, 44.

74. Schansberg, *Poor Policy*, 48.

75. Raymond de Roover, "Scholastic Economics: Survival and Lasting Influence from the Sixteenth Century to Adam Smith," *Quarterly Journal of Economics* 69 (May 1955): 186.

76. Pius XI, *Quadragesimo Anno* 79.

77. Joseph Zoric, "(re)Distributism (re)Considered," *The University Concourse*, March 7, 2000, at www.theuniversityconcourse.com/V,6,3–7–2000/Zoric.htm (accessed December 10, 2002).

78. Zoric, "(re)Distributism (re)Considered."

79. Stancioff, "Distributism," 14.

80. John A. Ryan, *Social Doctrine in Action: A Personal History* (New York: Harper, 1941), 242; see also Kevin E. Schmiesing, "Catholic Critics of the New Deal: 'Alternative' Traditions in Catholic Social Thought," *Catholic Social Science Review* 7 (2002): 145–59; Francis L. Broderick, *Right Reverend New Dealer: John A. Ryan* (New York: Macmillan, 1963).

81. Ryan, *Social Doctrine in Action*, 248.

82. Editors of IHS Press, "Introduction," 13.

83. Thanks to Professor Christopher Westley for this point.

84. Gary Dean Best, *Pride, Prejudice, and Politics: Roosevelt versus Recovery, 1933–1938* (New York: Praeger, 1991), 218.

85. Thomas E. Woods, Jr., "Great Depression: Ending," in *History in Dispute*, vol. 3, ed. Robert J. Allison (Detroit: St. James Press, 2000), 65–69. For a refutation of the widespread misconception that World War II lifted the United States out of the Great Depression and represented a time of economic prosperity, see Robert Higgs, "Wartime Prosperity? A Reassessment of the U.S. Economy in the 1940s," *Journal of Economic History* 52 (March 1992): 41–60; see also Reisman, *Capitalism*, 262, 592–93.

86. Richard K. Vedder and Lowell E. Gallaway, *Out of Work: Unemployment and Government in Twentieth-Century America* (New York: Holmes & Meier, 1993), 142.

87. Woods, "Great Depression: Ending," 65; Vedder and Gallaway, *Out of Work*, 137.

88. Vedder and Gallaway, *Out of Work*, 137; the authors cite Paul A. Samuelson and Robert M. Solow, "Analytical Aspects of Anti-Inflation Policy," *American Economic Review* 50, Supplement (1960): 177–94; Michael M. Weinstein, "Some Macroeconomic Impacts of the National Industrial Recovery Act, 1933–1935," in *The Great Depression Revisited*, ed. Karl Brunner (Boston: Martinus Nijhoff, 1981), 262–81.

89. Vedder and Gallaway, *Out of Work*, 141.

90. Thomas Aquinas, *Summa Theologica*, IIa, IIae, q. 66, art. 7.

91. Thus see Richard Tuck, *Natural Rights Theories: Their Origin and Development* (Cambridge, UK: Cambridge University Press, 1979), chs. 1 and 2.

92. Tuck, *Natural Rights Theories*, p. 22.

93. On Henry of Ghent, see Brian Tierney, *The Idea of Natural Rights: Studies on Natural Rights, Natural Law, and Church Law, 1150–1625* (Grand Rapids, Mich.: Eerdmans, 2001 [1997]), 78–89.

94. Leo XIII, *Rerum Novarum* 22 and 46.

95. Leo XIII, *Rerum Novarum* 22. Emphasis added. On Leo XIII's development of the idea of a natural right to property, see Ernest L. Fortin, "Sacred and Inviolable: *Rerum Novarum* and Natural Rights," in *Human Rights, Virtue, and the Common Good: Untimely Meditations on Religion and Politics*, ed. J. Brian Benestad (Lanham, Md.: Rowman & Littlefield, 1996), 191–222.

96. Murray N. Rothbard, *An Austrian Perspective on the History of Economic Thought*, vol. 1, *Economic Thought before Adam Smith* (Brookfield, Vt.: Edward Elgar, 1995), 115.

97. St. Thomas discusses human law in his "Treatise on Law," which can be found in questions 90 through 108 of the *Prima Secundae* (the first part of the second part) of the *Summa Theologiae*. Thus he writes, "Accordingly in human government also, those who are in authority, rightly tolerate certain evils, lest certain goods be lost, or certain greater evils be incurred: thus Augustine says [*De ordine* ii.4]: 'If you do away with harlots, the world will be convulsed with lust.'" II-II, q. 10, art. 11. St. Thomas argued that the state had to legislate for a great variety of men, who were by no means equal in virtue. The state does not engage in any fruitless attempt to perfect the vi-

cious (a lengthy process) but for the sake of the good of society seeks primarily to restrain those acts that directly threaten society itself. Thus St. Thomas: "Now human law is framed for a number of human beings, the majority of whom are not perfect in virtue. Wherefore human laws do not forbid all vices, from which the virtuous abstain, but only the more grievous vices from which it is possible for the majority to abstain; and chiefly those that are to the hurt of others, without the prohibition of which human society could not be maintained: thus human law prohibits murder, theft and suchlike . . . . The purpose of human law is to lead men to virtue, not suddenly, but gradually. Wherefore it does not lay upon the multitude of imperfect men the burdens of those who are already virtuous, viz., that they should abstain from all evil. Otherwise these imperfect ones, being unable to bear such precepts, would break out into yet greater evils." I-II, q. 96, art. 2.

98. Fred Foldvary, *Public Goods and Private Communities* (Aldershot, UK: Edward Elgar, 1994); see also *The Voluntary City: Choice, Community and Civil Society*, eds. David T. Beito, Peter Gordon, and Alexander Tabarrok (Ann Arbor, Mich.: University of Michigan Press, 2002).

99. See, for example, Rothbard, *Power and Market*; Hoppe, *Economics and Ethics of Private Property*; and Hoppe, *Theory of Socialism and Capitalism*.

100. Hans-Hermann Hoppe, *Democracy, the God that Failed: The Economics and Politics of Monarchy, Democracy, and Natural Order* (New Brunswick, N.J.: Transaction, 2001), 211.

101. Russell Hittinger, "The Problem of the State in *Centesimus Annus*," *Fordham International Law Journal* 15 (1991–92): 956.

102. Alfred F. Pollard, *Wolsey: Church and State in Sixteenth-Century England* (New York: Harper & Row, 1966 [1929]), 218.

103. Robert Nisbet, *The Quest for Community: A Study in the Ethics of Order and Freedom* (San Francisco: Institute for Contemporary Studies, 1990 [1953]), 99.

104. Bertrand de Jouvenel, *Sovereignty: An Inquiry into the Political Good*, trans. Daniel J. Mahoney and David DesRosiers (Indianapolis, Ind.: Liberty Fund, 1997 [1957]), 208.

105. On the many legal jurisdictions that existed during the Middle Ages, the classic study is Harold J. Berman, *Law and Revolution: The Formation of the Western Legal Tradition* (Cambridge, Mass.: Harvard University Press, 1983); on the premodern notion of law as discovered rather than made, see de Jouvenel, *Sovereignty, passim*; Bruno Leoni, *Freedom and the Law* (Indianapolis, Ind.: Liberty Fund, 1991 [1961]), esp. 83ff.; see also N. Stephan Kinsella, "Legislation and the Discovery of Law in a Free Society," *Journal of Libertarian Studies* 11 (Summer 1995): 132–81.

106. James Otis, "The Rights of the British Colonies Asserted and Proved," in *The American Republic: Primary Sources*, ed. Bruce Frohnen (Indianapolis, Ind.: Liberty Fund, 2002), 126.

107. A. R. Myers, *Parliaments and Estates in Europe to 1789* (New York: Harcourt, Brace, Jovanovich, 1975), 29; cited in Ralph Raico, "The Theory of Economic Development and the 'European Miracle,'" in *The Collapse of Development Planning*, ed. Peter J. Boettke (New York: New York University Press, 1994), 46.

108. De Jouvenel, *Sovereignty*, 226.

109. Norman F. Cantor, *Inventing the Middle Ages: The Lives, Works, and Ideas of the Great Medievalists of the Twentieth Century* (New York: William Morrow, 1991), 416; cited in Raico, "The Theory of Economic Development and the 'European Miracle,'" 46.

110. Peter J. Chojnowski, "Catholicism, Protestantism, and Capitalism, Part 2," *The Angelus*, November 1999.

111. Reisman, *Capitalism*, 653.

112. Thus Fr. James Sadowsky writes that on the market "[w]ealth is produced and wealth is exchanged. Period. So there are no distributors. If there is no distribution process on the market, how can there be an unjust process of distribution or—for that matter—a just process? Again, if there are no distributors, there can be no unjust distributors. The different holdings that result from the process of production and exchange will depend entirely on the justice of those processes." James Sadowsky, S.J., *The Christian Response to Poverty* (London: The Social Affairs Unit, 1985), 9.

113. Wilhelm Röpke, *Economics of the Free Society* (Chicago: Henry Regnery, 1963), 4.

114. Mises, *Human Action*, 193–94. Emphasis added.

115. Richard H. Tawney, *Religion and the Rise of Capitalism* (New York: New American Library, 1954 [1927]), 80.

116. Ryan journal, p. 43, in John A. Ryan Papers, Catholic University of America, Washington, D.C., Box 32.

117. Donald J. Boudreaux, "Equality and Capitalism," *Ideas on Liberty*, September 2002, 52.

118. Joseph A. Schumpeter, *Capitalism, Socialism, and Democracy* (New York: Harper & Bros., 1942), 144.

Chapter Seven

In Omnibus, Caritas

This book has attempted to vindicate the arguments of Catholics who support the free-market, private-property order. It shows that many of these arguments merely extend the insights of other great Catholics, particularly the late Scholastics of the fifteenth and sixteenth centuries. It also suggests that economics is a bona fide science, whose laws are binding whether we like them or not.

Therefore, if anyone suggests, for example, that living-wage legislation should be pursued in order to increase laborers' standard of living, we must first determine, equipped with the tools of economic analysis, whether the desired end will really be brought about by the means employed. If economic analysis should conclude that living-wage legislation would have consequences exactly contrary to the wishes of its proponents, and would in fact throw men out of work entirely, then *it should not be controversial to conclude that living-wage legislation cannot be a moral imperative.* It should also be obvious that this is not a question of dissent from Catholic doctrine, but a dispute involving the application of reason and logic.

Chapter 2 explained in detail exactly how wages rise, and how their rise can best be encouraged. I have the same desirable end in mind as the authors of the social encyclicals—the increased well-being of working people. But if I know that the path that the popes recommend for achieving that end will do no such thing, and that my morally licit alternative will yield a consistent rise in the standard of living, surely I am not guilty of "dissent" for saying so. As chapter 2 pointed out, Catholic critiques of the market have frequently been made on the basis of an economic assumption—namely, that in many cases wage rates could be increased by state edict without the appearance of any negative consequences worthy of moral analysis. What happens if this assumption is false?

However, there are plenty of commentators who cannot or will not make the kinds of distinctions I have made here, and I wish to refer to several of these as I draw my study to a close. For example, theologian Todd Whitmore has raised the question of whether the free-market positions adopted by Michael Novak "constitute formal dissent on Novak's part." "I believe that they do," he concludes.[1]

What neither Whitmore nor any other commentator has taken the trouble to answer is how it makes sense to speak of "dissent" from teaching one believes to be based on factual error on a matter on which the Church has been promised no divine protection from error. Had a series of popes said that two and two made five, it would not make any sense to call someone a "dissenter" who argued that in fact they made four, particularly since mathematics is not a discipline into which the popes have been granted any special insight. The very notion of dissent is obviously inapplicable in such a case.

This is precisely the nature of the critique offered by Novak and even more so by the present writer. We are not dealing here with the pertinacious denial of a solemn dogma believed by the Church for two thousand years, which the conscience is absolutely bound to accept, but rather with a good-faith effort on the part of loyal Catholics to amend certain economic positions and prudential judgments which, though advanced in the name of helping the poor or rectifying alleged injustice, must have the opposite effect.

As I noted in my introduction, if I can show—to take just one example among many—that coercive labor unionism must have the overall effect of impoverishing society more than in proportion to any "gains" won by unionized labor, and that even unionized labor would be better off in a society with a free labor market, I cannot be obliged in conscience to believe coercive labor unionism to be a good thing from the point of view of workers' economic well-being. We are dealing here with a matter of simple disagreement on a debatable point of fact—qualitatively different from the denial of the Virgin Birth, the Immaculate Conception, the equality of the three Persons of the Holy Trinity, or the absolute prohibition of abortion and euthanasia.

It is this distinction that many Catholic commentators on both the left and the right seem unwilling to make—to question any aspect of Catholic social teaching is, in their eyes, to be disloyal to the Church. "We need a Mandatum," say Mark and Louise Zwick, "to ensure that the economics taught in Catholic universities will reflect the social teaching of the Church."[2] Not only does such a demand constitute an outrageous offense against a legitimate sphere of academic freedom within the university, but it also reveals a profound confusion regarding the very nature of economics, not to mention the nature and scope of the Church's Magisterium.

Chapter 2 provided a praxeological demonstration of why labor unions cannot raise wages across the board, and explained what precisely it is that makes real wages rise. According to that analysis, coercive labor unionism must make some workers worse off. Empirical evidence exists to show, in addition, that labor taken collectively is considerably worse off than it would have been had a free labor market prevailed over the past half century. To be sure, that conclusion appears to contradict the implied conclusion of Catholic social teaching, that labor unionism is a legitimate means for workers to advance their interests, and one that Catholics should favor. Would praxeology therefore be forbidden in the Catholic university for which the Zwicks appear to pine? Will they, before firing me, at least do me the courtesy of explaining where my logic was mistaken, or am I simply to assume that logic is not welcome in their "Catholic" university, since its conclusions are disappointing from the point of view of the social teaching? Am I expected to perform my logical analysis over and over until it comes out "right" from their point of view?

Those of us within the Church who advocate the Austrian approach to economics are not demanding that the popes preach Austrian economics from the Chair of Peter. No one with any knowledge of the development of economic thought among churchmen over the centuries would dare to claim that a single view could constitute "Catholic economics." Against those who suggest that a Catholic may look at economic matters in only one way, Professor Daniel Villey reminds us that "Catholic theology does not exclude pluralism of opinions on profane matters."[3] We do not claim that ours alone is "Catholic economics," but merely that what we teach is not only not antagonistic to, but in fact is profoundly compatible with, orthodox Catholicism.

What we stand for, furthermore, is the legitimate liberty of opinion that is supposed to be permitted in matters that do not touch upon Catholic dogma, and on which men of good will may disagree. As St. Augustine is said to have remarked, "*In fide, unitas; in dubiis, libertas; in omnibus, caritas*" (in faith, unity; in doubtful matters, liberty; in all things, charity). Such liberty of opinion on economic matters is generally recognized in practice. No one is suggesting that the Spanish Scholastics be declared heretics for their economic views—though they certainly would be considered heretical had they denied an actual Catholic dogma: the Incarnation, the Trinity, the two natures in Christ, and so on. The Spanish scholastics remain profoundly admired by Catholics as the great intellects they were—unthinkable if they had pertinaciously taught perverse error.

When John Ryan put forth his moral arguments for a family wage for a head of household, he was criticized by some in Catholic scholarly circles, as I noted in Chapter 2. The *Catholic University Bulletin* published a lengthy critique of

Ryan in 1907—and as anyone familiar with that publication knows very well, its editors would never have published anything they believed to be in conflict with the tenets of the Catholic faith. That they nevertheless published critiques of Ryan reveals that they were able to make the elementary distinction between matters of Catholic dogma and matters which, by virtue of their reliance upon analysis borrowed from a secular discipline, are necessarily precluded from being infallible.

THE CATHOLIC ATTRACTION TO AUSTRIAN ECONOMICS

Over and against our critics, I am convinced that a profound philosophical commonality exists between Catholicism and the brilliant edifice of truth to be found within the Austrian school of economics. The Austrian method of praxeology should be especially attractive to the Catholic. Carl Menger, but above all Mises and his followers, sought to ground economic principles on the basis of *absolute truth*, apprehensible by means of reflection on the nature of reality. What in the social sciences could be more congenial to the Catholic mind than this?

Austrian economics reveals to us a universe of order, whose structure we can apprehend through our reason. As Jeffrey Herbener explains, "A causal-realistic approach to economics arose in Christendom because only there did scholars conceive of nature as an interconnected order, created in the flux of time by God out of nothing, and governed by God-ordained natural laws that human intellect could discover and use to comprehend nature, with the goal of ruling over it for God's glory."[4] The alternative is the world of John Stuart Mill, who posited that it was entirely possible that we might find some place in the universe where two and two did not make four—a view which, in Herbener's words, "is grounded in the metaphysical position that the universe is not an orderly creation." Which one is more compatible with Catholicism should not be difficult to discern.

Moreover, the Austrian School carries forward a great many of the economic insights of the late Scholastic theologians—a source of pride, not shame, for modern-day Catholics. The Scholastics perceived clear relationships of cause and effect at work in the economy, particularly after observing the considerable price inflation that occurred in sixteenth-century Spain as a result of the influx of precious metals from the New World. From the observation that the greater supply of specie had led to a decline in the purchasing power of money, they came to the more general conclusion—an economic law, as it were—that an increase in the supply of any good will tend to bring about a decrease in its price.[5]

The Austrian School also shows what reason, properly exercised, can accomplish, and surely this is something that Catholics, who have always granted reason its rightful due, ought to appreciate. The great economic treatises of Mises and Rothbard begin with the action axiom I discussed in chapter 1, and proceed to deduce an entire economic system from this simple, irrefutable premise and a few subsidiary postulates. Austrians reject the mathematization of the discipline that other paradigms have encouraged, and dismiss artificial models that reduce man to a mere atom. They insist that the study of man, who unlike animals and inanimate things is endowed with reason and free will, is something unique, whose study is conceptually distinct from the study of the physical universe, and criticize those who would fashion economics along the model of physics and the hard sciences. And they perceive a fundamental order to the universe that renders social phenomena intelligible.

This, clearly, is a system that is eminently congenial to the Catholic mind.[6]

Economics does not contain all the answers of life, nor does it claim to. It does, however, show how the morally acceptable desire for profit leads to spontaneous social cooperation that obviates the need for a bloated state apparatus to direct production. It shows us the fascinating mechanisms by which peaceful social cooperation, without the initiation of physical force, leads to overall prosperity. This means less disease, more leisure time to spend with our families, and greater opportunities to enjoy the good things of civilization. This, stated simply, is why so many orthodox Catholics can be found on the side of private property, sound money, and the free market.

NOTES

1. Todd David Whitmore, "John Paul II, Michael Novak, and the Differences Between Them," *Annual of the Society of Christian Ethics* 21 (2001): 230.

2. Mark and Louise Zwick, "G. K. Chesterton and Dorothy Day on Economics: Neither Socialism nor Capitalism," *Houston Catholic Worker*, September–October 2001.

3. Daniel Villey, "The Market Economy and Roman Catholic Thought," *International Economic Papers* 9 (1959): 108.

4. Jeffrey M. Herbener, "The Austrian School in the Liberal Arts" (paper presented at the Ludwig von Mises Institute's Twentieth Anniversary Conference, October 18–19, 2002).

5. Herbener, "The Austrian School in the Liberal Arts."

6. Readers whose interest in economics has been piqued by what I have had to say may wish to continue reading within the Austrian tradition. The best introduction to Austrian economics, in my opinion, is Gene Callahan's *Economics for Real People: An Introduction to the Austrian School* (Auburn, Ala.: Ludwig von Mises Institute,

2002). Callahan writes in a crisp, clear, and engaging manner, and his thoroughly enjoyable presentation demonstrates why we Austrians find economics so fascinating. Indeed, Austrian economics is every bit as fascinating as "mainstream" economics is dry, mathematical, and unrealistic.

With equal enthusiasm do I recommend Mises.org, without a doubt the best and most comprehensive website dedicated to Austrian economics.

Thankfully back in print is Alejandro Chafuen's outstanding study of the late scholastics, now available in a second edition as *Faith and Liberty: The Economic Thought of the Late Scholastics* (Lanham, Md.: Lexington Books, 2003). Chafuen's book makes an overwhelming case that the late scholastic theologians should be considered proto-Austrians in their economic views, from prices and wages to subjective value and monetary theory.

Bibliography

Ashton, T. S. *The Industrial Revolution 1760–1830*. Oxford: Oxford University Press. 1947.

Baeck, Louis. "Spanish Economic Thought: The School of Salamanca and the *Arbitristas*." *History of Political Economy* 20 (Autumn 1988): 381–408.

Bandow, Doug and Ian Vásquez, eds. *Perpetuating Poverty: The World Bank, the IMF, and the Developing World*. Washington, D.C.: Cato Institute, 1994.

Bastiat, Frédéric. *Economic Harmonies*. Edited by George B. de Huszar. Irvington-on-Hudson, N.Y.: Foundation for Economic Education, 1997.

———. "What Is Money?" *Quarterly Journal of Austrian Economics* 5 (Fall 2002): 87–105.

Bauer, P. T. *Equality, the Third World, and Economic Delusion*. Cambridge, Mass.: Harvard University Press, 1981.

Bauer, Peter. *From Subsistence to Exchange and Other Essays*. Princeton, N.J.: Princeton University Press, 2000.

Bellante, Don and Roger W. Garrison. "Phillips Curves and Hayekian Triangles: Two Perspectives on Monetary Dynamics." *History of Political Economy* 20 (Summer 1988): 207–34.

Belloc, Hilaire. *Economics for Helen*. London: J. W. Arrowsmith, 1924.

———. *An Essay on the Restoration of Property*. Norfolk, Va.: IHS Press, 2002 [1936].

———. *The Servile State*. Indianapolis, Ind.: LibertyClassics, 1977 [1913].

Beito, David T. *From Mutual Aid to the Welfare State: Fraternal Societies and Social Services, 1890–1967*. Chapel Hill: University of North Carolina Press, 2000.

Beito, David T., Peter Gordon, and Alexander Tabarrok, eds. *The Voluntary City: Choice, Community, and Civil Society*. Ann Arbor: University of Michigan Press, 2002.

Benedict XIV. *Vix Pervenit*. 1745.

Bennett, James T. and Thomas J. DiLorenzo. *Official Lies: How Government Misleads Us*. Alexandria, Va.: Groom Books, 1992.

Berman, Harold J. *Law and Revolution: The Formation of the Western Legal Tradition.* Cambridge, Mass.: Harvard University Press, 1983.

Best, Gary Dean. *Pride, Prejudice, and Politics: Roosevelt versus Recovery, 1933–1938.* New York: Praeger, 1991.

Bethell, Tom. *The Noblest Triumph: Property and Prosperity through the Ages.* New York: St. Martin's, 1998.

Bittle, Celestine N., O.F.M.Cap. *Reality and the Mind: Epistemology.* New York: Bruce Puiblishing Co., 1936.

Blevins, Sue A. "The Medical Monopoly: Protecting Consumers or Limiting Competition?" Cato Policy Analysis No. 246, December 15, 1995.

Block, Walter. "Coase and Demsetz on Private Property Rights." *Journal of Libertarian Studies* 1 (Spring 1977): 111–15.

———. "Ethics, Efficiency, Coasian Property Rights, and Psychic Income: A Reply to Demsetz." *Review of Austrian Economics* 8, 2 (1995): 61–125.

———. "Private Property Rights, Erroneous Interpretations, Morality, and Economics: Reply to Demsetz." *Quarterly Journal of Austrian Economics* 3 (Spring 2000): 63–78.

Block, Walter and William Barnett II. "The Living Wage: What's Wrong?" *Ideas on Liberty*, December 2002. <http://www.fee.org/vnews.php?nid=5288> (July 8, 2004).

Boettke, Peter J., ed. *The Collapse of Development Planning.* New York: New York University Press, 1993.

Böhm-Bawerk, Eugen von. *Capital and Interest.* 3 vols. Translated by George D. Huncke and Hans F. Sennholz. South Holland, Ill.: Libertarian Press, 1959.

Bostaph, Samuel. "The *Methodenstreit*." Pp. 459–464 in *The Elgar Companion to Austrian Economics*, edited by Peter J. Boettke. Cheltenham, UK: Edward Elgar, 1994.

Boudreaux, Donald J. "Equality and Capitalism." *Ideas on Liberty*, September 2002, 51–52.

Brinkley, Alan. *Voices of Protest: Huey Long, Father Coughlin, and the Great Depression.* New York: Random House, 1982.

Broderick, Francis L. *Right Reverend New Dealer: John A. Ryan.* New York: Macmillan, 1963.

Burton, Katherine. *Leo the Thirteenth: The First Modern Pope.* New York: David McKay Co., 1962.

Callahan, Gene. *Economics for Real People.* Auburn, Ala.: Ludwig von Mises Institute, 2002.

Carlson, Allan. "What Has Government Done to Our Families?" *Essays in Political Economy*, Ludwig von Mises Institute, November 1991.

"A Catholic Economics." *The Angelus*, June 1997, 28–40.

Chafuen, Alejandro A. *Christians for Freedom: Late Scholastic Economics.* San Francisco: Ignatius Press, 1986.

Chamberlin, Edward H. *The Economic Analysis of Labor Union Power.* Washington, D.C.: American Enterprise Association, 1958.

Chojnowski, Peter J. "Catholicism, Protestantism, and Capitalism, Part 2." *The Angelus*, November 1999, at www.sspx.ca/Angelus/1999_November/Catholicism_Protestantism_and_Capitalism.htm (accessed July 8, 2004).

Coase, Ronald. "The Problem of Social Cost." *Journal of Law and Economics* 3 (October 1960): 1–44.

Coughlin, Charles E. *Money! Questions and Answers*. Royal Oak, Mich.: National Union for Social Justice, 1936.

Cox, W. Michael and Richard Alm. *Myths of Rich & Poor: Why We're Better Off than We Think*. New York: Basic Books, 2000.

Crafts, Nicholas F. R. *British Economic Growth during the Industrial Revolution*. Oxford: Clarendon, 1985.

Cruz, Lucía Santa. "Etica y Capitalismo: Entrevista a James Sadowsky, S.J." *El Mercurio*, November 22, 1987.

De Jouvenel, Bertrand. *Sovereignty: An Inquiry into the Political Good*. Translated by Daniel J. Mahoney and David DesRosiers. Indianapolis, Ind.: Liberty Fund, 1997 [1957].

De Roover, Raymond. "The Concept of the Just Price: Theory and Economic Policy." *Journal of Economic History* 18 (December 1958): 418–34.

———. "Joseph A. Schumpeter and Scholastic Economics." *Kyklos* 10 (1957): 115–46.

———. *San Bernardino of Siena and Sant'Antonio of Florence: Two Great Economic Thinkers of the Middle Ages*. Boston: Baker Library, 1967.

———. "Scholastic Economics: Survival and Lasting Influence from the Sixteenth Century to Adam Smith." *Quarterly Journal of Economics* 69 (May 1955): 161–90.

De Soto, Jesús Huerta. "New Light on the Prehistory of the Theory of Banking and the School of Salamanca." *Review of Austrian Economics* 9, 2 (1996): 59–82.

Dempsey, Bernard W. *Interest and Usury*. London: Dennis Dobson, 1948.

Demsetz, Harold. "Block's Erroneous Interpretations." *Review of Austrian Economics* 10, 2 (1997): 101–9.

———. "Ethics and Efficiency in Property Rights Systems." Pp. 97–125 in *Time, Uncertainty, and Disequilibrium*, edited by Mario Rizzo. Lexington, Mass.: Lexington Books, 1979.

DiLorenzo, Thomas J. "Franklin Roosevelt's New Deal: From Fascism to Pork-Barrel Politics." Pp. 425–51 in *Reassessing the Presidency*, edited by John V. Denson. Auburn, Ala.: Ludwig von Mises Institute, 2001.

———. "The Origins of Antitrust: An Interest-Group Perspective." *International Review of Law and Economics* 5 (June 1985): 73–90.

———. "Ron Brown's Corporate Welfare Scam." *The Free Market*, June 1996, at www.mises.org/freemarket_detail.asp?control=182 (accessed July 8, 2004).

Dorn, James A. "Economic Development and Freedom: The Legacy of Peter Bauer." *Cato Journal* 22 (Fall 2002): 355–71.

Dorn, James A., Steve H. Hanke, and Alan A. Waters, eds. *The Revolution in Development Economics*. Washington, D.C.: Cato Institute, 1998.

Doyle, William. *The Oxford History of the French Revolution*. Oxford: Oxford University Press, 1989.

Durant, Will. *The Age of Faith*. New York: MJF Books, 1950.

Ebeling, Richard M. *Money, Method, and the Market Process: Essays by Ludwig von Mises*. Boston: Kluwer, 1990.

Fahey, Rev. Denis. *Money Manipulation and Social Order*. Dublin: Browne & Nolan, 1944.

Flynn, John T. *The Roosevelt Myth*, 50th anniv. ed. San Francisco: Fox & Wilkes, 1998 [1948].

Foldvary, Fred. *Public Goods and Private Communities*. Aldershot, UK: Edward Elgar, 1994.

Folsom, Burton W., Jr. *The Myth of the Robber Barons: A New Look at the Rise of Big Business in America*. Herndon, Va.: Young America's Foundation, 1991.

Fortin, Ernest L. "Sacred and Inviolable: *Rerum Novarum* and Natural Rights." Pp. 191–222 in *Human Rights, Virtue, and the Common Good: Untimely Meditations on Religion and Politics*, edited by J. Brian Benestad. Lanham, Md.: Rowman & Littlefield, 1996.

Friedman, Milton and Rose Friedman. *Free to Choose: A Personal Statement*. New York: Avon, 1979.

Garrison, Roger W. "Business Cycles: Austrian Approach." Pp. 64–68 in *An Encyclopedia of Macroeconomics*, edited by Howard Vane and Brian Snowden. Aldershot, UK: Edward Elgar, 2002.

———. *Time and Money: The Macroeconomics of Capital Structure*. London: Routledge, 2000.

Gordon, David. *The Philosophical Origins of Austrian Economics*. Auburn, Ala.: Ludwig von Mises Institute, 1993.

Grant, Edward. *The Foundations of Modern Science in the Middle Ages: Their Religious, Institutional, and Intellectual Contexts*. Cambridge, UK: Cambridge University Press, 1996.

———. *God and Reason in the Middle Ages*. Cambridge, UK: Cambridge University Press, 2001.

Green, John and Kevin E. Schmiesing. *The State of Economic Education in United States Seminaries*. Grand Rapids, Mich.: Center for Economic Personalism, 2001.

Grice-Hutchinson, Marjorie. *Early Economic Thought in Spain, 1177–1740*. London: George Allen & Unwin, 1978.

———. *The School of Salamanca: Readings in Spanish Monetary Theory, 1544–1605*. Oxford: Clarendon Press, 1952.

Gronbacher, Gregory M. A. "Economic Personalism: A New Paradigm for a Humane Economy." In *Centesimus Annus: Assessment and Perspectives for the Future of Catholic Social Doctrine*, edited by John-Peter Pham. Vatican City: Libreria Editrice Vaticana, 1998.

Haberler, Gottfried. *International Trade and Economic Development*. San Francisco: International Center for Economic Growth, 1988.

Hamowy, Ronald. "The Early Development of Medical Licensing Laws in the United States, 1875–1900." *Journal of Libertarian Studies* 3 (1979): 73–119.

Hartwell, R. M., ed. *The Industrial Revolution*. New York: Barnes & Noble, 1970.

———. *The Industrial Revolution and Economic Growth*. London: Methuen & Co., 1971.

Hayek, F. A., ed. *Capitalism and the Historians*. Chicago: University of Chicago Press, 1954.

———. *Unemployment and Monetary Policy: Government as Generator of the "Business Cycle."* Washington, D.C.: Cato Institute, 1979.

Hazlitt, Henry. *Economics in One Lesson*. New York: Crown, 1979 [1946].

Henderson, David R. "The Case for Sweatshops." Hoover Institution Weekly Essays. February 7, 2000, at www-hoover.stanford.edu/pubaffairs/we/current/henderson_0200.html (accessed October 10, 2003).

Herbener, Jeffrey M. "The Austrian School in the Liberal Arts." Paper presented at the Ludwig von Mises Institute's Twentieth Anniversary Conference, October 18–19, 2002.

———. "Calculation and the Question of Arithmetic." *Review of Austrian Economics* 9, 1 (1996): 151–62.

Hittinger, Russell. "The Problem of the State in *Centesimus Annus.*" *Fordham International Law Journal* 15 (1991–92).

Hoppe, Hans-Hermann. *Democracy, The God that Failed: The Economics and Politics of Monarchy, Democracy, and Natural Order*. New Brunswick, N.J.: Transaction, 2001.

———. *The Economics and Ethics of Private Property*. Boston: Kluwer Academic Publishers, 1993.

———. "How Is Fiat Money Possible? — or, the Devolution of Money and Credit." *Review of Austrian Economics* 7, 2 (1994): 49–74.

———. *A Theory of Socialism and Capitalism: Economics, Politics, and Ethics*. Boston: Kluwer, 1989.

Horwitz, Steven. "Inflation." Pp. 402–7 in *The Elgar Companion to Austrian Economics*, edited by Peter J. Boettke. Aldershott, UK: Edward Elgar, 1994.

Hufton, Olwen H. *The Poor of Eighteenth Century France, 1750–1789*. Oxford: Oxford University Press, 1974.

Hülsmann, Jörg Guido. "Facts and Counterfactuals in Economic Law." *Journal of Libertarian Studies* 17 (Winter 2003): 57–102.

Hutt, W. H. *The Strike Threat System*. New York: Arlington House, 1973.

Jaki, Stanley L. *Science and Creation: From Eternal Cycles to an Oscillating Universe*. Edinburgh, Scotland: Scottish Academic Press, 1986.

John Paul II. *Centesimus Annus*. 1991.

———. *Laborem Exercens*. 1981.

Kerby, William J. "Atheism and Socialism." *Catholic University Bulletin* 11 (July 1905): 315–26.

Kinsella, N. Stephan. "Legislation and the Discovery of Law in a Free Society." *Journal of Libertarian Studies* 11 (Summer 1995): 132–81.

Kirshner, Julius, ed. *Business, Banking, and Economic Thought in Late Medieval and Early Modern Europe: Selected Studies of Raymond de Roover*. Chicago: University of Chicago Press, 1974.

Klein, Peter G. "Economic Calculation and the Limits of Organization." *Review of Austrian Economics* 9, 2 (1996): 3–28.

Kohler, Thomas C. "Quadragesimo Anno." Pp. 27–43 in *A Century of Catholic Social Thought: Essays on 'Rerum Novarum' and Nine Other Key Documents*, edited by George Weigel and Robert Royal. Washington, D.C.: Ethics and Public Policy Center, 1991.

Kohr, Leopold. *The Breakdown of Nations*. New York: Rhinehart & Co., 1957.

Kolko, Gabriel. *The Triumph of Conservatism: A Reinterpretation of American History, 1900–1916*. New York: Free Press, 1963.

Krauss, Melvyn. *Development without Aid: Growth, Poverty, and Government*. New York: McGraw-Hill, 1983.

Lavey, Patrick Bernard. "William J. Kerby, John A. Ryan, and the Awakening of the Twentieth-Century American Catholic Social Conscience, 1899–1919." Ph.D. diss., University of Illinois, Urbana-Champaign, 1986.

Lawson, Robert A. "We're All Rawlsians Now!" *Ideas on Liberty*, June 2002, 49–50.

Leef, George C. "The Lawyer Cartel." *The Free Market*, November 1998, at www.mises.org/freemarket_detail.asp?control=51 (accessed July 8, 2004).

Leeman, Wayne A. "The Limitations of Local Price-Cutting as a Barrier to Entry." *Journal of Political Economy* 64 (August 1956).

Leo XIII. *Longinqua*. 1895.

———. *Quod Apostolici Muneris*. 1878.

———. *Rerum Novarum*. 1891.

Leoni, Bruno. *Freedom and the Law*. Indianapolis, Ind.: Liberty Fund, 1991 [1961].

Lindsey, Brink. *Against the Dead Hand: The Uncertain Struggle for Global Capitalism*. New York: John Wiley & Sons, 2002.

Luckey, William R. "The Intellectual Origins of Modern Catholic Social Teaching on Economics: An Extension of a Theme of Jesús Huerta de Soto." Paper presented at the Austrian Scholars Conference, Ludwig von Mises Institute, March 23–25, 2000.

Magnet, Myron. *The Dream and the Nightmare: The Sixties' Legacy to the Underclass*. San Francisco: Encounter Books, 2000 [1993].

Mariana, Juan de, S.J. "A Treatise on the Alteration of Money." Translated by Patrick J. Brannan, S.J. *Journal of Markets & Morality* 5 (Fall 2002).

Matusow, Allen J. *The Unraveling of America: A History of Liberalism in the 1960s*. New York: Harper & Row, 1984.

McGee, John W. "Predatory Price Cutting: The Standard Oil (N.J.) Case." *Journal of Law and Economics* 1 (April 1958): 137–69.

McShane, Joseph M., S.J. *"Sufficiently Radical": Catholicism, Progressivism, and the Bishops' Program of 1919*. Washington, D.C.: Catholic University of America Press, 1986.

Mises, Ludwig von. *Economic Calculation in the Socialist Commonwealth*. Auburn, Ala.: Ludwig von Mises Institute, 1990 [1920].

———. *Epistemological Problems of Economics*. Translated by George Reisman. Auburn, Ala.: Ludwig von Mises Institute, 2003 [1960].

———. *The Historical Setting of the Austrian School of Economics*. Auburn, Ala.: Ludwig von Mises Institute, 1984 [1969].

———. *Human Action: A Treatise on Economics*, Scholar's edition. Auburn, Ala.: Ludwig von Mises Institute, 1998 [1949].

———. "Inflation and You." In *Economic Freedom and Interventionism*, edited by Bettina Bien Greaves. Irvington-on-Hudson, N.Y.: Foundation for Economic Education, 1990, at www.mises.org/efandi/ch18.asp (accessed July 8, 2004).

———. *Planning for Freedom*. South Holland, Ill.: Libertarian Press, 1952.

———. "Small and Big Business." In *Economic Freedom and Interventionism: An Anthology of Articles and Essays*. Irvington-on-Hudson, N.Y.: Foundation for Economic Education, 1990, at www.mises.org/efandi/ch45.asp (accessed July 8, 2004).

———. *Socialism: An Economic and Sociological Analysis*. Indianapolis, Ind.: Liberty Classics, 1981 [1922].

———. *The Theory of Money and Credit*. Translated by H. E. Batson. Indianapolis, Ind.: LibertyClassics, 1981 [1912].

———. *The Ultimate Foundation of Economic Science: An Essay on Method*. Princeton, N.J.: D. Van Nostrand, 1962.

Murray, Charles. *Losing Ground: American Social Policy 1950–1980*. New York: Basic Books, 1984.

National Center for Policy Analysis. "Religious Hostility to the Free Market." August 16, 2001, at www.ncpa.org/pd/social/pd081601e.html (accessed July 8, 2004).

Nisbet, Robert. *The Quest for Community: A Study in the Ethics of Order and Freedom*. San Francisco: Institute for Contemporary Studies, 1990 [1953].

Noonan, John T., Jr. *The Scholastic Analysis of Usury*. Cambridge: Harvard University Press, 1957.

North, Gary. *An Introduction to Christian Economics*. Nutley, N.J.: Craig Press, 1976.

———. *Salvation through Inflation: The Economics of Social Credit*. Tyler, Tex.: Institute for Christian Economics, 1993.

———. "Undermining Property Rights: Coase and Becker." *Journal of Libertarian Studies* 16 (Fall 2002): 75–100.

Olsen, Mancur. *The Rise and Decline of Nations: Economic Growth, Stagflation, and Social Rigidities*. New Haven, Conn.: Yale University Press, 1982.

O'Neil, Patrick M. "A Response to John T. Noonan, Jr., Concerning the Development of Catholic Moral Doctrine." *Faith & Reason* (Spring/Summer 1996).

Osborne, Evan. "Rethinking Foreign Aid." *Cato Journal* 22 (Fall 2002): 297–316.

Otis, James. "The Rights of the British Colonies Asserted and Proved." Pp. 119–34 in *The American Republic: Primary Sources*, edited by Bruce Frohnen. Indianapolis, Ind.: Liberty Fund, 2002.

Paul VI. *Octogesima Adveniens*. 1971.

———. *Populorum Progressio*. 1967.

Payne, James L. *Overcoming Welfare*. New York: Basic Books, 1998.

Pelzman, Sam. "Toward a More General Theory of Regulation." *Journal of Law and Economics* 19 (August 1976): 211–40.

Pesch, Heinrich. *Liberalism, Socialism and Christian Social Order*. Book 1: *The Philosophical Roots of Economic Liberalism*. Translated by Rupert J. Ederer. Lewiston, N.Y.: Edwin Mellen Press, 2000.

Peterson, Robert A. "Lessons in Liberty: Hong Kong, 'Crown Jewel' of Capitalism." Pp. 103–13 in *The Industrial Revolution and Free Trade*, edited by Burton W. Folsom, Jr. Irvington-on-Hudson, N.Y.: Foundation for Economic Education, 1996.

Petro, Sylvester. *The Labor Policy of the Free Society*. New York: Ronald Press, 1957.

Pius XI. *Quadragesimo Anno*. 1931.

"Politics without Economics." *The Economist*, August 6, 1988, 8.

Pollard, Alfred F. *Wolsey: Church and State in Sixteenth-Century England*. New York: Harper & Row, 1966 [1929].

Porter, Roy. *The Creation of the Modern World: The Untold Story of the British Enlightenment*. New York: W. W. Norton, 2000.

Reed, Lawrence W. "Labor Freedom Makes Sense." *Ideas on Liberty*, February 2003, 14–15.

Reisman, George. *Capitalism*. Ottawa, Ill.: Jameson Books, 1996.

——. "The Free Market and Job Safety." Mises.org. January 22, 2003, at www.mises.org/fullarticle.asp?control=1143 (accessed January 23, 2003).

——. *The Real Right to Medical Care Versus Socialized Medicine*. Laguna Hills, Calif.: Jefferson School, 1994.

Reynolds, Morgan O. *Making America Poorer: The Cost of Labor Law*. Washington, D.C.: Cato Institute, 1987.

Ritenour, Shawn. "Praxeology as Christian Economics." Paper presented at the Baylor University conference "Christianity and Economics," November 7–9, 2002.

Rockwell, Llewellyn H., Jr. "Medical Control, Medical Corruption." *Chronicles*, June 1994, at www.lewrockwell.com/rockwell/medical.html (accessed July 8, 2004).

Rogge, Benjamin. *Can Capitalism Survive?* Indianapolis, Ind.: Liberty Fund, 1979.

Röpke, Wilhelm. *Economics of the Free Society*. Chicago: Henry Regnery, 1963.

Rose, Jim. "Child Labor, Family Income, and the Uruguay Round." *Quarterly Journal of Austrian Economics* 1 (Winter 1998): 75–92.

Rothbard, Murray N. *An Austrian Perspective on the History of Economic Thought*. Vol. 1: *Economic Thought before Adam Smith*. Hants, England: Edward Elgar, 1995.

——. *The Case against the Fed*. Auburn, Ala.: Ludwig von Mises Institute, 1994.

——. "In Defense of 'Extreme Apriorism.'" *Southern Economic Journal* 3 (January 1957): 314–20.

——. "Economic Depressions: Their Cause and Cure." Pp. 65–91 in *The Austrian Theory of the Trade Cycle and Other Essays*, compiled by Richard M. Ebeling. Auburn, Ala.: Ludwig von Mises Institute, 1996 [1978].

——. "The End of Socialism and the Calculation Debate Revisited." *Review of Austrian Economics* 5, 2 (1991): 51–76.

——. *The Ethics of Liberty*. Atlantic Highlands, N.J.: Humanities Press, 1982.

——. *Individualism and the Philosophy of the Social Sciences*. San Francisco: Cato Institute, 1978.

——. "Law, Property Rights, and Air Pollution." *Cato Journal* 2 (Spring 1982): 55–99.

——. *The Logic of Action One: Method, Money, and the Austrian School*. Gloucester, UK: Edward Elgar, 1997.

——. *Man, Economy, and State: A Treatise on Economic Principles*. Auburn, Ala.: Ludwig von Mises Institute, 1993 [1962].

——. "Mises and the Role of the Economist in Public Policy." Pp. 193–208 in *The Meaning of Ludwig von Mises: Contributions in Economics, Sociology, Epistemology, and Political Philosophy*, edited by Jeffrey M. Herbener. Boston: Kluwer, 1993.

——. *The Mystery of Banking*. New York: Richardson & Snyder, 1983.

——. *Power and Market: Government and the Economy*. Kansas City, Mo.: Sheed Andrews and McMeel, 1970.

——. "Toward a Reconstruction of Utility and Welfare Economics." Pp. 224–62 in *On Freedom and Free Enterprise: Essays in Honor of Ludwig von Mises*, edited by Mary Sennholz. Princeton, N.J.: D. Van Nostrand, 1956.

——. *What Has Government Done to Our Money?* 4th ed. Auburn, Ala.: Ludwig von Mises Institute, 1990.

Ryan, John A. *A Living Wage: Its Ethical and Economic Aspects*. New York: Macmillan, 1906.

——. Papers. Catholic University of America, Washington, D.C.

——. *Social Doctrine in Action: A Personal History*. New York: Harper, 1941.

Sadowsky, James, S.J. *The Christian Response to Poverty*. London: The Social Affairs Unit, 1985.

Sadowsky, James A. "Capitalism, Ethics, and Classical Catholic Social Doctrine." *This World* 6 (Fall 1983): 115–25.

Sauvage, George M. Review of *A Living Wage*, by John A. Ryan. *Catholic University Bulletin* 13 (July 1907): 470–75.

Schansberg, D. Eric. *Poor Policy: How Government Harms the Poor*. Boulder, Colo.: Westview Press, 1996.

Schmiesing, Kevin E. "Catholic Critics of the New Deal: 'Alternative' Traditions in Catholic Social Thought." *Catholic Social Science Review* 7 (2002).

Schumpeter, Joseph. *Capitalism, Socialism, and Democracy*. New York: Harper & Bros., 1942.

——. *History of Economic Analysis*. New York: Oxford University Press, 1954.

Searle, George M., C.S.P. "Why the Catholic Church Cannot Accept Socialism." *Catholic World* (July 1913): 449–50.

Sennholz, Hans F. *Age of Inflation*. Belmont, Mass.: Western Islands, 1979.

——. *The Politics of Unemployment*. Spring Mills, Pa.: Libertarian Press, 1987.

Sharpe, John. "Liberal Economics vs. Catholic Truth." November 3, 2002, at www.seattlecatholic.com/article_20021103_Liberal_Economics_vs_Catholic_Truth.html (accessed November 4, 2002).

Shostak, Frank. "Expectations and Austrian Cycle Theory." Mises.org. January 6, 2003, at www.mises.org/fullarticle.asp?control=1131&id=69 (accessed January 7, 2003).

Smith, Ted, III, ed. *In Defense of Tradition: The Shorter Essays of Richard M. Weaver.* Indianapolis, Ind.: Liberty Fund, 2000.

Stancioff, Marion Mitchell. "Distributism." *The Angelus*, July 1998, 10–16.

Stern, Charlotta. Review of David T. Beito, *From Mutual Aid to the Welfare State. American Journal of Sociology* 106 (May 2001): 1834.

Stigler, George. "The Theory of Economic Regulation." *Bell Journal of Economics and Management Science* 2 (Spring 1971): 3–21.

Stringham, Edward. "Kaldor-Hicks Efficiency and the Problem of Central Planning." *Quarterly Journal of Austrian Economics* 4 (Summer 2001): 41–50.

"Study Discovers Swedes Are Less Well-Off than the Poorest Americans." Reuters, May 5, 2002.

Tanner, Michael. *The End of Welfare: Fighting Poverty in the Civil Society.* Washington, D.C.: Cato Institute, 1996.

Tawney, Richard H. *Religion and the Rise of Capitalism.* New York: New American Library, 1954 [1927].

Taylor, Jared. *Paved with Good Intentions: The Failure of Race Relations in Contemporary America.* New York: Carroll & Graf, 1992.

Taylor, Thomas C. *An Introduction to Austrian Economics.* Auburn, Ala.: Ludwig von Mises Institute, 1980.

Telser, Lester. *A Theory of Efficient Cooperation and Competition.* Cambridge, UK: Cambridge University Press, 1987.

Thomas Aquinas. *Summa Contra Gentiles.* Translated by Vernon J. Bourke. Notre Dame, Ind.: University of Notre Dame Press, 1975.

———. *Summa Theologica.* Translated by Fathers of the English Dominican Province. New York: Benziger Brothers, 1948.

Tierney, Brian. *The Idea of Natural Rights: Studies on Natural Rights, Natural Law, and Church Law, 1150–1625.* Grand Rapids, Mich.: Eerdmans, 2001 [1997].

Tindall, George Brown and David Emory Shi. *America: A Narrative History*, vol. II, brief 5th ed. New York: W. W. Norton, 2000.

Tuck, Richard. *Natural Rights Theories: Their Origin and Development.* Cambridge, UK: Cambridge University Press, 1979.

Tucker, Jeffrey A. and Llewellyn H. Rockwell, Jr. "The Cultural Thought of Ludwig von Mises." *Journal of Libertarian Studies* 10 (Fall 1991): 23–52.

"U.S. Bishops Urge More Foreign Aid to Help Ensure Peace." Zenit, April 4, 2003.

van Dun, Frank. "Human Dignity: Reason or Desire? Natural Rights versus Human Rights." *Journal of Libertarian Studies* 15 (Fall 2001): 1–28.

Vásquez, Ian. "Poor Country Debt Relief, Rich Country Shenanigans." Cato Institute. July 30, 2001, at www.cato.org/dailys/07–30–01.html (accessed October 29, 2002).

Vedder, Richard K. and Lowell E. Gallaway. *Out of Work: Unemployment and Government in Twentieth-Century America.* New York: Holmes & Meier, 1993.

Vermeersch, A. "Interest." *Catholic Encyclopedia*, 2nd ed., 1913.

———. "Usury." *Catholic Encyclopedia*, 2nd ed., 1913.

Villey, Daniel. "The Market Economy and Roman Catholic Thought." *International Economic Papers* 9 (1959).

Waite, Linda J. and Maggie Gallagher. *The Case for Marriage*. New York: Doubleday, 2000.

Waterman, A. M. C. "The Intellectual Context of *Rerum Novarum*." *Review of Social Economy* 49 (Winter 1991): 465–82.

———. "Property Rights in John Locke and in Christian Social Teaching." *Review of Social Economy* 40 (October 1982): 97–115.

Waters, Alan. "In Africa's Anguish, Foreign Aid Is a Culprit." *Heritage Foundation Backgrounder*, August 7, 1985.

White, Lawrence H. "The Methodology of the Austrian School Economists." 1988, at www.mises.org/mofase.asp (accessed July 8, 2004).

Whitmore, Todd David. "John Paul II, Michael Novak, and the Differences between Them." *Annual of the Society of Christian Ethics* 21 (2001): 215–32.

Williams, Walter. "The Role of Profits." June 26, 2002, at www.townhall.com/columnists/walterwilliams/ww20020626.shtml (accessed October 28, 2002).

———. *The State against Blacks*. New York: McGraw-Hill, 1982.

Woods, Thomas E., Jr. *The Church Confronts Modernity: Catholic Intellectuals and the Progressive Era*. New York: Columbia University Press, 2004.

———. "Great Depression: Ending." Pp. 65–69 in *History in Dispute*. vol. 3. edited by Robert J. Allison. Detroit: St. James Press, 2000.

Zanotti, Gabriel J. "Fundamentos Filosóficos Epistemológicos de la Praxeología." *Libertas*, no. 13 (October 1990); manuscript in possession of the author.

———. "Misesian Praxeology and Christian Philosophy." *Journal of Markets & Morality* 1 (March 1998): 60–66.

Zmirak, J. P. "Honor Thy Fathers." *The American Conservative*, June 16, 2003.

Zoric, Joseph. "(re)Distributism (re)Considered." *The University Concourse*. March 7, 2000, at www.theuniversityconcourse.com/V,6,3–7–2000/Zoric.htm (accessed December 10, 2002).

Zwick, Mark and Louise Zwick. "G. K. Chesterton and Dorothy Day on Economics: Neither Socialism nor Capitalism." *Houston Catholic Worker*, September–October 2001, at www.cjd.org/paper/roots/rchest.html (accessed July 8, 2004).

Index

agriculture, 167, 187–88, 205
Aid to Families with Dependent Children (AFDC), 156
Albertus Magnus, 34, 39n67
American Bar Association, 184, 186
American Medical Association, 184–85
antitrust law, 176–77
Aristotle, 6, 16, 28, 34, 126n69
Ashton, T. S., 173–74
Augustine, 215
Austrian School of economics: business cycle theory of, 100–106; as compatible with Catholicism, 8, 16, 19, 216–17; described, 7–8; fractional-reserve banking and, 93, 125n39; inflation and, 96; methodology of, 15–19, 28, 69, 216, 217; on money supply, 100; praised by Heinrich Pesch, 84n72; realistic philosophy and, 38n50
Azpilcueta, Martin de, 50, 98, 117

Bandow, Doug, 138
Bangladesh, 135
banking, 89–100; business cycle and, 101–6; central, 94–98; fractional-reserve, 89–93, 97–100; free, 89–90; origins of, 89. See also Federal Reserve System

barter, 87–88
Bastiat, Frédéric, 14–15, 42, 100, 189
Bauer, Peter, 4, 129–30, 132, 133, 135, 139; on *Populorum Progressio*, 134, 142, 144n24, 145n58, 145n59
Beito, David, 148
Belloc, Hilaire, 107, 157, 163, 167–68, 176, 178; on distributism, 161–62, 165–66, 190; on interest, 117–21
Benedict XIV (pope), 120
Bethell, Tom, 131
Biel, Gabriel, 98
blacks, 154, 155
Block, Walter, 26
Böhm-Bawerk, Eugen von, 8, 163–64
Bostaph, Sam, 28, 38n49
Boston Compact, 152
Bourke, Vernon, 34
The Breakdown of Nations, 170
Britain, 169–74
Buridan, Jean, 93
Burke, Edmund, 157
business cycle: moral analysis and, 104–5; theory of, 100–106

Cairnes, John, 69
Calle, Luis Saravia de la, 98
Cantillon, Richard, 94, 107
Cantor, Norman, 201

231

About the Author

Thomas E. Woods Jr. is Assistant Professor in the Department of History at Suffolk County Community College, State University of New York.